Tina Schula

About the Author

RACHEL SHUKERT is the author of *Have You No Shame? And Other Regrettable Stories.* Her writing has appeared in numerous publications, including *McSweeney's, Heeb*, Salon, Gawker, the Daily Beast, and Nerve, as well as on National Public Radio. She has contributed to a variety of anthologies, including *Click: Young Women on the Moments That Made Us Feminists* and *Best American Erotic Poetry: 1800 to the Present.* Shukert is also a performer and playwright. She was born and raised in Omaha, Nebraska, and now lives in New York City with her husband and their bipolar cat.

Everything Is
Going to
Be Great

Also by Rachel Shukert

Have You No Shame? And Other Regrettable Stories

HARPER PERENNIAL

NEW YORK • LONDON • TORONTO • SYDNEY • NEW DELHI • AUCKLAND

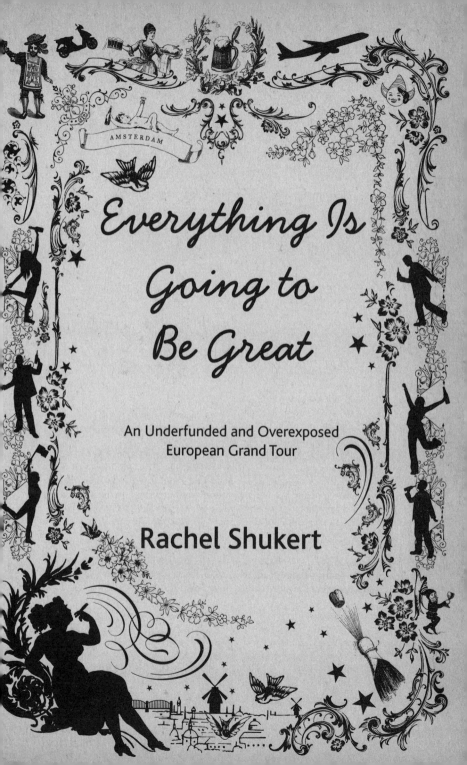

Everything Is Going to Be Great

An Underfunded and Overexposed European Grand Tour

Rachel Shukert

914
S56 2

HARPER ● PERENNIAL

EVERYTHING IS GOING TO BE GREAT. Copyright © 2010 by Rachel Shukert. All rights reserved. Printed in the United States of America. No part of this book may be used or reproduced in any manner whatsoever without written permission except in the case of brief quotations embodied in critical articles and reviews. For information address HarperCollins Publishers, 10 East 53rd Street, New York, NY 10022.

HarperCollins books may be purchased for educational, business, or sales promotional use. For information please write: Special Markets Department, Harper-Collins Publishers, 10 East 53rd Street, New York, NY 10022.

Designed by Justin Dodd

Library of Congress Cataloging-in-Publication Data is available upon request.

ISBN 978-0-06-178235-0

10 11 12 13 14   OV/RRD   10 9 8 7 6 5 4 3 2 1

For my parents, who still speak to me.
And also for the boys of East Seventy-fourth Street.

CONTENTS

HOW TO USE THIS BOOK

There are many wonderful ways to use this book.

For example, if you are removing a hot casserole dish from the oven and have misplaced all your trivets, you could use this book instead. Perhaps you happen to be entertaining a great number of alcoholics: several copies of this book could make an adorable set of substitute coasters. Or say you are camping, stranded in a war zone, or in hiding in the Belorussian forest from a band of genocidal maniacs bent on eradicating your kind. Thank God then, that before you fled from your home in terror, you grabbed your copy of this book, whose pages can easily serve as Kleenex, toilet paper, kindling, or, if carefully folded to the proper shape and thickness, a sanitary napkin.*

Other helpful features of this book include its flimsy paperback cover and thin pages, which are ideal for tearing, shredding, and burning; very handy when you are having a tantrum and looking for something inexpensive and easy to destroy. I personally have massacred many copies of my books in crazed fits of rage and despair. You can always go back to the bookshop and buy ten or fifteen more copies to have on hand the next time the mean reds strike, but

---

* While I understand that for many women, the "napkin" can be an impractical and cumbersome menstrual choice, I am uncomfortable explicitly endorsing this product for bodily insertion, uncertain as I am of the safety of any chemical additives in the paper, dyes, or inks. Should you contact the customer service line at HarperCollins, I am sure they will be able to advise you.

don't go overboard—buy too many extra copies and my next book might actually have a chance in hell of coming out in hardcover, which is much sturdier and more difficult to demolish.

Of course, some of you may actually read this book. There may be a handful of you who will even enjoy it. And of that handful, there may be a tiny sliver (as I'm told sometimes happens with travel books of this nature) who will decide to re-create my adventures as your own (a) in hope of finding some sense of clarity and purpose; (b) in hope of parlaying that sense of clarity and purpose into a book deal of your own; or (c) because you are completely mental.

Whatever your motives, I am in your corner. I have no doubt that you too can turn up in Europe with no money, work at terrible jobs, eat horrible food, and experience a variety of disconcerting sexual encounters with possible sociopaths. You might even learn some things about the world and yourself, which is after all the ostensible (and treacly) point of travel.

However, should you choose to undertake such an, um, *undertaking*, I find it incumbent upon me to smooth your way, which is why throughout this book I have included for your benefit a variety of helpful essays, observations, and travel tips. You will recognize these special features because they will look totally different from the rest of the book, and because they are strategically placed at points where even I am tired of hearing about myself.

En avant!

Preparing the Preparations

In the Olden Days, when wealthy young English gentlemen stormed the immoral European continent in order to shake off the last libidinous and homosexual vestiges of boarding school before settling down to the business of siring heirs and murdering wildlife, travel preparations could take months. Lucky for you, embarking upon Rachel Shukert's The Grand Tour™ requires far less time and expense.

Step 1: Assemble Your Rachel Shukert Costume

If you want to travel like Rachel Shukert, you'll need to look like Rachel Shukert. Your Rachel Shukert Costume™ (circa 2003) should ideally include the following:

- One shoulder-length dark brown wig with bangs. You may use your own hair, but you'll want to cut the bangs yourself, as a professional will leave you looking far too presentable. Children's safety scissors or the herb shears that are often included in basic kitchen knife sets are optimal for the look you are trying to achieve. For the most accurate color, use a variety of medium to dark brown shades of drugstore hair dye. Don't be afraid to experiment. Remember: You're not trying to look polished or even attractive. You're trying for a look that says: "I have no money, and I'm trying to cover up my premature grays."
- One oversized T-shirt or sweatshirt, preferably emblazoned with ridiculous slogan or embarrassing/wonderful tourist destination (for example: Dollywood).
- One short skirt. Flounced or cheerleader styles are fine. Should be about two inches too short to be appropriate and/or flattering; think sudden growth spurt. *Variation:* One pair seersucker shorts, to be worn regardless of the weather; should also be inappropriately short.

- One pair boy-cut underpants. The frequency with which these are washed is up to you; however, for true period verisimilitude, a liberal attitude toward personal hygiene is encouraged. Should you find yourself in a situation where acts of intimacy seem impending, simply repair to the nearest bathroom, remove and discard the indecorous panties, and thoroughly wash and dry the affected area with hand soap from the wall dispenser. Avoid brown, recycled paper towels when drying, as these can leave telltale and unsightly fibers adhering to thighs and labia. *Note*: If you are a biological male, then for best results in this costume element you will need to tuck. Diagram is below:

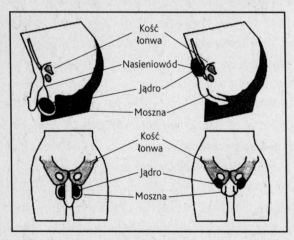

I found this on the Internet. The parts are labeled in Polish, but you get the idea.

- One compact pink blush, to approximate rosacea/alcoholic flush.
- One hip flask.
- One small mirror for handy admiration of oneself and one's "pain."
- *A simple variation*: Should you lack the time and/or initiative to assemble the entire Rachel Shukert Costume™, included opposite is a Rachel Shukert Mask™.

Simply enlarge to desired sized, cut out eye and mouth holes, and hold constantly in front of face. You are now guaranteed to be found sexually attractive by everyone you meet.

Step 2: Alienate Your Family

- Phone at odd hours with strange requests. For example: Ring up at two a.m. demanding an explanation of the theory of relativity, or the name of the moose from *The Get Along Gang*. While the family member is disoriented and struggling to figure out if you are on drugs, burst into tears and beg them to tell you why they never loved you as much as your sister.
- Make outrageous accusations. For example: If a family member hazards an opinion about your personal life, yell: "OH YEAH? JUST BE-CAUSE YOU'RE A HERMAPHRODITE!" For an opinion about politics or an otherwise sensitive subject, retort: "OH YEAH? JUST BECAUSE YOU'RE A RACIST!" If they mention to you that maybe you should think about getting a job someday, cry.

xviii   HOW TO USE THIS BOOK

- Live your life in direct opposition to the guiding principles of theirs. For example: If you come from a family of evangelical social conservatives, participate in as many indiscriminate sex acts as you can, and don't be shy about sharing: "You know, Grandma, when Hector rammed his huge cock into my ass for the first time, I felt like I finally understood how you feel about Jesus." If you come from a liberal, tolerant family, consider actually joining the NRA, the Teabaggers, or some other such repellent organization. When confronted, become irate, then cry.
- When in doubt, cry.

Step 3: Empty Your Bank Account

If you need my help with this, you are not a patriotic American.

Congratulations! You are now ready to embark on your ill-advised voyage of personal discovery! Good luck, and bon voyage!

Everything Is Going to Be Great

I AM NOT EVEN WASHING THE UNDERPANTS OF ME

I have to tell you: I love looking at myself in the mirror.

I realize that coming from a person who has published two memoirs before the age of thirty, this admission is about as shocking as a teenage boy owning up to a furtive wank into a brittle notebook during an undersupervised study period. But all is not as simple and self-regarding as it seems. While I'm certainly helpless to resist the affirming charms of a freshly polished shop window, and loath to sit opposite a reflective surface in a restaurant lest my dining companion bear witness to a narcissism so overwhelming it overshadows even the elemental impulse to feed, the truth is that my favorite time to look at myself is when something horrible has happened.

When a boyfriend does a runner, when a family member dies, when a doctor who clearly doesn't know the kind of suggestible maniac he is dealing with mentions that a seemingly benign skin rash on my forearm is a potential symptom of a rare form of lymphoma, I rush at once to the nearest glass in order to admire the bloodshot eyes, the swollen features, the shadowy streaks of mascara trailing unsteadily from cheek to chin like some faded penmanship of woe.

It is in these moments of despair that I think I feel most alive. This, I think as I gaze upon my mournful countenance with quiet pride, is not a person who goes quietly, measuring out her life in uncomplaining coffee spoons, hiding away her feelings behind a suffocating veil of politesse. This is a person of exquisite sensitivity. A person who sees, who senses, who feels deeply. Some people might say that such a person is histrionic and insufferably tiresome, but I like to think that such a person is, at least in some small part, special and destined for great things.

Unfortunately, what I seem most destined for is repeatedly smashing into things and breaking my face. I've been doing it with alarming frequency throughout my histrionic, insufferable, and tiresome life.

When I was seven, hopped up on three Cokes and a giant Rice Krispies treat, I smashed my face into the cement floor of a Schlotzky's deli in Omaha: the result of an ill-advised gymnastics demonstration on a pommel horse constructed of two metal chairs. My teeth hit the ground first, nearly severing half my upper lip. I had to be rushed to the emergency room to have it reattached. Perhaps this was the catalyst for my curious rapture in observing my own misery, for in the weeks that followed, I found myself glued to the full-length mirror in my parents' bedroom, watching with cheerful fascination as my lip evolved from a seeping chancre laced with blood-encrusted stitches to something resembling the sickly pulp of a rotten grape.

"I never thought you'd turn into one of those girls who is always staring at herself in the mirror," my father said, his voice tinged with wounded bewilderment. "I just didn't think you were the type."

"Well," I lisped through the pain, "I gueth you thwought wrong."

The injuries continued at such a rate it's a miracle I didn't graduate from high school looking like Mickey Rourke. At nine I caught a fly ball with my eye socket, at ten an ice skating mishap left me with a vicious slash across my temple and minor nerve damage in the pad of my right hand. I lost track of the number of times the annual French Club ski trip to Nebraska's single fake mountain ended in a stinging haze of iodine and a smear of fresh blood on the manufactured snow. When I was a college sopho- more, a full-height subway turnstile locked and retracted with- out warning, leaving me with a black eye that lasted for weeks. I camped out in the bathroom on the third floor of the Arts and Sci- ences building, delighting in the ever-changing sunrise of violets, mustards, and fuchsias that danced around my eye socket, until a well-meaning janitor slipped me the number of a domestic vio- lence hotline. Some months later a midnight hula-hoop contest and a pitcher of Long Island Iced Teas had ended with me waking up on a stretcher at the NYU hospital downtown. As I had been in an alcoholic blackout at the time, the attending physician could only postulate I had been hit by a car. A close shave, but boy, was it worth it—the wall of gritty facial abrasions that greeted me in the morning looked like an abstract rendering of the Battle of Corregidor.

Yet none of those various manglings had prepared me for what stared back at me in the mirror the day our story begins, bathed in a drowsy stream of soft Parisian light.

It was the summer before my junior year of college. I was one of sixteen NYU acting students deemed promising enough for par- ticipation in an eight-week experimental theater intensive in Am- sterdam. Each morning, we wrapped ourselves in loose, shapeless clothing—oversized T-shirts and soft trousers, the sort of pants an infant might wear—and noisily mounted our secondhand bicycles for the chilly ride to class, garnering curious stares from the lanky

Dutchmen on their way to work. Throughout the day, we lay in darkened studios, contorting our bodies into unseemly shapes; we thrust our hindquarters into the air and tried to feel the workings of our kidneys; we let out feral, wordless cries to symbolize rage and bellowed strings of rapid gibberish to approximate joy. We thought we were geniuses.

Even better, we were rich geniuses. In New York, we might sleep in some windowless storage space in Bushwick with room-mates who found it perfectly fine to pee in the kitchen sink or hoard their menstrual blood for use as plant fertilizer, but in Amsterdam, where the dollar was strong and the euro just an avaricious gleam in the World Bank's beady eye, we spent like sheiks. In the evenings, when classes had ended, we cut a wide swath through the city's shops and descended on its restaurants, gorging ourselves on Kobe beef, giant prawns, desserts thick with chocolate and cream, and when the night's feasting was over, we gathered in our common room to smoke enormous amounts of marijuana and congratulate one another on our general excellence. We were golden children, shining beacons of untapped talent and unending youth, and one day soon we would all be stars.

When our first free weekend arrived, we were eager to reward ourselves for our hard work. A large group had decided to visit a mountain town in the Swiss Alps, where in exchange for money one could jump out of an airplane. I thought this sounded like fun, until it dawned on me that the jumping would occur while the airplane was actually in the air, and I realized everyone around me was out of their fucking mind. I would no sooner jump willingly out of a plane than insert shards of broken glass into my anus. The world was already fraught with danger. Why ask for more trouble?

"Dude, I can't *wait* for that shit." An enormous wave of curling smoke drifted out of Jason Barnsdorf's mouth and over the bong, like a sheet of clouds around the roof of a lighthouse. "To be in the sky like that? Like some kind of fucking *immortal*, man."

"Like a god." Todd Beckerman pumped his arms in the air and bent backward at the waist, displaying the flexibility newly honed in our daily Ashtanga class. He had already removed his pants for the night, and at the hem of his jockey shorts I could plainly see one of his testicles, straining dangerously against its taut wrapping of hairy flesh. "Like a Greek fucking god."

Four feet eleven inches tall, and bedecked in Tiffany hearts and chains and knots that I assumed had been draped ritualistically on her person at the time of her Bat Mitzvah, Stacey Seligmann hailed from Great Neck, New York—a place I had never visited but believed to be peopled with those who felt the same way I did about voluntarily plummeting to one's death in some godforsaken corner of Switzerland.

"Fuck that," said Stacey delicately, surveying our companions with a look of practiced disdain. "I want to stay in a nice hotel and go *shopping*. I want to wear pants with a zipper and feel like a human being again."

I said, "I just don't want to die."

And so two interminable days later, Stacey Seligmann, Stacey Seligmann's Louis Vuitton Classic Monogram Carryall, and I arrived at the Gare du Nord in Paris. Our heavily discounted train tickets had taken us on a circuitous route, including several uninteresting and unannounced stops in rural Belgium, and by the time we arrived we were dirty, tired, and cranky, just like real Parisians.

It was July 14, exactly 211 years to the day since a mob of revolutionaries had stormed the fortress of the Bastille. As I watched Stacey's kinky blond ponytail bob determinedly before me, I thought that now, as then, France might never be the same.

We took a taxi to our hotel to drop off our things and wandered over to the Place Vendôme. The statue of Napoleon on top of the famous bronze column glittered softly in the midday sun, as men in gray jumpsuits were setting up long tables along the street. On the tables sat plump bottles of red wine, spaced in clusters every few feet. Two of the men careened past us, carrying an enormous bench, and Stacey jumped out of the way to avoid being knocked to the ground.

"It must be for Bastille Day," I said, sweeping my hands awkwardly in the air. "It's today. *Le quatorze de juillet.* I was here for it before, when I was in high school." The summer between my sophomore and junior years of high school, I'd spent several weeks in a small village in the southwest of France as part of an exchange program I had signed up for with three clearly defined goals in mind: (1) to learn to speak perfect French; (2) to shed my last stubborn pounds of pubescent baby fat; and (3) to finally experience the love of a man: that is, the kind of love that can be shown with a penis. My abject failure to achieve any of these at the time (although, in the interim, I had at least managed to accomplish the last two) was in large part the motivation for my decision to take this summer semester abroad: I wanted another chance to do things right.

Stacey pursed her small mouth thoughtfully. "It's like the French Fourth of July, right?"

I nodded. "It's a lot the same. There are fireworks, picnics, things like that. And I guess we must have missed it, but in the morning there's a big parade down the Champs-Élysées."

"Like Macy's? Cartoon floats and things?"

"No. It's an army parade, and very solemn. Every branch of the military marches: the navy or the air force or . . . whatever, in these ceremonial outfits, you know, like with swords and epaulettes and big ostrich plumes. Christian Lacroix designs all the dress uniforms of the French military," I remembered suddenly. "It's all very gay and ornate."

"Lacroix." Stacey rolled the word over her tongue. "How do you know that?"

"The father of my French exchange family told me." The family had taken advantage of the holiday to take a weekend trip to the Futuroscope, a sort of stunningly dull Gallic Epcot Center just outside Poitiers. On the journey north, we had driven for miles through commercial sunflower farms. Accustomed to the unrelieved dullness of cornstalks and grain silos that formed the similarly agricultural landscape of Nebraska, I thought the bursting fields of towering golden blossoms were one of the most beautiful things I had ever seen. On the morning of Bastille Day, the other children and I gathered in front of the ancient television set in one of the dingy hotel rooms their parents had rented, to peer at the endless stream of soldiers loping crisply down the boulevard, perfect and splendidly dressed as expensive toys in a glass case. I was enthralled, and nearly jumped out of my skin when the father (whose penis, incidentally, was the only one I saw during my stay, a fleshy, purple Twinkie bobbing gelatinously against his inner thigh as he changed clothes at the beach) surprised me from behind, grunting in English: "Regard them. They lose every war for five hundred years, but how *magnificent* their vestments."

Stacey Seligmann narrowed her eyes. "My cousin Jonathan went to join the Israeli Army after he graduated high school. Now he's superreligious and he won't talk to his parents. His wife wears a wig, and they already have like thirteen kids, and my aunt and uncle have never met any of them. My mother says it's a cult."

"I've decided to raise my kids Catholic," I said. "It's also a cult, but at least they'll get to wear cute uniforms. I always wanted to be a Catholic because of the uniforms."

"Why didn't you just go to a private school, then?" Stacey asked.

"We don't have them in Omaha," I said. "I used to ask to go to boarding school, but my mother said we were too poor."

Stacey quickly changed the subject. Even a facetious reference to poverty seemed to make her uneasy. "Would you ever date an Arab guy?"

"Maybe," I said. "Would you?"

"What's the point? Your family would never speak to you again, and your kids would just end up looking Jewish anyway." I was beginning to enjoy Stacey Seligmann. "Do you think they'll hang out in the streets tonight?" she asked. "Like a block party or something? Is that what these tables are for?"

I eyed one of the men in the gray jumpsuits, who stood scowling at the far end of the nearest table as he smoothed the creases from the tablecloth, a cigarette dangling out of the corner of his mouth. "I'll find out."

Americans love to moan about the rudeness of the French, but I've found that any effort to communicate with them in their native tongue, no matter how poor or grammatically ludicrous, eases one's way considerably. It allows the French to change their attitude toward you from revulsion to pity, and it's hard to be truly hostile to someone you feel genuinely sorry for. You might, for example, be annoyed with an ill-mannered child in a fancy restaurant, but when you realize the child is severely retarded, that changes things. If you want to get anywhere with the French, you have to become that retarded child.

After a few dribbling starts, the man grudgingly informed me that yes, there would be a celebration in the streets that night. The tables were set up for people to come with picnic suppers to watch the fireworks. The tables, like the wine, were provided by the government.

Stacey was somewhat less impressed by the idea of government wine than I was. "Really?" She squinted, adjusting the Pucci-print scarf tied round her head. "You want to hang out all night in the street with a bunch of strangers? I thought we were going to have dinner at that Japanese restaurant we saw in the guidebook."

"You can get sashimi in New York!" I cried. "We're in Paris! It's so beautiful! We'll party with French people. We'll meet hot guys. Where's your sense of adventure?"

"But I don't speak French."

"Don't worry," I said. "I'll take care of everything. Just leave it to me."

Sometimes I have dreams in which I become extraordinary, capable of extraordinary things. I dream I am a professional ballet dancer or an Olympic gymnast or an M-to-F transsexual married to Joe Biden (actually, this last was rather upsetting, as none of the other Georgetown wives would have lunch with me once they'd heard I had a penis) and I feel small and empty when I wake up to discover that I am still just me.

The Bastille Day party was like one of those dreams made real. After a mere six to eight glasses of government wine, I was speaking French with an eloquence and fluency I have never achieved before or since, and the more I drank, the better I got. Unlike government cheese, which gives you stomach cancer and, when squashed into spherical form, provides a handy and biodegradable alternative to a Super Ball, government wine was an elixir of verbosity and insight. This, I thought, was the wine of philosophical discourse and political debate, the wine of Voltaire and Descartes, of Sartre, Derrida, Foucault, and Debord.

"If only they'd served this wine in the exam room of my SAT IIs, I might have had a real chance at life," I said. Sadly, I chugged the rest of my glass, spilling some of the dark purple liquid down my neck.

"Take it easy," said Stacey. "It's eight o'clock, and we haven't eaten anything."

"Eaten?" I shrieked. "Who needs to eaten? I'm *fiiiine*. Better than fine. I'm *formidable*. This bottle is gone. I better go *cherche* for another one."

About halfway through *bouteille nombre deux,* I struck up a conversation in French with a group of equally sozzled graduate students.

"Speak not of Simone de Beauvoir to me!" The force of my exhortation caused me to teeter slightly. Serge, one of the students, was standing beside me. I grabbed his shoulder for support, and the top of his balding head grazed my clavicle. There are two major types of Frenchmen, I've found: the heartbreakingly gorgeous Alain Delon types, whose bee-stung lips and limpid eyes leave them with few options in life other than posing languidly in Versace ads and illegitimately impregnating people like Halle Berry; and then there are these crinkly little Ewok people who have no compunction about dandling their nicotine-stained fingers in and around your cervix in public, preferably without your consent. My French "father" from my previous sojourn, for example, fell squarely in the latter category, as did my new friends, apart from Fabrice the dental student, who was easily six foot nine with a face like Andre the Giant. But they were friendly, they had somehow commandeered a full case of magical wine, my cervix had as yet remained unfondled, and I was on a roll: "It is Gustave Flaubert who is the one true writer of feminism of France. Yes, it is true, he is making the punishment on top of Emma Bovary, but also he is saying it is the bad of the society that he is making atop her this punishment. It is necessary for one to wait for the writer who calls himself Ibsen for to allow the sin of a woman it is to be also her salvation. But too bad!

All the men of Scandinavia are being very terrible in the doing of the sex." Triumphant, I let go of Serge's shoulder and lurched back against the railing of the bridge.

Serge laughed. "Okay. But, *chérie*, we are all mathematics students. We aren't studying literature."

I scoffed. "This is nothing to me." I pulled the cork out of another bottle of red wine and poured about a third of the contents down my throat. "But I have more to be talking. Simone de Beauvoir, she is talking very beautiful about the feminism. But in the true life? She is washing the underpants of Sartre and then she is making of the tears when he is doing the sex with the others of the women." Even in French, I was beginning to detect in my speech the vaguely Southern twang that creeps into my voice when I am very, very drunk. How I came upon this affectation is a mystery to me—I think it has something to do with some atavistic association of Southerners with gentiles, and gentiles with drunkenness. "A woman who is true feminist, she is not doing of this. Hear me, Benoit! Me, I do not care if you are erotic"—Benoit had tiny eyes, set high in his forehead like a Modigliani painting, while the tip of his nose almost reached his chin—"but I am not doing the washing of the shit from the underpants of a man!" I finished the rest of the wine and smashed the empty bottle against the cobblestones, for punctuation. The shattered glass sprayed my legs, leaving a spatter of tiny red spots of blood against my bare skin. "I am not even washing the underpants of me!"

"Are you okay?" asked Stacey.

"Are you kidding? I'm just getting started," I proclaimed. "Now, which one are you going to fuck? I think I'll take the little one, unless you want him. You know, since you're both small." She stared at me strangely. "No," I amended, "you're right. We should be in love with them first."

I don't know how long we stood drinking on the bridge, but around bottle number six, I hit the wall. By the time it was agreed we should be moving on, I had lost my full command of any language.

"Where?" I slurred, for the fourteenth time, as we descended the steps into the Metro, sloshing wine from a paper cup down the front of my sundress. "Where we go to?"

"We are going to the ball," said Benoit, in English. "The ball, the party of the . . . the man of fire. You know? With the water, he extinguish of the fires . . . from the trees he is rescuing the small poor kittens . . ."

"I think we should go back to the hotel," said Stacey. "We can just get a cab."

"No!" I shouted. My cup was empty now. The spilled wine stung the tiny cuts the broken glass had left on my legs. "Don't be crazy! This is what we're here for. We're going to the fucking ball!"

I knew I was naked before I knew I was awake. Naked and swathed in a coarse fabric of an unfamiliar blue. Oh God. What the hell was the matter with me? I hadn't actually meant to sleep with that tiny Frenchman. It was supposed to be a joke, just a joke, like the time at dinner when I said I would do four shots of balsamic vinegar, no hands, for fifteen dollars. Although afterward, when I lay moaning in agony on my bare mattress as the acid churned mercilessly through my insides, that hadn't seemed so funny either.

Alors. One must persevere, even though it sometimes seems most practical to kill oneself. I propped myself up slightly on an aching elbow and scanned the ground for my clothes. The floor was linoleum, gleaming whitely under the glare of reflected fluorescent light. That was unexpected—unless you lived in a nursing home, who had linoleum in their bedroom? Or fluorescent lighting? And who slept in a bed that was this narrow? Or this high off of the ground? Or on wheels?

The sheet was tucked up tightly under my armpits, smooth and uncreased as though done with great care. At the top, stamped in fuzzy black ink, was a name: Hôtel-Dieu de Paris. Hotel? This was not our hotel. The hotel I had checked into had carpeting and was lit by floor lamps with soft, flattering bulbs. Had we changed rooms? Outraged, I sat all the way up and lunged for the phone by the bedside, intending to call down to the front desk to complain.

That was when I noticed the IV sticking out of my left hand.

"Elle se réveille!" A woman, dressed all in white, was charging down the corridor. Her features were small and clenched, as though someone had pulled a string and gathered them tightly together in the center of her face, like the puckered folds of a drawstring purse. *"La petite Américaine qui a bu trop!"*

She was at my bedside now, forcing me back down against the sheets, shoving a thermometer under my tongue. A man in a white lab coat materialized at her elbow. He was bearded, his sleepy eyes ringed with shadows the color of a Kalamata olive. It took me a couple of minutes to realize they were speaking to me. I had no way to answer them. My miraculous French had disappeared completely, a dream forgotten before waking. All I could pick out was a scolding refrain: *Tu as bu trop. Tu as bu trop.* You drank too much.

They're using the familiar, I thought wildly. Why don't they show some respect?

The nurse produced a syringe. "Please," I croaked in terror, desperate for them to understand. "No medications . . . *pas de* . . . penicillin, *pas de . . . de* sulfa . . . I'm allergic, *allergique,* I . . ." Suddenly, I was blanketed in sick. The vomit was heavy and thick, and for a moment I was surprised at how nice it felt, as though someone had spread hot oatmeal over my bare chest. I was very sleepy. I would go back to sleep, I thought. When I woke up, I would be somewhere else, somewhere familiar and safe.

The Emergency Room

Here is a fact: Being in foreign countries makes you clumsy. American feet unaccustomed to cobblestones are forced to lumber gingerly through the streets. You don't know where anything is, so you have to keep retracing your steps, seeking out inscrutable signage, wandering around looking sweet and befuddled, which makes you an easy mark for bullies, criminals, and the perpetually annoyed. Making a phone call from a public telephone becomes an insurmountable feat. The money is unfamiliar, so buying anything takes forever, to the undisguised annoyance of your fellow shoppers. In short, to visit a foreign country is to know what it's like to be a very old person holding up a grocery store queue at rush hour, vaguely aware of the storm cloud of hatred lurching in your direction but powerless and too arthritic to fling yourself from its merciless path.

This, in combination with the activities most people like to engage in while on vacation, such as the drinking of alcohol, the doing of drugs, and the sexing of dubious strangers, means there is approximately a 115 percent chance of you or one of your party landing in the emergency room sometime during your stay.

Fear not! Despite what you may have heard some asshole in a bad toupee say on C-SPAN, America does NOT in fact have the best health care system in the world. Every Western European country is ranked higher than the United States in overall health care, and most Central European ones as well. (You know who's last? Myanmar. Don't get drunk and break your nose in Myanmar, unless you want to wake up in a vat of raw sewage with someone else's severed hand sewn to your face.)

However, just because the doctors and nurses across the pond are pretty much guaranteed not to let you die in the emergency room because you don't have the right piece of laminated cardboard, or to present you with an itemized bill totaling $148,000, including twelve dollars per sheet of Kleenex used to mop the blood and/or vomit from your neck and clavicle, it doesn't mean things can't go wrong. Still, an emergency room visit can be one of the grandest highlights of Rachel Shukert's The Grand Tour™ if you simply follow the Three P's: Politesse, Preparedness, and Prescience.

Be Polite
Apart from a serial killer whose trailer you have unwittingly just entered, there is nobody with more godlike control over your body and well-being than a medical professional about to insert an IV or other such implement into your vein. Now is not the time to say things like: "If it weren't for us, you'd all be speaking German right now," or "Tell me, Herr Doktor, what were your parents doing during the war?"

Be Prepared
It's more than likely you will be unconscious or insentient for at least the beginning part of your hospital stay. If you are, by some unfortunate mistake, conscious and sentient, remember it is by no means guaranteed that your caregivers will speak English: For example, you could find yourself in a hospital in the former East Germany, where people learned Russian in school instead of English, or in France, where people speak English but are sadistic assholes. Therefore, I have whipped up these helpful badges. Simply cut out, fill in the blanks with the appropriate responses, and keep fastened to your person at all times.

ENGLISH

HELLO!
My name is

_____

I am an American who speaks only English.
I am allergic to the following medications: _____
In the event of my death, please contact: _____
He/She is my: _____
Thank you! I love you!

FRENCH

BONJOUR!
Je m'appelle

_____

Je suis un(e) américain(e) qui parle seulement anglais.
Je suis allergique à les médications suivant: _____
Si je vais mourir, vous téléphonez s'il vous plaît: _____
Il/Elle est mon/ma: _____
Merci bien! Je t'aime!

GERMAN

HALLO!
Ich heisse

_____

Ich bin eine Amerikanerin und kann nur Englisch sprechen.
Ich bin allergisch gegen die folgenden Medikamente: ___
Im Falle meines Todes, wenden Sie sich bitte an: _____
Er/Sie ist mein/meine: _____
Danke schön! Ich liebe dich!

SPANISH

HOLA!
Mi nombre es

_____

Soy uno(a) americano(a) que sólo habla inglés.
Soy alérgico a los siguientes medicamentos: _____
En caso de muerte, por favor contacto: _____
El/Ella es mi: _____
Gracias! Te amo!

ITALIAN

CIAO!
Mi chiamo è

_____

Sono un(a) americano(a) e parlo solamente inglese.

Sono allergico a queste medicinali: _____

In caso di morte, per favore contattare: _____

Lui/lei è mio/mia: _____

Grazie! Ti amo!

POLISH

WITAM!
Nazywam sie

_____

Jestem amerykanin(ka) i mówię tylko po angielsku.

Jestem uczulona na następujące lekarstwa: _____

W razie mojej śmierci, proszę skontaktowa ć się z: _____

On/ona jest moim/moja: _____

Dziękuję! I kocham was!

If you are conscious, you will likely be in far too agitated a state to memorize and deliver long phrases in what is to you, essentially, gibberish. However, here is a small list of words and gestures that might help you to convey just what has happened to you.

- *Drunk/Ivre/Betrunken/Borracho/Ubriaco/Pijany*
  (Mime lifting glass to lips, pouring down shirt.)
- *Hit by car/Frappé par une voiture/Von einem Auto angefahren/ Arrollado por un coche/È stato investito da un'automobile/Uderzony przez samochód*
  (Mime driving, make sound of explosion, fall to floor.)
- *Drug overdose/L'overdose de la drogue/Drogenüberdosis/Sobredosis de la droga/Overdose di droga/Przedawkowanie narkotykami*
  (Mime tapping for a vein and injecting contents of syringe, fall to floor.)
- *Terrorist attack/L'attaque terroriste/Terroranschlag/Atentado terrorista/Attacco terroristico/Atak terrorystyczny*
  (Mime long beard, make sound of explosion, fall to floor.)
- *Food poisoned/L'intoxication alimentaire/Lebensmittelvergiftung/ Intoxicación alimenticia/Avvelenamento da cibo/Zatrucie jedzeniem*
  (Mime eating, vomit on yourself.)
- *Rape/Le viol/Vergewaltigung/Violación/Sono stata violentata/Gwalt*
  (Point wildly to vagina and/or anus, then slide index finger of one hand back and forth through circle made with thumb and index finger of other hand.)

Be Prescient
A stitch in time saves nine, and a tumor spotted now is a tumor less likely to kill you six months on! As long as it's free, take advantage! Have that CAT scan! Finally figure out what that thing on your neck is! A coronary thrombosis can take up to seventy-two hours to fully manifest, plenty of

time to hop on the next flight to Paris to get taken care of on the socialist's dime!

True Story Treehouse: My friend Lauren, who was living in Los Angeles, wisely waited until she had arrived in Edinburgh to suffer a massive cerebral hemorrhage, and enjoyed National Health Service benefits all the way through major neurosurgery, six weeks in intensive care, and learning how to speak again. If you ask her now, she'll tell you she wouldn't have it any other way (of course, she'll tell you this with a slight Scottish accent!).

I opened my eyes again and I was standing up, dressed in a loose white smock with garlands of flowers of an indecisive blue printed on the cotton, faded like old tattoos on wrinkled flesh. The nurse with the drawstring face was supporting my back with her hand as she guided me slowly down the corridor into the X-ray room. As we entered, the young technician sprang up from a small desk in the corner and arranged me against a whitewashed expanse of wall, carefully aligning a heavy black apparatus suspended from the ceiling against the side of my face. He tilted my chin upward slightly as he did this, and shyly, I looked into his face. He was very handsome, with clear hazel eyes and rumpled gold hair that fell carelessly over his forehead. I smiled at him. He looked startled and murmured something to me in French. I didn't understand what he had said. I decided to pretend it was "I love you." A bright white light flashed close to my eyes. Overcome with dizziness, I crumpled to the floor, a stream of purple bile pouring from my mouth. This time, it didn't feel so good.

• • •

Sunlight streamed through an open window, prying open my eyes. I was lying in a regular hospital bed, in what appeared to be a private room. The IV was gone. The throbbing in my temples was gone too, but the rest of me was in excruciating pain.

"Hello?" I called as loud as I could, hoping someone, anyone in the corridor would hear me and be able to explain what horrific thing I had done to myself this time. "Hello? Can anybody hear me?"

A dark-haired woman in a white coat opened the door. "Hello," she said. "I see you are awake."

"You speak English?"

"But of course. I think it must have been a bit difficult for you before I arrived, no?"

"Oui," I said. "Very difficult."

She smiled. "Good. You are seeming a little more like a human being." She pointed at her name tag. "My name is Dr. Ginzburg, and I am the . . . ah . . . attending physician for you today. How are you feeling?"

"I'm in a lot of pain."

"Yes," Dr. Ginzburg said seriously. "I think this is true. We will give you some capsules after we can be sure that all of the alcohol is cleared from your bloodstream. Now, please, regard." She switched on the lamp at my bedside and held an X-ray up to the light. "Here is your nose, and here," she continued, pointing to a small dark spot near the top, "it is broken."

"Broken?" I echoed. "My nose is broken?"

"Cassé," she said, frowning. "Broken."

No, I thought. Not broken. This was a catastrophe. I had always been inordinately proud of my nose, a pert Aryan wonder that had long been an object of speculation and envy among relatives and friends. For the first time since this whole nightmare started, I began to weep. "Will I . . . will it look the same?"

"We have set the bone and disinfected the wound," Dr. Ginzburg said matter-of-factly. "It is not so very large a break. It is a small . . . how do you say it? The fracture. A small fracture. And it is at the very . . . ah, top of the nose, so I do not think it will affect the shape. But the wound is very . . . deep. I expect there will be some small scar, between the eyes."

I settled contentedly back against my pillow. "A small scar. I can live with that."

Dr. Ginzburg laughed. "You have a friend waiting to see you. I will have her come in? She has been very worried, I think."

The doctor disappeared into the hallway, and after a moment, Stacey entered, white-lipped and bedraggled. Without makeup, she looked about ten years old.

"Hi!" I said brightly. "Have you been waiting all this time?"

The light rap of knuckles against wood broke Stacey's silence. In the doorway, smiling anxiously, stood a tiny man in a short-sleeved yellow sport shirt, neatly pressed. In one hand he carried a small bouquet of pink flowers.

"Serge!" I cried gaily. "Come in!"

Serge ventured a few steps into the room. "You . . . remember me?" he asked shyly. His eyes were different than I remembered them, tilted like little upside-down smiles. He looked like a nice person.

"Of course I do," I assured him warmly. "But I'm sorry, I can't do . . . *français* . . . anymore. *J'ai* too *mal . . . à la tête* . . ."

He chuckled. "But of course. We speak in English. It is no problem."

"Really?" I giggled. "Just like that? Well, the next time I hear some American complaining about the French pretending not to understand them, I'll be like, dude, all you have to do is black out, smash your face in, and wake up naked and covered in vomit on a stretcher in a public hospital. *C'est facile!*"

Serge laughed. I laughed. Stacey didn't laugh. "This is very good hospital," Serge said. "It is the . . . most old hospital in all of Paris. The man who begin it, he is a . . . saint."

"Oh, I bet," I said breathlessly. "My grandmother does a lot of volunteer work at Children's Hospital in Omaha. She runs the Christmas Bazaar every year."

Serge frowned and shook his head. "I am sure your grandmother is a very gentle woman. But this man, he is a real saint. Saint Landry. He is bishop of Paris, after the Roman Empire, it collapse. This hospital, I see on the outside . . . the . . . the . . ."

"Cornerstone?" I nudged helpfully.

"No, no . . ."

"Keystone."

"*Non.* It is . . . upon the wall . . ."

"Plaque," said Stacey, curtly.

"Ah, *oui*, plaque! The same word in French, *plaque*. Plaque. On the plaque it is saying that *l'hôpital* is first begun by Saint Landry in 651. It is almost fourteen hundred years old," Serge finished.

"You see, Stacey!" I exclaimed. "That's what I love about Europe. There's just history everywhere. You don't get that in the States."

Serge nodded proudly. *"Voilà."* He held out the spray of pink flowers.

"For me? That's so sweet of you. Pink is my favorite."

"In Paris, one buys flowers in all one color. And I think, for such a pretty girl, a pretty pink."

"Pretty," I snorted. "I can't even imagine what I look like."

"Not good," said Stacey. "Like, really not good." She shoved a soft bundle at me. Inside were my clothes, freshly laundered and pressed in a neatly folded stack. "Get dressed. They're sending you home."

"Already?"

"You've been here for almost forty-eight hours."

Serge scrambled hastily to his feet, saying he'd wait for us at the checkout desk. Stacey turned to leave as well.

"Stacey?"

She stopped. "What?"

"I . . . I'm sorry I ruined your trip," I said finally.

She looked at me with a mixture of compassion and disgust. I knew this expression; I had felt my own face take its shape the time I had been asked politely for change on a subway platform by a man with a black gaping hole where his eyeball should have been. "Just get dressed," she said.

There were no curtains to draw over the windows facing the hallway, so I dragged myself into the bathroom to change and eagerly turned my face toward the small mirror above the sink.

It wasn't as bad as I was expecting. It was worse.

My right eye was bloody, my left swollen shut, and both of them magnificently orbited in varying shades of uncooked organ meats—liver, kidneys, tripe—except for the brow bone, which was streaked with a vivid, sickly yellow. My poor lip, already beset by more than its fair share of deformity, looked like someone had excised a tumor from a cancerous lung and affixed it there like a hideous corsage. There was a large violet bruise adorning my cheekbone; my jawline was laced with angry-looking scrapes and contusions. And my nose, my beautiful nose, was hidden by a metal splint and swathed in bandages that seemed to be held in place by an ocher trickle of pus.

I had come to Europe to grow up, to fall in love, to become the kind of person that I wanted to be. But the person I was becoming was destroying the person that I already was.

I looked away. Slowly, I zipped my dress; tied my shoes; gin-gerly, painfully, drew my arms through the sleeves of my jacket. Finally, I turned back to the mirror to gaze one last time at my bloody, ruined reflection, and made myself a promise.

"Sometime, somehow, I am going to come back."

Europe would just have to sit tight.

Two

HELLO FROM BETSY WALDBAUM ABRAMSON

At the end of summer, when I was small, I would wait outside for hours for the mailman to deliver the annual list from my elementary school, informing me of the school supplies I was required to have for the upcoming year. First graders received a blue paper, the second grade yellow, the third grade pink. Printed next to each item was a small blank box, which could be satisfyingly slashed with a thick black checkmark once the requirement of number two pencils, safety scissors, or felt-tip pens had been fulfilled.

The selection of school supplies provided me with a degree of autonomy unmatched by any other kind of shopping. I was denied sugary breakfast cereals, and my mother shuddered when I pointed out a flounced pink bikini, saying it reminded her of Jodie Foster in *Taxi Driver*, but when it came to colored pencils and Trapper Keepers, there were no rules. Drunk with power, I floated through the aisles in our local Target, savoring the scent of new erasers and caressing the unspoiled glass jars of rubber cement. My mother would park herself outside the ladies' room on a red plastic chair, like a high school debate moderator ready to hear the arguments of the day. Did the presence of a sharpener in my regulation box of sixty-four

Crayola crayons preclude the purchase of an additional pencil sharpener in the shape of a puppy? Was a single five-subject notebook the equivalent of five separate single-subject notebooks, which would provide a greater variety of colors? Her answer was always the same: "Get whatever you want and let's get the hell out of here."

On the first day of school, I arranged my pristine treasures in my desk and locker and would fuss over them for weeks. Markers were neatly capped and replaced in their unwrinkled box, arranged according to their place in the color spectrum. I cleared the viscous residue from the orange nipple of my glue bottle as gently as if it were my own child's tears. The inside of my pencil box was immaculate, free from any careless scrawls of graphite or ink. My teachers were awestruck, predicting great things from a student so careful, so conscientious. I soaked up their warm approval like a flower turning to the sun.

And every year around the first week of October, things completely fell apart.

It began innocently enough—a stray smudge of crayon, a hastily discarded bit of gum—but once set into motion, the ruin was rapid and complete. Uncapped markers went dry, erasers turned to gummy stubs, blackened and shredded like clumps of decomposing flesh. I was not unaware of the disappointment and disgust on my teachers' faces as I presented them with the crumpled wad of filthy paper that was my math worksheet or scraped the putrid remains of an unattended sandwich out of the soggy bottom of my backpack, but there was simply nothing I could do.

Years later, it has become clear to me that the decline into squalor of my third-grade desk provides an ominous metaphor for my entire life. In the words of Chinua Achebe, things fall apart.

Junior high imploded when I fell victim to one of the Stalinist purges that periodically occurred in the uneasy coalition of cheerleaders, heiresses, and future real-estate agents that an eighty-five-pound megalomaniac named Brianna ruled with an iron fist. High school was a fresh start, but soon deteriorated in a haze of marijuana smoke and missed classes. My teachers said they expected more from me. I was never sure what I had done to give them the impression that I had anything more to offer. Just once I wanted to look one of them square in the face—the student teacher who mispronounced every French name in *A Tale of Two Cities*, the rumored former Chippendale dancer who spent most of the time he was supposed to be teaching us social studies asleep at his desk, smelling faintly of Southern Comfort—and say, "And I expected so much more from *you*." I never did.

Despite my abysmal GPA, I was accepted into the drama program at NYU. It was the only school to which I had applied, and I vowed I would make it count this time. I was in my dream school, in my dream city, in my dream program. Failure was not an option. I was serious about this; so serious I wrote it on the back of a business card given to me by a pimp I met on the subway—"Failure Is Not an Option"—and tucked it inside my wallet.

Then I lost my wallet.

Still, the first two years of my university career were marked by an uncharacteristic streak of excellence. I showed up to class on time, assignments completed and lines learned. I was cast in productions, earned accolades from my teachers and peers and received some of my first A's since elementary school. But without my ever knowing quite what had happened, it all disintegrated into a frustratingly preventable miasma of eating disorders, depression, and a kind of juvenile alcoholism not quite severe enough to arouse pity but sufficiently obnoxious to alienate friends, destroy a fragile record of achievement, and generally lay waste to any and all short-term goals.

"I know what's wrong with me," I said to the student psychiatrist the university had provided for my care. "Don't think I don't know. My gargantuan sense of entitlement is matched only by my formidable laziness. I have no self-discipline. My eyesight is bad and I hate my boobs. I habitually shoplift small and valueless objects such as nondairy coffee creamer and premade California rolls. I am paranoid, insecure, and pathologically jealous of what other people have—for example, parents who are rich and powerful. I yearn for the approval of others, even though I don't think I like other people very much, apart from the uninterested men with whom I periodically become obsessed. I am addicted to Diet Coke, which I'm told will give me neurological problems and bladder cancer. I'm a terrible hoarder. The only thing I seem able to get rid of is alcohol, which goes down my throat, even though my mother keeps telling me that Jews don't drink."

The psychiatrist said, "I think you're afraid of success."

I said, "Here is a list of the things I am afraid of: elephants, flying, terrorists, sexually transmitted diseases, credit card statements, Poles, ballet teachers, and failure, which is generally agreed to be the opposite of success. Unless you're trying to practice some kind of reverse psychology on me, in which case you can go and fuck yourself."

The psychiatrist sat back in his chair. "Do you think your self-criticism is motivated by an underlying fear of rejection, requiring you symbolically to reject yourself?"

"I have to leave now," I said. "I'm drunk and I have to throw up."

So that was college. At the end, I was rewarded for surviving four expensive and puke-sodden years with a sheet of paper certifying me to be an actor, but I had no agent, no jobs, and no discernible prospects of either on the horizon. My mother, smelling blood, began to pepper her daily phone calls with sinister hints about my returning to Omaha.

"You could work at a restaurant!" she exclaimed. "That's what Michael Friedlander is doing. You know, Grandma's friend Dorothy Schneiderman's nephew's grandson, who was a couple years ahead of you, and he had that sister Erica, who married the Italian guy at the church and now they have a deaf baby?"

I said, "I have no memory of any of those people."

She was unfazed. "Well, apparently, he's doing *very* well. There's nothing wrong with being a waitress"—here she paused for emphasis, although which of us she was trying to convince was unclear—"nothing at all. You could save some money. New York will always be there."

"If I have to come back to Omaha," I said, "I guarantee in three months I will be dead, or you'll wish I was."

She gasped, as if in pain. "How can you say that? *How can you say things like that?*"

"I'm sorry," I said instantly, and meant it.

Sensing weakness, my mother switched tacks. "You know," she said, "I don't know what you think you're accomplishing here, trying to . . . to *blackmail* us with your overdramatic *bullshit*. It's really *very* unattractive." Privately, I agreed with her, but now was not the time.

"I think I'd really like to go to Europe for a while," I said.

"Yeah? So would I," said my mother. "I'd also like to be a gorgeous, six-foot, twenty-two-year-old member of the Swedish Bikini Team, but like your grandfather always said, if my aunt had balls, she'd be my uncle."

"I'm serious. Maybe I'll . . . I don't know . . . *find myself.*"

"Are you missing? Should I put your picture on a milk carton?"

"Why do you treat me like this?" I wailed.

"Like what?"

"I don't know," I said. "Like a joke."

My mother sighed. "We've already sent you to Europe. Once in high school and once in college. That's two more times than I'd been when I was your age. If you didn't find yourself then, you probably aren't there." We fell silent. Finally, she said: "Do you remember little Jeremy Rosen? Richie and Janet Rosen's little boy? His grandfather played golf with Grandpa until he had the stroke a couple years ago, and he was the one who bit your friend Andy Melnick on the neck that time during Rosh Hashanah services and then kicked him in the balls? The little boy, that is, not the grandfather. Well, *I* always thought Jeremy was probably autistic, and it turns out he is! He's totally nonverbal now, his IQ is so low it's off the charts, and they're sending him off to some special place in New Mexico for kids with neurological problems. What do you think of that?"

"I guess not everyone can be a genius," I said.

"You're right," she said, her voice pregnant with meaning. "That's absolutely true. And that's *fine*."

My adult life stretched out before me, a limitless expanse of nothingness. I filled the days as best I could. I invented meaningless errands: trips to the drugstore to buy unneeded and inexpensive household items, pointless job interviews, drinks parties with other recent graduates of drama school, where we would gather and share our bewilderment at being confronted at last with the specter of our vast, terrifying ordinariness. Nobody seemed to understand quite how this had happened. Just a few short months ago we had been so sure of the glorious destiny that awaited us; fame and fortune seemed encoded in our DNA as surely as the color of our hair or our underlying propensities toward paranoid schizophrenia. Now, through an act as simple as walking across a stage and collecting an empty plastic folder representing a degree, our stock had plummeted to nothing, the wretched leavings of some cosmic Ponzi scheme. A lifetime's worth of planning and training and delusion gone with the wind. Some of us were moving home to live free of charge in our parents' guest rooms, or if we were thin enough, heading west to try our luck in Los Angeles; others, to our collective horror, were being forced to work at actual jobs.

As it turned out, I was one of the lucky ones.

A couple of months before graduation, I had managed to wangle myself an audition with a famous theater director who often cast in his work young actors just out of school, usually in background, nonspeaking roles. My friend and classmate Connor had successfully auditioned for him a few weeks earlier, and when he mentioned over burritos in the common room one afternoon that the director was still looking for people for his latest show, I begged him to put me in touch.

"It's easy," said Connor. "He'll pretty much see anyone. You just have to phone him. His number is listed in the book."

"Under what?"

"Under his name. Seriously. I mean, he's famous to us, but not, like, to *real* people."

I was nervous, but after reminding myself that there were people my age currently embedded in combat convoys in the mountains of Tora Bora, I somehow found the courage to place the call, and the director immediately assigned me a time to come to his apartment, a converted loft space in lower Manhattan, for an audition. When I arrived, he greeted me perfunctorily at the door, and I followed him silently down a dim corridor lined with framed prints of mysterious and archaic maps, and into a room at the end of the hall. The room was enormous, smelling strongly of sawdust, and was filled with a truly awe-inspiring number of books, enough to fill the shelves of a medium-sized public library, all neatly labeled by subject and arranged in a forest of gleaming, cantilevered book-shelves. Apart from a couple of ancient sofas bearing a collection of brocade cushions, there was no other furniture.

The director motioned for me to sit down. I perched nervously at the edge of one of the sofas as he asked me a few preliminary questions: Where had I gone to school? Was I familiar with his work? He had a soft voice and his manner was not unkind, yet I had the distinct feeling that my comfort—or lack thereof—mattered not to him in the slightest. It was as if I had turned up to repair his dishwasher or install his blinds; he had no cause to be unfriendly, but I could assume there would be no unnecessary pleasantries. After I answered his questions, he explained a bit about what he was asking of me, should I be chosen. The play would be very hard work and would require my entire attention for more than a year. I would have no lines and be unable to take on other projects or even part-time work, a potential worry, as there would be little in the way of compensation, financial or professional. I nodded eagerly, in the dopey, puppyish way that people have when they are at-tempting to give the impression of listening intently. When he had finished, the director removed his thick, black-rimmed glasses and rubbed them several times with a soft, checked cloth. "All right," he said. "The audition has begun."

He gave me a string of simple directions. I was to get up from my seat and walk very slowly to one of the bookshelves. I was then to select a book. I was not to pause or deliberate or try to choose something that I thought would impress him. Then I was to walk back over to him and silently attempt to get his attention—an at-tempt he would defy until the proper time.

"Then, once you've finally gotten me to look up, I want you to open the book to a random page, point to the first sentence you see, and show it to me. But when you show it to me, I want you to imagine that it reads differently than it actually does, and that that's the message you are trying to convey."

"What should I pretend that it says?" I asked.

He replied, "I want you to pretend that it says, 'You are the biggest asshole that ever lived. I want you to eat my shit, you total fucking moron motherfucker.' Begin."

I stood up in what I hoped was a graceful manner and crossed to the shelves, acutely conscious of his huge, magnified eyes fixed on my back. Hastily, I selected *Nadja*, by André Breton, a book I actually happened to have read. A semi-autobiographical account of the author's ten-day relationship with a mental patient in Paris, it had (perhaps predictably) made the rounds through my group of college girlfriends, who for the most part also had emotional problems and fancied themselves troubled muses with fern-colored eyes—a worldview that sadly seemed to lead us directly into the arms of unemployed singer-songwriters with commitment issues and minor venereal diseases. Staring now at the familiar cover, I wondered if it was a wise choice. What would he think it said about me? What would he think I was trying to say about myself? That I was crazy, or liked to pretend I was? That I was a female version of those boys who talk about re-creating the trip in *On the Road* (except for the gay sex parts) and pretend that they didn't give you crabs and eventually wind up, age forty, serving cappuccinos somewhere in Austin, covered in whimsical/meaningful tattoos and telling pretty twenty-year-old girls about how much it meant to them when their son was born, even though they split with the mother right afterward and now she lives in the suburbs with some I-banker, but it's cool and he just figures it's his responsibility to make sure the kid grows up knowing the right bands?

"No, no, no!" cried the director. "That isn't the action I described at all. Bring the book over to me *without hesitation*."

I started to walk over to him.

"Start over," he barked. "Go back to the bookshelf, choose the same book, and bring it over to me. And remember, I'm a worm. I am a fetid smear of day-old excrement on the heel of your shoe. I am lower than dirt, and when you look at me you feel nothing but disgust. You would defecate on my face, but it's far more than I deserve. Begin."

Cheeks burning with shame, I retraced my steps and presented *Nadja* to him. He averted his eyes, playing his part. I opened the book, and shoved it under his nose, pointing fiercely to a random sentence, or rather an exchange. It seemed serendipitously apt: *"I want to ask one question that sums up all the rest . . . who are you? And she, without a moment's hesitation: I am the soul in limbo."*

The director nodded. "You can leave now." He didn't say goodbye.

A couple of months after graduation, as I was seated on the floor of my bathtub struggling to free a foot-long tangle of hairy scum from the drain, the phone rang.

"I'd like you to be in the play," the director said. "If you're still interested." It was obvious from the timing of his call and the tone of his voice that I was far from his first choice for this position, but I didn't care. I wanted to be an actor. Dignity is not part of the job description.

"Of course I'm still interested!" I squealed.

"All right, that's fine," he said. "But before you get too excited, I need to reiterate a couple of things . . . I know we discussed this before, but . . ." He took a deep breath. "There's no money. You won't be able to be in the play without an alternate source of income. I want to make sure that's very clear."

"Understood," I said. I was sure I could get my parents to kick up, just for a few more months. Over the past year, as I had watched less-talented but better-connected classmates sail confidently toward the television and high-profile film careers that were theirs by birthright, I had inwardly cursed my parents for their utter use-lessness. Sure, I had grown up in a stable, two-parent household. Sure, I never had to introduce people to my nineteen-year-old stepmother, or explain why my father had lost his ability to speak intelligibly and my mother no longer had any of her original skin. Sure, they "loved" me. Big deal. Love is cheap. A ferret can love. Being equipped from birth with an agent, a SAG card, and a trust fund that can get you through the canceled series/cocaine years: These are the gifts that keep on giving. However, the silver lining to my underprivileged life was that my parents were ludicrously easy to impress. If I told them I had been cast in a show in which I would have no lines and for which I would be paid no money, but which was directed by a person whose name they had once read in the *New York Times* Arts and Leisure section, it would not occur to either of them to suggest, even in the gentlest way, that it might be a total fucking waste of time.

"All right," said the director. "We rehearse six days a week, from ten to six. There will be no acceptable conflicts, no sick days. If you can't abide by these requirements, you'll have to quit. It will be grueling."

He wasn't kidding. Rehearsal was exhausting and endless. The sole bright spot, the lonely light at the end of the tunnel, was the prospect of a European tour at the end of our New York run. The thought sustained me. As I staggered home exhausted at the end of the day to open up another can of tuna for another meager supper, I repeated over and over to myself, like a mantra, the names of the places we might go. Barcelona. Berlin. Florence. Stockholm. Düsseldorf. Wherever it was, I thought as I looked around the bleak little flat I shared in Brooklyn with two strangers—a pair of sullen girls who rarely spoke to me except to criticize the scouring job I had done on a borrowed skillet or accuse me of leaving minute tufts of pubic hair on one of their towels (an utterly specious charge, although the more I was accused the more the idea of doing so tempted me)—would be a welcome change. Wherever it was, it wouldn't be here.

At last the schedule was set. We would spend three weeks in Vienna, another three in Zurich, and then at last we could go our separate ways. After months of anticipation, the abbreviated nature of the trip was a bit of a letdown, but my yearning to escape was stronger than ever. True to form, things had begun to go south for me. I jokingly referred to my role in the play as a sort of "avant-garde chorus girl," but in truth my duties were more akin to a minor stagehand, only much less glamorous and accorded far less respect—after all, stagehands had a union, while I had only the shaky rule of law to shield me from physical or emotional abuse. And besides, what was I going to do? Press charges? I'd never work in experimental downtown theater again! What was even more degrading was that the director had made it clear that he considered me one of the "male" versions of whatever it was we were supposed to be, as opposed to the two "females," a pair of leggy six-foot blondes costumed in thigh-high stockings and vinyl hot pants. As a male, my face was painted red, like a satanic mime. I was dressed in several layers of shapeless woolen rags, an enormous pair of boots that gave me the shuffling, jerky gait of a heavily sedated mental patient taking his first tentative steps into the common room after a recent lobotomy, and, to top it all off, a black rubber hat that made it look as though someone had squatted over me, lowered his pants, and dropped an enormous coiled shit on the top of my head.

As I glanced up into the house toward the huge, unblinking eyes impassively surveying his lumbering creation, I knew exactly who it was.

We males were required to wear the poop hat at all times, during every minute of every rehearsal. The hat gave me dandruff, and after a few weeks, my hair began to fall out on the left side of my head. When I complained, I was told that the constant presence of the hats was the only way our director, a man whose career in the theater had spanned four decades and garnered him nearly every conceivable international honor save a Nobel Prize (an oversight, it should be noted, he found particularly difficult to accept), could properly design a lighting plan for the stage. I pointed out that it was more than four months before the schedule called for any lighting implements to be put into place.

"If you don't like it," snapped the technical manager, "we can find someone else. A million kids would kill to do this job."

"Fine," I wanted to say. "Find one of them, and I'll go work for somebody reasonable, like Mullah Omar or Anna Wintour."

"The guy's a hack," said BJ, tipping his poop hat off his forehead in order to scratch an angry-looking scaly patch at the crown of his head. A fine crust of moist white flakes formed under his fingernails, and he flicked them into the air for the rest of us to breathe. BJ was my best friend, but our relationship had suffered of late. In the same way Connor had recruited me into the service (my colleagues and I often used military terms when discussing our plight), it was on my recommendation and encouragement that BJ had enlisted. At the time, I thought I was doing him a great favor, giving him direction and purpose in a senseless universe. Now I spent most of our conversations in tearful apology, like a cinematic action hero begging forgiveness from a dying comrade who has just been crushed by a falling building. "A total fucking hack. The emperor has no clothes, and he knows it. This is how the Nazis got started. And I would think you of all people, Rachel, would be sensitive to that."

BJ took great satisfaction in pointing out my Jewishness whenever the opportunity arose. He claimed that growing up in rural Texas as "a faggot named BJ" had accorded him the right to say anything he wanted for the rest of his life, no matter whom he offended. Any attempt to debate him on this point would be met with a tremendous retaliatory fart of such pungency and length it would totally disarm its victims, if not asphyxiate them completely. He called this "biological warfare." In our circle, we often hypothesized that BJ's ability to produce, seemingly at will, farts of such sustained and inhuman gruesomeness had to be the result of years of diligent study, a careful calibration of diet, intent, and sublime muscular control. It seemed more than likely, as BJ took an eager, if not entirely wholesome, interest in the doings of his digestive tract. During our senior year he had sent away for a special stool that fitted around the base of his toilet, enabling him to squat above the bowl as he defecated, and of this special pooping stool he was exceedingly proud. Visitors to his home were often treated to a real-time demonstration, the bathroom door ajar while their host, half-naked atop his plastic perch, explained how such a position was superiorly natural and healthful, preventing hemorrhoids, impactions, and every variety of complication that might prevent the act of emptying one's bowels from being the transcendent pleasure our Creator had intended it be. "In some cultures," said BJ, "shitting is accorded the same kind of mystical reverence as childbirth."

"What cultures?" I scoffed, but my skepticism was drowned out by the thunderous splash of another enormous baby delivered safely to the comfort of his underwater crib.

The stench of this rebuke still fresh in my sense memory, I spoke cautiously. "Well, he's not the most *lovable* person . . . but I don't know if it's really fair to compare him to a Nazi . . ."

"Oh, don't give me any of your Jewish bullshit," BJ snapped. "And stop making excuses for him just because you're so desperate to be liked. I've been around bullies my whole miserable life. I don't care if he lives in a loft the size of Miami and gets grant money from Jesus fucking Christ himself, that man's a bully, plain and simple. Nothing would give me more pleasure than hearing he dropped dead tomorrow and went straight to hell."

You can't argue with crazy, my mother likes to say, and you can't argue with the truth. And the truth was our director was a tyrant. The theater was his fiefdom, no less an autocracy than tsarist Russia or the court of Saddam Hussein (whom we were currently being told had weapons of mass destruction no less deadly than BJ's farts, a revelation that would probably lead to war). Like courtiers of some medieval despot, expected to let the vengeful monarch beat them at tennis or sodomize their wives without a word of complaint, we were expected to flatter him, cajole him, and accept every humiliation or insult he chose to inflict on us with an obsequious smile. To fall out of favor with the king meant total ostracism. From the start, I hadn't been one of the cool kids in this particular high school, but my status as a social leper was cemented, perversely and typically, by what I had meant as a gesture of friendship.

One day, bubbling over with good intentions (you know, what they pave the road to hell with) I approached the director. "Does the name Edie Waldbaum mean anything to you?"

I had never seen him speechless before. His eyes, already enormous behind his Coke-bottle glasses, widened with something akin to real fear. "What?" he blustered. "How did you . . . where did you hear that name?"

"Her younger sister runs the sisterhood gift shop at my parents' synagogue." I smiled artlessly. "You know, Betsy—Betsy Abramson now. My mother was in there the other day buying a Bar Mitzvah present for somebody and she was telling Mrs. Abramson about me being in the play and Mrs. Abramson said she went to high school with you, in Short Hills, and that you took her sister Edie to the prom."

"I . . . I what?" All around us, the other actors stared on in horrified awe. Connor had clasped one hand over his mouth and the other to his heart, and Kevin, the stage manager, desperately shook his head from side to side, begging me not to go on.

It was too late to turn back. "Edie Waldbaum. You took her to the prom, in Short Hills. Mrs. Abramson told my mother that you were the chairman of the prom committee that year. She said it had a tropical island theme, and the decorations were so beautiful that even then they all knew how talented you were. And she asked my mother to ask me to say hello to you from her. So, hello from Betsy Waldbaum Abramson," I finished lamely. "And also she said to tell you that she was sure that Edie would want to send her regards as well, but she died six years ago from ovarian cancer. Mrs. Abramson thought you'd want to know. She said the two of you were very close."

He sat back in his chair, staring intently at the stage. A few rows back, BJ was convulsing with soundless laughter, literally foaming at the mouth. Everyone else stood motionless, stunned and silent. Finally, the director spoke. "Well," he said. "Well. I don't remember anything about that. Actors, onstage. We'll pick it up from where the giant baby flies through the window."

From then on, I could do no right. In a perfect dictatorship, I would have simply been executed without trial; instead, I was criticized constantly for the smallest error or infraction. I tried to play along, as though it were all part of the game, hoping to somehow get back in my director's good graces. When he berated me for thirty minutes straight, screaming that there must be something wrong with my brain for failing to hold a painted screen straight (ignoring the fact that the screen, at his instruction, had been cut in the shape of a parallelogram), I laughed it off. On New Year's Eve, while we were out on dinner break, he went into my bag, took the dress I had intended to wear to a party later, and used it to puff up a rubber prop head he had deemed insufficiently round; I good-naturedly pretended it was a colossal joke. But the trickle-down effect of being a permanent object of blame and derision proved too much to bear—when one of the main actors, someone I had previously regarded as an ally, berated me cruelly outside the theater one night, I crumpled to the flagstones in humiliated tears. My crime? I had swung my legs while sitting on a chair backstage. The actor had found this distracting and blamed me for ruining his performance. I am not especially thin-skinned (I publish things on the Internet for a living), but I thought he, at least, was vaguely on my side, that he was kind of a friend. But I was wrong, and BJ, as usual, was right. I was desperate for people to like me. It was all I had ever wanted. And once again I had ruined everything. Later in the run, I was temporarily relieved of my post as resident punching bag when BJ announced he would not be doing the tour. After months without pay, he had totally depleted his savings, and had been offered a proper job. He offered his assistance in finding a replacement, at which time he was escorted to the dank back office, where our enraged director gave him the dressing down of a lifetime. Spitting with fury, the director called my friend "morally bankrupt" and an "irresponsible liar," and told him that doing the show was a "moral imperative." BJ, never a shrinking violet, replied that it was also a moral imperative to treat one's fellow human beings with understanding and respect, at which point the director may or may not have thrown a wall clock at BJ's head.

I was devastated by the news. Not only was BJ an ally and confidant in an endlessly hostile environment, he was also my best friend, and I was terribly disappointed he wouldn't be coming on the trip. For months we had bubbled with excitement over our impending adventure: the sights, the food, the men. Still, his absence would make it easier for me to distance myself from the entire affair. I would show up and do my job to the best of my ability, and that was it. I wanted nothing to do with any of these people ever again. I would be alone, a single entity, and in the anonymity of a foreign country, I would be able to disappear and not return until fully renovated. New York, and everything in it, all the thwarted hopes and broken hearts, would fade from view. I would be free.

We stood for almost an hour in the customs line in Vienna, waiting to get our passports stamped. Behind the smudged Plexiglas of the office window, Kevin the stage manager was having a tense-looking word with a uniformed official, who stabbed a long finger in our direction. But Kevin emerged smiling, and an incredible thing happened. The customs official, with a casual wag of the hand, waved us all through.

"Don't you need to—" I held out my passport as I passed the booth.

"No, no," said the official. "You are all here together, so it's fine. Please step through, I must process the next transport."

This is a chilling phrase to hear spoken with an Austrian accent, but I scarcely noticed as I passed through the portal into the fluorescent light of the terminal. It is a satisfying thing to have a passport stamped, to hear the affirmative clunk of ink to paper, to have the tangible evidence that one has been somewhere, done something; it's a lot like admiring a nascent scar in a mirror. But as I stood at the baggage claim, forlornly looking at the empty page in my brand-new passport where my stamp should have been, it began to dawn on me just what its absence meant. There was no visible record of my entering the European Union. When I returned, if I returned, there would be no record of how long I had been away. I was suddenly an undocumented visitor, an illegal, a faceless statistic.

I could stay here forever, if I wanted to.

If I could keep it all from falling apart, I could have a whole new life.

Three

IN VIENNA, EVERYONE LOOKS LIKE YOUR THERAPIST

The Hotel Kummer was a very dark place.

The paneling was dark. The upholstery was dark. The dark stains on the dark carpet hinted at dark acts. The dark entrance hall was surrounded on all sides by heavy doors of dark wood, slightly ajar, leading to an endless web of dimly lit rooms, each grimmer and more oppressive than the last. In thickly gilded frames on the oak-paneled walls hung oil paintings depicting an assortment of nineteenth-century figures in varying states of misery—heavy-lidded matrons gazing mournfully into the distance; an impressively decorated officer whose tufted eyebrows lent a fearsome look to his otherwise anguished countenance; a pale young beauty with a brackish veil settling about her narrow shoulders like a shadow of death. The paintings were individually lit by a series of small brass lamps mounted to the wall. These were the only source of light.

Through one of the open doors, I glimpsed a flicker of movement as an ashen-faced waiter in a maroon jacket gingerly prodded some silverware into place on a round table. He must have felt me staring, for he slowly drew himself up to full height and regarded me for a long while, long enough for me to note the gleam on his black shoes, the knife-edge crease in his navy slacks, the metallic slashes of silver glinting dully from the neat part in his hair. He studied me with similar intensity and I felt a flash of shame at what he saw—an untidy thicket of streaky hair, cheeks laced with the sticky remnants from the bag of sweets I'd devoured on the plane, eyes flashing with a disgusting mix of eagerness and fear, like a once-despised girl on her first day at a new school. He turned impassively back to his forks.

Apparently, I was checking into *The Night Porter*.

Apart from me, Connor was the only one of us left to check in; he collected his key swiftly and started down the darkened passageway to the elevator without a second glance. Feeling suddenly very alone, I lugged my two enormous suitcases to the front desk, where a uniformed attendant stood at attention before a wall of cherry wood cubbyholes. He was a tall man with a spare build and sharp cheekbones forming a set of neatly angled quotation marks upon which rested a pair of round spectacles, the style favored by glamorous fashion icons like John Lennon and Heinrich Himmler.

The man spoke. *"Darf ich Ihnen helfen, Fräulein?"*

"What?"

He pressed his lips together slightly. "May I help you?"

"Oh! Yes," I said. "I need to check in."

"Of course," he said.

"I'm so sorry," I hurtled forth, unable to raise the force field fast enough to avoid utter humiliation. "I don't understand German. I took French in school, but sometimes I think I should have gone for German instead. I mean, we should all be learning Chinese, right? But after all, some of my family was from Austria. Or maybe it was Germany. Or Poland. You know, the Austro-Hungarian Empire. There's that joke, you know, about the man who was born in Austria, grew up in Poland, got married in the Soviet Union, and died in the Ukraine? And the punch line: He lived all his life in the same town! Anyway, what I'm trying to say is"—I staggered, bloodied, to the finish—"that I think there's something about Europe that makes Americans"—bring it home, *Fräulein,* bring it home—"all Americans, somehow feel like failures. We may seem arrogant, but that's because we have a huge inferiority complex. Look at Bush. He's so insecure. It's why he started the war." And with that final profundity, at last I was silent.

The man gazed at me intently through his tiny glasses. His expression was nearly identical to that of the silver-haired waiter just moments earlier: unblinking, keen yet impassive, perceptive yet unfixed, revealing nothing of the one who wore it, and yet possessed of a strange power. It was an expression to which one might confess one's greatest secret, one's deepest shame.

The man behind the desk spoke. "May I have your last name, please?"

"Sure," I replied nervously. "But my last name isn't Austrian, it's actually . . ."

"Excuse me, but this is an irrelevance," he interrupted. "I require your last name only so that I can access your reservation and begin the check-in process."

"Oh." I flushed. "It's Shukert."

"Can you spell it please?" He smacked his lips slightly, glancing down at what I saw to be a computer keyboard, a concession to modernity tastefully hidden behind the polished mahogany countertop. I obeyed.

"Very well," he said. "I have retrieved your reservation. You will be placed in room 305, which is on the third floor, but as an American, you will assume it is the fourth floor. Please operate the buttons of the lift accordingly. You are lucky to have a corner room, which means it is larger than the other rooms of its floor and receives rather more sunlight than the others. I assume you will be comfortable, *Fräulein*, but if there is anything else you require, do not hesitate to contact me. My name is *Herr* Winkler. You may call me *Herr* Winkler."

Winkler, I thought. Like the Fonz.

The Fonz rang a small bell, and another uniformed man materialized at my elbow, dragging my luggage behind him. "Abdul will take care of your valises," the Fonz continued, and produced a curlicued metal object, which he pressed into my hand. "Here is your key. If you like, you can leave it at the desk for safekeeping as you come and go. Many guests believe this is the best way, as there can be no replacements should it become lost."

"Well, I'll try not to lose it," I said.

"I would advise you to do more than try," said the Fonz. "I would advise you to leave it here for safekeeping when you leave the hotel. Good day to you, *Fräulein*."

"But if I do lose it . . ." I began.

"Good day, *Fräulein*."

Despite this rather icy welcome, the days leading up to the opening were surprisingly pleasant. The theater where the play would run was in the Museumsquartier, an enormous square of raked pink gravel flanked on all sides by former royal residences that now housed some of the greatest art treasures in the world. Pale benches like fat pastels peppered the square; on the stone terraces of posh restaurants cultural grandees presided over it benevolently, sipping sweet white wine and coffee with whipped cream.

"It's civilized," we said, taking in the Hapsburg splendor, the sleek cafés, the parade of people in avant-garde eyeglasses strolling purposefully but unhurriedly to their destinations. "This is what 'civilized' means."

The theater itself was a majestic marble edifice, flooded nightly with footlights that imparted the stone façade with an otherworldly glow. The lobby was a pristine Bauhaus wonderland of glass and leather; the house could seat three hundred in plush covered seats. By any reasonable standards, it was a palace; compared to the freezing, airless, joyless black box in which we had spent nearly all our waking hours for the past nine months, it was heaven itself. When the cheerful wardrobe assistant showed me to my private dressing room, which was equipped with a wall of softly lit mirrors, a sink, and a beribboned package from the producers of the festival containing a T-shirt, chocolates, and a laminated map of the city, I actually cried.

Even our director seemed to manifest the change. At first, I assumed he had been subdued by jet lag and would be back to his horrible self in no time, but as the days went on, it seemed his change of attitude was genuine. Removed from his natural habitat, he was a mellow, charming, decent human being.

Opening night was its usual tumult—the dash to get dressed, the perfunctory hugs of the players exchanged backstage, the low hum of the well-heeled audience settling into their seats.

About five minutes in, we had our first walkout, a woman and her companion who shuffled quickly through the row and up the aisle. Reflexively, I glanced toward their empty seats (the director liked to keep the houselights up during the performance, so we could watch the audience watching us) and noticed for the first time the man who had been sitting beside them. I didn't know how I had missed him before. In a sea of dark opera coats and black turtlenecks, he was a flash of color, dressed in what looked like a woman's blouse from the 1970s, a geometric pattern of reds and oranges and flecks of deep blue. His face was deeply tanned, and his eyes were dark, ringed with friendly-looking creases that oddly made him seem younger, as though his face were pressed in a permanent smile, and I realized with terror that he was staring at me with an expression at once probing, bemused, shrewd. It was the same look I had seen back at the hotel on the faces of the shadowy Night Porter and the Fonz. With a shudder, I knew where else I had seen it before.

In Vienna, everyone looks like your therapist.

Given the kind of irreproachable emotional stability you've seen me display thus far, I'm sure you'll be shocked to discover that men were kind of a tricky subject for me. My college boyfriend Sam and I had broken up a few months after graduation in a toxic haze of infidelity (mine), rage (mine), and recrimination (ours!), after which he had fled immediately to California, wisely refusing to have anything more to do with me. When the initial grief had waned (as had the dramatic dent made to my sexual confidence by being referred to as a "male" every day for eight months), I joylessly embarked on a series of increasingly random and ludicrous one-night stands. The last one was a couple of weeks before we left for Vienna. I had gone out drinking that night with my friend Tommy, a fellow borderline alcoholic with whom I had forged a strong bond over our shared talent for disappointing people. We had showed up uninvited at the trendy Lower East Side restaurant where our friend Bart had recently gotten a job as a barback and sat there for hours, tossing back cheap Scotch and fiddling with our overpriced plates of macaroni and cheese. At four a.m., Bart came over to our table and told us it was time to go. Tommy swore at him violently before passing out on the floor, his face nuzzled against a grimy pool of melting ice. Bart promised to take care of him, shooing me out the door before he could get in trouble with his manager, and I walked up Ludlow Street alone. It was just beginning to feel like spring. The night air was warm and welcoming, shyly fragrant with the fresh smell of newly flowering trees. The streets were teeming with people: kissing couples, bartenders getting off work, groups of friends spilling out of bars, hanging onto one another in tipsy solidarity, searching for an empty cab. I felt a pang of envy; I could no more afford to take a cab back to Brooklyn than I could afford to buy the Brooklyn Bridge. I continued uptown for another block or so and hung a left on East Fifth. Most of the windows were dark, their occupants down for the night, but a bit further down the block, a dim light flickered on the third floor of an old tenement building. Music pulsed through the open window, and a couple of girls about my age leaned over the sill, drinking out of red plastic cups and calling down to the group of boys standing on the sidewalk outside, huddled over a joint like hobos around a trash fire.

Feeling brave, I nodded casually at the boys and walked through the open door into the building, following the music up the stairs. The apartment was empty of furniture apart from an abandoned DJ stand in the corner where a lonely light flashed, shadowing the walls with forlorn streams of colored half-light. A makeshift bar was set up on a card table by the door, littered with several mostly empty handles of vodka and gin. On the marbleized counter of the kitchen were some plastic cups in a short stack. I grabbed one, checking it for visible stains or cigarette ash before I dropped a handful of tepid ice inside, followed by a splash of warm gin and a drizzle from a spent two-liter bottle of flat 7-Up, and made my way into the living room.

The party was winding down, and the guests who remained were fading fast, swaying alone to the music, hunting for purses and jackets, slumped against each other in corners, heatedly winding up negotiations over the night's sexual arrangements. No one took any notice of the stranger in their midst; they were probably strangers to one another. Over the rim of my cup I noticed a dark-haired guy standing alone near the hallway. A stream of light from the DJ stand fell over his face, and I could see his eyes were a clear light green. He smiled.

"Hi," I said.

"Hi," he said. "Did you just get here?" His voice was low and husky. I detected a slight accent—distinctly foreign, but brushed with London vowels, the way Europeans speak when they have learned English from a British teacher.

"Yeah," I said. "Only just."

"Do you go to Parsons?" he asked. "Are you a friend of Jake's?"

"No," I said. I was too drunk to tell anything but the truth. "I don't know anyone here. I was out with a friend, and he passed out, and I was just passing by and the door was open, so I just walked in. I'm not a crazy person," I continued, "I just didn't want to go home yet." I paused, weighing the significance of these words. "I didn't want to be alone."

The boy laughed. "So you crashed a party by yourself at five in the morning." He had a light checked scarf wound around his throat, the ends falling on either side of the V-neck of his T-shirt, like curtains framing a window of hairy chest. I wanted to rub my face in it.

"I think men should wear more accessories," I said.

He glanced at his watch. "It's late. I think I'd better head out."

"Yeah," I said. "I guess I should too."

"Can I put you in a cab?"

"I can't afford to take a cab."

"I'll give you the money."

"You don't have to do that."

"Please," he said urgently. "Let me be a gentleman."

"Okay," I said. "If you insist."

He grabbed his bag from one of the bedrooms, and we picked our way through the carpet of discarded cups and splatters of vomit on the stairs. He walked behind me, a protective hand just grazing the small of my back. I wondered if I seemed drunker than I felt. On the landing was a spray of broken green glass. I turned to warn him. The turn was all it took. He pulled me close, pressing his lips against my open mouth.

"I thought you were gay," I said.

"Why?"

"Because of your little scarf."

He grinned. "Couldn't you tell I was going to kiss you?"

"So? You wouldn't be the first gay guy I've kissed."

When I left his apartment a couple of hours later, he was asleep, his black briefs still askew around his hips from when he had groggily pulled them back in the darkness. I was halfway down the block, searching for a subway stop, when I glanced at my cell phone and noticed the date. It was my birthday. None of my friends had remembered, and I had forgotten to remind them. I was twenty-three years old.

About a week later, I was at the bodega methodically working my way through a stack of scratch-off lottery tickets when I ran into my friend Daphne with a cute guy in tow.

"I think we've met before," he said.

"It's possible." I wrinkled my nose cutely, wishing I weren't wearing the sweatpants with the period stain across the back. "Although I can't think where. I get around."

"I guess *so*," he said.

They paid for their drinks and left the shop. About an hour later my phone rang.

"Do you remember yet how you know my friend?" Daphne asked.

"No," I said, "but he's cute."

"I'm glad you think so," said Daphne, "because he said he fucked you a couple of weeks ago."

"Guys don't fuck me," I said haughtily. "I fuck them."

"I realize you have your feminist principles," said Daphne, "but he told me that you crashed some party he was at in the middle of the night, went home with him after five minutes, and snuck out in the morning before he woke up. Are you saying you didn't do it? Because that sounds like you."

"It wasn't him," I said. "It couldn't have been."

"You left your driver's license at his house," Daphne continued. "He found it on the floor of his bedroom. He said it must have fallen out of your purse when you were looking for a condom."

"We used a condom?" I said. "That's good news."

"Apparently, it happened on your birthday," Daphne continued. "He knew when he saw your driver's license. He thought it was kind of weird you didn't say anything."

I felt queasy. "The guy I slept with had an accent. I swear to God he had a European accent."

Daphne snorted. "He does have an accent. From Dallas."

"I can't believe this," I said. "I'm sure I asked him if he was European. This is terrible."

"What are you upset about?" Daphne pressed. "Because you didn't recognize him, or because he isn't European?"

I said nothing.

"Oh my God," she hooted. "Oh my God! That's why you slept with him, isn't it?" Daphne continued. "Because you thought he was European?"

"I liked his chest hair," I said defensively. "But mostly, yes. This news is extremely disquieting. I wonder if it's time to finally seek some kind of in-patient psychiatric care."

Daphne sighed. "Do you want me to try to get your license back before you leave?"

I told her not to worry about it. I don't really know how to drive anyway.

The opening night party after the show was lovely, full of flowing wine and tempting snacks and laughing strangers. Connor grabbed my arm with violent glee, and shoving our way through the crowd, we managed to commandeer a bottle of iced champagne, a tray of canapés, and a table.

I shoved a handful of smoked trout with crème fraîche into my mouth. "Do you think anyone can tell I haven't had a shower in a couple of days?"

Connor's mouth was full of deviled egg, a fine jam of yolk, paprika, and mayonnaise frothing creamily over his lips. "Why didn't you take one in the dressing room?"

"I didn't want to be late. I thought all the food would be gone."

"Skip this one." Connor pointed at a slab of mini schnitzel, slathered with something creamy and mushroom-like. "It's mostly gristle. And the gravy is just weird."

I buried my nose in my armpit for a moment and inhaled deeply. "Eh, I think I'm okay. It's not a bed of roses in there, but it could be worse."

Connor reached for the champagne and filled both of our flutes for the third or seventh time. "I'm sitting next to you and I can't smell you. So who cares? Who's going to get close enough to you to notice?"

I raised an eyebrow. "You never know."

A heavyset blonde materialized at our table. By her side was my friend from the audience, still wearing his bright blouse and a rumpled grin.

"Hello!" the woman bellowed. "My name is Hilda Bormann. I'm one of the officials of the festival, and I wish to be grateful to you for making your performance here in Vienna!"

"You're welcome," said Connor, snapping to attention and quickly dabbing at his chin with a napkin. "It's our pleasure."

"Hello," said the man. He made a little bow. "My name is Berthold."

"Berthold?" I repeated dumbly. I had spent an hour having eye-sex in a poop hat with a person named Berthold?

"Berthold," said Hilda helpfully. "Like the great writer of Germany named Brecht."

"Right," I said. "Of course."

Berthold was shorter than I had expected, only an inch or two taller than me. He was also quite a bit older than he had looked from the stage—the lines around his eyes deeper, his face more determinedly weathered, but artfully so, like one of those distressed handmade journals bought in overseas marketplaces by people who are very serious about properly poeticizing their self-absorption; for example, people like me. As we stood there beaming idiotically at one another like befuddled dignitaries determined not to cause offense, I wondered if Berthold might not serve the same purpose as such a journal—a sort of talismanic shortcut to authenticity, a leathery foreign object suitable for display in dimly lit cafés, telegraphing my literary ambitions, my credibility, my admirable commitment to tasteful pretension. I also wondered if there was a way to find out just how old he was, without sounding like a second grader.

Berthold finally spoke. "I'm sorry," he said. "We will speak slowly? My English is not so excellent."

"It's okay," I said quickly. "Neither is mine."

His eyes, I noticed, were a beautiful, liquid golden brown, like a stream of perfectly brewed tea. He blinked several times before he spoke again, and I could almost see him carefully formulating the English words before he said them aloud, taking care not to make a silly mistake. "So," he said finally. "You are from New York City?"

"Yes," I said. "I mean, no. I mean, yes, I live in New York City. But I'm not from there originally. I grew up in Omaha. In Nebraska."

"Nebraska?" He frowned. "What is it?" This is, I am afraid to say, not an unfamiliar question. With none of the annoyance that I display when asked the same thing by people who have spent their entire lives in the northern suburbs of New Jersey, I explained very nicely that Nebraska was a Midwestern state, smack in the middle of America and, when asked, that it was a major producer of beef, corn, and soybeans; that the list of famous natives included Fred Astaire, Marlon Brando, and Dick Cheney; and that, no, Nebraskans had never legally owned slaves.

Berthold reached for a strand of my hair, wrapping it gently around his forefinger. "Your hair. It is so dark. You are a red Indian?"

"Nope," I said cheerfully. "I just drink like one."

Berthold replaced my hair against my shoulder and bent to light the cigarette he held cupped in his hand. "What about you?" I asked. "Did you grow up in Vienna?"

He shook his head. "I am from a small town in the south of Oster . . . ah . . . Austria. It is very close to Italy. The culture and the people"—he gestured vaguely around the room—"are more Italian."

"Oh!" I exclaimed. "Well that explains . . ." *why you're so short*, I was about to say.

"Explains?" he asked encouragingly.

"Why I like you so much," I finished lamely. "I've always liked Italians. And Italian food!"

"Yes," he said seriously. "It is very delicious. And Vienna? You are finding Vienna . . ."

"I love it," I assured him. "It's like Paris, but sinister."

His face lit up. "You are a joke-maker!"

"It's important to have a sense of humor in life," I said. "Right?"

Berthold narrowed his eyes and let out a low hiss, curls of blue smoke unfurling from his flared nostrils, and inclined his head in the direction of the director, who was clutching a glass of wine and talking animatedly with a couple of tall bald men in heavy turtle-necks. "This man, he is your *Direktor?*"

"Yes," I said. "They say he's a genius."

Slung over Berthold's shoulder was a small leather bag. I had noticed this earlier, assuming it to be some sort of troubling European man-purse, and had tactfully averted my eyes; I figured that this, like strange sandals and bikini underwear, was just the sort of thing a person had to overlook if she ever wanted to fuck someone who wasn't from the suburbs of San Antonio. Now, to my relief, I saw it was actually a boxy camera case, from which Berthold extracted a handsome Polaroid camera, the old-fashioned kind, trimmed in chrome and covered in brown Naugahyde. Deftly, he unfolded it and jammed a dusty-looking cartridge into the film slot. "I am photographer," he said. "You are joke-maker. Shall we make a joke together?"

"Sure," I said.

"Gut," he said. "Let us hide ourselves beneath the table, and take one Polaroid color photograph of the ass of your director."

I said, "That would be a pretty good joke."

Several bottles of wine later, Berthold pressed me against an ancient wall in a cobblestone alley and crushed his mouth onto mine. His breath tasted sour, of cigarettes and liquor, and he forced my jaw open to accept his tongue, which wriggled thick and slightly cold in my mouth, like a slab of reanimated sashimi. It took up a lot of space, and uneager to suffer an undignified death by double-lingual asphyxiation, I was forced to store my own tongue in his mouth, pressing it somewhere between his undulating dorsum and the wet inside of his cheek. Berthold took this simple safety precaution for a show of passion and clamped both his hands on the back of my head, smashing his mandible into mine. Our incisors met with a crunch, faint but sickening all the same, like a greasy butter knife scraping against a china plate. I dislike this kind of aggressive tooth-kissing, as it reminds me of the wee, fist-like monster that gnawed through John Hurt's stomach in *Alien*, so I pulled away for a moment, pretending to catch my breath.

"Look at this wall," I murmured. "It's so old. Imagine. Mozart probably peed against this wall."

Berthold kneaded my neck hard with his chin. "Please," he whispered throatily. "Come please with me now, to my home." His arms snaked inside my jacket and wrapped warmly around my waist.

It felt nice to be held, at least. I rested my head on his shoulder for a moment, breathing in the scent of his warm neck, the light smell of detergent on his blouse. The horrible kissing aside, I was tempted. I liked being with him—from what I could tell from our brief acquaintance, he was funny (no small feat, with the language barrier), generous (we had gone to a bar afterward with several other cast members and he had been accommodating almost to the point of profligacy, ordering bottles of wine for the table, offering cigarettes to anyone who wanted them), and kind (he had listened sympathetically, if not entirely comprehendingly, to my tales of woe from the past year, and done his best, in his halting, Teutonic way, to reassure me of my essential worth as a human being). I knew his last name (Krüger); I knew his age (forty-six); I knew his occupation (commercial and artistic photographer). I was convinced that he was neither a thief nor a serial killer, nor was he planning to abduct me in order to conduct grisly acts of medical experimentation and/or cannibalism. He was a friend of Hilda, the festival official, who radiated the scrubbed good sense of a young Angela Merkel. I had gone home with many, many, many young men about whom I knew a lot less—and when what I did know was a lot less encouraging. But that night, something held me back. Somehow, I wasn't prepared to go home and have sex with an Austrian stranger named Berthold who was old enough to be my father.

He seemed to understand. "It is my wish that you will be safe. I will please take you to your hotel." It was a declarative statement, and one to which I was happy to acquiesce. He was a gentleman. He was *civilized*.

"I'm staying at the Hotel Kummer," I said. "Do you know it?"

He nodded solemnly. "It is very near."

We walked in silence down the Mariahilferstrasse, the flounced miniskirts and bright vests in the windows of H&M and Mango in odd dissonance with the carved limestone façades and Hapsburg flourishes that surrounded them. The new world can never truly escape the old. When we reached the iron doorway of the hotel, Berthold kissed me formally on both cheeks.

"The Hotel Kummer," he said softly. "Do you know what it means, Kummer?"

I shook my head.

"Sorrow," he said. "The Hotel Sorrow."

"Well," I said. "The lobby is awfully depressing."

"The Hotel Sorrow," he repeated, gazing past me into the lightless void of the welcome hall. "Maybe next time I see you, you have no more sorrow, Rachel." The lines around his eyes deepened; his tea-colored irises glistened moistly in the streetlight. It was the first time he had said my name.

• • •

That night, I couldn't sleep. After a week and a half, I hadn't entirely gotten over my jet lag, but the unease that kept me awake was something else—a vague, nagging feeling that I had lost something. I checked my handbag for my passport and the closet for the envelope that held my ready cash. I rifled quickly through my suitcases. Nothing seemed to be missing. Now, fully awake, I wished I could call Berthold back, and I wondered, crazily, if he was still out there, standing on the hotel steps, gazing up at the windows, looking for a sign that I had changed my mind. Before I quite knew what I was doing, I jerked my raincoat on over my pajamas and ran down the carpeted steps of the entry hall to the stoop outside.

It was empty.

There were a few loose euro coins in the pocket of my raincoat, so I walked to the all-night *Käsekrainer* stand across the street. The *Käsekrainer* is unique to Vienna; it is a special kind of sausage about a foot long, thicker than a broomstick, and cooked in a rotisserie-style oven. Once the crisped skin has turned a mottled pinky brown and is heavily beaded in hot fat, it is placed inside a long, dense roll, made hollow by impalement on one of the long metal spikes that line the counter. The hole is specially lubricated with a choice of slippery condiments—mustard, ketchup, curry sauce—to keep the toasted bread from drying out as the sausage is inserted. About an inch of pink, slightly wrinkled meat peeks temptingly out of its yeasty cubby. You bite off the inch, and a piping hot gusher of runny white cheese coats your tongue, singeing the roof of your mouth and any other parts of your body on which it may happen to land. From the first time I saw it, it was immediately clear to me that this beloved snack was the apotheosis of the Freudian (and peculiarly Viennese) conflict

between Eros and Thanatos, sex and death. The sexual compo-
nent was obvious, and I felt quite sure that improper consumption
of the *Käsekrainer* could actually kill you. At this very stand, on
my first night in town, I suffered a direct hit of cheese to the eye.
I screamed in pain, but my cries were quickly drowned out by a
chorus of cruel laughter from a pair of young skinheads standing
next to me. The skinheads reeked of alcohol, and for a moment I
felt afraid, but they quickly lost interest and went back to inhaling
their thick sausages. I guess they just couldn't get enough of that
hot meat in their mouths. One of them reeled back and threw up
a little down his front. A long strand of sticky white clung to the
crooked swastika scrawled in black Sharpie on the front of his T-
shirt. Then it was my turn to laugh.

That night, the skinheads were back. I stepped up to the
counter and ordered a beer, trying not to call attention to myself.
Several of the skinheads had terrible acne, and one of them had
missed a spot while shaving—there was a small patch of matted
yellow fuzz at the back of his head, like the greasy feathers of a
just-hatched chick. They were very young, teenagers probably.
I drank my beer and looked at the laces of their boots. Someone
had told me once that you could tell from the color of the shoe-
laces which skinheads were the racist kind, but I couldn't remember which color meant what. I wondered if they were even
really skinheads. Maybe I had imagined the Sharpie-d swastikas
on their shirts. Maybe they hadn't even meant to shave their
heads at all. Maybe they were a band of juvenile cancer patients
trying to enjoy a final night on the town. I remembered when
I was little, my parents used to get fund-raising letters from
the Anti-Defamation League. On the outside of every envelope
was a black and white picture of two angry-looking skinheads,
dressed in leather jackets and scowling in front of a Nazi flag.

The picture frightened me. From the dining room table, where the mail was usually stacked, I felt as though the skinheads were following me with their eyes, and whenever one of the letters came, I would try to throw it away before my mother saw it. In retrospect, it seemed unlikely to me that the ADL had managed to coax two genuine skinheads into posing for photographs for their fund-raising campaign. They were probably just two regular guys, actors maybe, dressed as skinheads. But I had been frightened all the same. I wondered if this was my sorrow, like Berthold had said. To always see skinheads where there were none.

The next day I spent sightseeing and came back to the Hotel Sorrow late in the afternoon, planning to take a short nap before I was due at the theater. At the front desk, the inimitable *Herr* Winkler cleared his throat loudly. "A message was left for you, *Fräulein*," he said. He reached into one of the cubbyholes behind him and removed a bright blue envelope, which he handed to me. It bore no name.

"Are you sure it's for me?"

"Room 305. The American girl." The Fonz sneered.

Inside the envelope were two things: a Polaroid photograph of a man's behind, swathed in threadbare black fabric, and a small piece of thin cardboard, about the size of a postcard. On one side of the card was pasted a colored map of Nebraska, cut perfectly to fit. On the other, printed carefully in neat black ink, was a long number. I showed it to the Fonz.

"Is this a telephone number?" I asked.

"*Ja.*"

"Who dropped this off?" I demanded.

The Fonz lowered his glasses slightly, so that he could be sure

I would get the full hypothermic effect of his glare. "A gentleman. I assumed at first he was your father, but his German was perfect. Perhaps he is some . . . older relation? An uncle, perhaps?"

I told him I didn't care for his insinuation. He just smirked.

Berthold was already at the restaurant when I arrived after the show that night, drinking a gin and tonic at a table near the window. He motioned for the waiter to bring one for me as well, along with a bottle of cold white wine. We ordered two plates of Wiener schnitzel, accompanied by creamy mounds of potato salad and buttered spaetzle, little handmade noodle dumplings that melted in my mouth. The schnitzel was delicious, washed down with the crisp, sweet wine, and Berthold showed me how to eat it the traditional way, slathered with fresh blackberry jam that was served in a little glass pot alongside the plate. Like my French, his English became more fluent as the wine took hold, and as we ate, he told me about himself. He had grown up in a small Alpine town near the Italian border, the youngest child of a policeman father and a housewife mother. His parents were badly suited, and to escape their constant arguments, Berthold had fled to the slopes. He spent most of his teens training to be a championship skier, until he was derailed by an injury just before the Olympic trials and found that after his leg had healed he had no desire to continue. As he explained it, the arbitrariness of sport, the realization that all he had worked for could be undone in a matter of seconds by a burst of wind, a poorly fastened boot, became intolerable to him. If it was all luck, then why bother? He had always liked to draw, and during his long convalescence he had taken up painting in earnest and was accepted into art school in Salzburg. A year later, frustrated with painting, he had drifted into photography, which appealed to his newfound democratic streak.

"To make a painting, one must create something with what is not there," Berthold said. "To make a photograph, one must understand what is. One must create with what *is*."

There had been a Spanish woman with whom he'd been involved for a number of years, but things had ended when, in a spasm of Catholicism, she insisted they marry. Berthold didn't believe in marriage. He had seen what it had done to his parents. He preferred to keep himself disentangled from commitment. He wanted to feel young.

"Is that why you spend your time chasing young American innocents abroad?" I asked, a little drunkenly.

He stubbed out his cigarette against the word "Cinzano," printed in blue at the bottom of the ashtray, and reached across the table to touch my face. Softly, he murmured something in German.

"What did you say?" I asked.

"I say: You are a beautiful child."

If ten thousand chimpanzees, injected with the cloned genetic material of Casanova and Sigmund Freud, were gathered in a vast laboratory and chained to typewriters, with the voice of God reading my psychiatric records over the cosmic loudspeaker, in seventy years or more they could never come up with a line that would get my clothes off faster. When Berthold kissed me outside the café, there was none of the unpleasant choking wetness of before, and when we broke apart and he asked me, again, to come home with him, this time I didn't refuse.

Berthold put some Strauss on the stereo and produced some sweet white wine in a beautiful bottle of blue glass. The wine, he told me, was a special kind, made from tiny grapes that grew wild under the snow in the Alps. He poured it over my body, and licked it off the tops of my breasts.

I was beginning to feel like the disembodied hand an indeterminately accented Christopher Walken attempted to ply with champagne and erotic massage in that old *Saturday Night Live* sketch, but I decided to go with it. He half-carried me into the bedroom and lay back on the bed. I smiled and, feeling drunk and generous, curled between his legs to take him into my mouth. There was a strange rubbery band gathered around the base of his penis. Loose and almost viscous, it flapped impotently against my lips, like a deflated balloon someone had tied loosely around a broom handle. Startled, I spat it out discreetly, in order to properly assess the situation. The skin was just too big. It was like one of those plastic surgery makeover shows in which sad people had large amounts of fat forcibly sucked out of them instead of going to therapy, and were left with grisly wings of emptied skin hanging over their bodies like a shameful cloak. Perhaps, I thought, something similar had happened to Berthold? Perhaps he had recently lost a great deal of weight . . . from his penis? And suddenly, it hit me, like a bacon truck colliding with a Lubavitch Mitzvah Mobile. This little roll of rubbery flesh was a *foreskin*.

I almost had to call a halt to the proceedings right then and there. This must be a European thing. Why had no one told me? After all, it was practically a matter of public record in the States that European women didn't shave their armpits, use deodorant, or perform other acts of hygienic sterilization necessary to make intimidated American men sexually comfortable. Did it never occur to anyone to mention that European men have an inch and a half of extra skin wrapped around their dicks like a cowl-necked sweater? Where was that little tidbit in the conversation that the pervy older brothers were having in *Home Alone*?

Berthold moaned.

"What?" I whispered, hoping the strangulation in my tone sounded seductively kittenish, instead of like I was having my windpipe crushed by an epidermal garrote.

"I say you give me much pleasure," he sighed and, to my enormous relief, reached into a small tin box for a condom.

Foreskin FAQs

Look, I don't know who you are. You probably already know all about foreskins. You may even have one yourself. But in light of my previous tirade, I feel I cannot in good conscience let this opportunity go by to share my hard-earned cultural knowledge with you.

What does a foreskin look like? Contrary to how I pictured it, the foreskin is not a flap of unaffiliated skin that hangs off the penis like one of those dangly things on the sleeve of an ice dancing costume. The foreskin is a loose sheath of skin that covers the head of the penis, ending over the urethral opening in a circular pucker that looks like a wrinkly Cheerio, or maybe a hemorrhoid cushion for a dollhouse.

Who has them? Biological males who are uncircumcised. Circumcision is most prevalent in North America, Australia, Africa, and the Middle East, and rarest in Europe, Central and South America, and Asia. Worldwide, the World Health Organization estimates a rough 30 percent circumcision rate. A similar study conducted by the author of the population of Zionist summer camps in the metropolitan area of Ocmonowoc, WI between the years 1993 and 1998 found a circumcision rate of exactly 100 percent.

What do you say when you see one? Nothing! Believe it or not, men are very touchy about what you think of their penis—especially if your observations are prefaced by "ewww" or "weird." Such an outburst may subject you to an uncomfortable line of questioning about American "mutilation" practices, which you will be forced to answer by saying that the overwhelming prevalence of circumcision in the United States is a plot by the evil Jewish doctors to ensure a steady stream of future patients for the evil Jewish psychiatrists.

Is it clean? Generally, yes. While smegma—which sounds like the name of a cat-suited administrative assistant/concubine to an alien warlord but is actually a substance made from discarded skin cells and sebaceous fluid—can accumulate under the foreskin, unless you're in bed with that kid from gym class who never takes a shower you should be fine.

Fun Fact: The term "smegma" comes from the Greek word for "soap"! Sexy!

Will it make sex better? Maybe. But you'll be using a condom (won't you, young lady?), so it won't matter anyway.

I woke that morning to the light touch of a hand on my forehead. Berthold, fully dressed, was sitting on the edge of the bed. He told me he had to go out to work now, but I was welcome to stay as long as I liked. I nodded and pretended to go back to sleep, but as soon as I heard the front door click behind him, I sprang out of bed as if it were on fire, throwing on my clothes and beginning the tidying process. I always liked to straighten things up after a one-night stand, to fold blankets, fluff pillows, to stack, to smooth, to sweep, to leave the campsite better than how I found it. I supposed it would be a fairly simple matter for analysis—a need to be nice after being naughty, to bring physical order to emotional chaos, to play the dutiful girlfriend before sneaking out the back door sweaty and still half-drunk and having to figure out what fucking part of Queens I was stranded in this time—but the main reason was that it gave me an excuse to snoop around the apartment, gleaning information about its occupant that I may have failed to collect the night before. While I was emptying the ashtrays and folding the jeans, I could check out the titles on the bookshelf, glean a last name and address from a stack of unopened mail. Dropping off the wad of semen-streaked T-shirts in the bathroom hamper made it easy to have a look in the medicine cabinet to see if there was anything I should know about (Valtrex, Risperdal, methadone) or anything I should steal (Valium, Percocet, Adderall). After I had a quick shower and a good look around, admiring the high ceilings, the parquet floors, and the beautiful view of the Secession hall from the picture window, I gathered up the contents of my purse (which I had dumped out on the floor, searching for a cigarette lighter), retrieved the rumpled condom packets from their perch atop *The Collected Works of Joseph Beuys*, and generally made the place presentable.

Berthold was a nice guy, I reflected on my walk back to the Kummer, a really nice guy, and I could hardly wait to turn this into a good story, to tell all my friends at home about the middle-aged Austrian photographer who had seduced me. My escapades never really felt real until I had told someone about them. I needed other people to prove to myself that I existed. I knew this wasn't healthy, but it also wasn't healthy to spend an entire year as a poop-hat-wearing slave to a narcissistic megalomaniac. It wasn't healthy to eat sausage every night at four in the morning in the company of possible neo-Nazis. It wasn't healthy to be constantly running away from things, people, places. We're born sick, and life is the impossible struggle to get well.

I was hiding in my hotel room, eating mustard out of the tube and watching the making of Beyoncé's "Crazy in Love" video on German MTV, when the phone rang.

"*Fräulein*, this is *Herr* Winkler at the front desk. I have a telephone call for you, may I put it through?"

"Sure," I said in surprise, a daub of mustard-colored spit falling out of my mouth and settling itself on my chin.

"Rachel? This is Berthold."

I spit out the rest of the mustard. "Oh . . . hi. *Hi*. Um . . . how are you?"

He paused for a moment before he continued. "You left with such speed this morning. I had hoped you would still be there when I am returned. I am only away for a couple of hours."

"Oh," I said, lamely. "I just had a few things I had to do. E-mails . . . you know."

"Yes," he said. "I also." He paused again. "I am telephoning to tell you—I have found on the floor your passport."

"Oh," I said. "Shit."

"I am thinking you will maybe need this back?"

"Yeah," I said. "I guess I do."

"Rachel," Berthold said urgently. "If you do not wish to see me, then this is how it will be. But I have your passport. And I like you very much. Of all the girls I have made sex with, you are the only one who makes back the bed. I like this. It is an American custom?"

"No," I said. "It's something I picked up in the army."

There was a quizzical silence on the other end. "You are joking," he said finally.

"Yes. Stupidly."

"It is interesting, the way you are always making the jokes. Why do you think that is?"

"Well," I said darkly, "if you get me on your couch again maybe we can figure it out."

He chuckled. "Then I guess I must make it last one hour."

"Fifty minutes is fine," I said. "You'll need the last ten for notes, before your next patient."

We made plans for a late dinner.

Four

THE SECOND DISTRICT

I was sitting alone in a café outside the theater one afternoon, trying to squeeze in a last coffee before reporting for duty, when I overheard a conversation between a couple of American tourists at the next table.

"You know," said the man, a bluff fellow in a beige polo shirt with the name of a construction company embroidered over his left nipple, "ever since we've been here, I just keep noticing how everyone looks just like us! I mean, damn, it's like a Hauser family reunion or something. Goddammit, Cathy, it's like a whole country full of Hausers!" He rested both his hands on the swell of his gut and chortled, delighted with himself.

His wife looked thoughtful as she fanned her plump neck with a beer mat. "Mmmm. I've noticed that too. It was the same thing when we were in Germany . . . maybe even more so. We are a German family, after all."

"Everywhere I go," said the man, "people immediately speak to me in German. Like I'm a native."

"I know it isn't, I don't know, *politically correct* to say so," said the woman, "but there really is something to the blond hair and blue eyes. Like, it really is a genetic trait, like a *race*, you know? Not that there's anything wrong with being a different race"—she lowered her voice and glanced furtively around, as I expect she did back in Tucson whenever she said the word "Mexican" in public—"but dammit, I'm proud. These are our people, Dwight. This is *what we are.*"

Suddenly, I remembered the day in the seventh grade when my friend Amy Finnegan sat down next to me at the lab table we shared in biology and announced she didn't like me anymore.

"Why?" I gasped. The abrupt withdrawal of friendship was woefully common among girls in junior high, but until that moment, I had never imagined it would happen to me. I took great care not to do anything that might cause offense. I no longer volunteered answers in class or mentioned my inclusion in the Gifted and Talented Program; I had learned not to talk about anything I found interesting, such as Douglas Sirk, the British peerage, or rare genetic diseases; and, while Amy often treated me with blithe cruelty, happily informing me that my jeans were too tight or my hair looked dirty, she was still my best friend. The kind of best friend who would prank call your house or start a whisper campaign about you masturbating with a tampon in the locker room, but a best friend nonetheless.

"Why?" I asked again, plaintively. "What did I do?"

Amy took a small hairbrush from her purse and began to scrape her thick blond hair into a ponytail, fastening it with the checked blue scrunchie that dangled from her wrist. "It's not what you did, it's what you *are.*" She drew from her backpack a library book with a cracked plastic cover and pointed at the title. *The Great Irish Potato Famine: 1845–1849.*

"I've been reading this book for my social studies project," Amy continued, "and I'm feeling pretty Irish. And you're English, which pretty much makes us enemies forever. You wouldn't believe some of the horrible things the English did to the Irish. They threw them out of their houses and let them starve to death, and they put them in these ships called 'coffin ships' that were supposed to go to America or whatever, but the ships sank on purpose and everybody drowned. Thousands, maybe millions of Irish died horrible, horrible deaths"—she had slipped her hair out of its ponytail and was brushing it again, the constant preening of a plain girl convincing others she was pretty—"all because of English people like you."

Let me explain about the English thing.

At the tiny private elementary school I had attended before starting junior high that year, it was simple: We were all Jewish. No one ever wondered why you only ate Hydrox cookies and never Oreos, or why you took so much allergy medication, or why you had hair like a black person even though you were white. The answers were obvious, plain as the beaky nose on your sallow little face. Now, in the glamorous world of Gentiles, where I had met twelve-year-olds who were taller than any adult member of my extended family and the only people who had hair like black people were actually black, the gene pool had radically increased, and it was something of a fad for my classmates to compare their ethnic origins as a means of sizing each other up.

"I'm Polish, German, Irish, and one-sixteenth Lakota Sioux Indian," Nicole Detweiller would announce proudly, crossing her arms over her training bra in a stony imitation of Sitting Bull.

"Well, my mom is Swedish, Norwegian, and Czech," Megan Jankovic would reply, "but my dad is full-blooded Serbian."

"No way, you're Serbian?" exclaimed Jason McElroy. "So am I! Also Scottish, Irish, English, Danish, Greek, Polish, Lithuanian, and Irish."

"You already said Irish," I would point out.

"Yeah, 'cause I'm super fucking Irish," Jason would say. "As soon as I turn eighteen, I'm going to get this rad tattoo across my back of a leprechaun, only instead of a shamrock, he's going to be holding this giant bud leaf, and instead of a person face, he's going to have a dragon head. It's going to be pretty fuckin' sweet."

"They're always after me Lucky Charms!" Nicole Detweiller cried out in a grotesque Irish brogue, and I laughed along with the others, although Lucky Charms would never be found in my house in a million years. My mother's creative but unyielding interpretation of the laws of kashrut was basically organized around Lenny Bruce's Jewish/*goyische* dialectic, and along with mayonnaise, ranch dressing, Pop-Tarts, Velveeta, fudge, and Mountain Dew, the paranoid leprechaun and his delicious marshmallow rainbow fell squarely in the forbidden category.

"That's so funny," I said, just to make sure the Gentiles knew I was in on the joke. "That's hilarious." Then I sang the entire jingle, with full vibrato.

"Wow." Nicole Detweiller wrinkled the nonexistent bridge of her tiny nose as if I had just slurped down a juice box of my own urine. "I guess you really like Lucky Charms."

"Yeah," I said. "It's pretty much all I eat. That and Pop-Tarts. And cheese from a can. And um . . . ham and pork chops and pigs' feet and lobsters and, like, pheasants and stuff."

"Does your dad hunt?" asked Jason McElroy.

Hunt? The only thing anyone in my family had ever hunted for was a suit that came with two pairs of pants.

"Oh yeah," I said. "All the time. He's killed, like, a ton of wild animals who were just minding their own business not hurting anyone. He shoots them with his guns."

Jason raised his eyebrows. "That's pretty sweet. Does he have a lot of guns?"

"Oh my God," I said. "So many. Our house is, like, full of guns."

This statement, I told myself, was absolutely true, if by "guns" you meant "different-colored satin yarmulkes with the dates of people's Bar Mitzvahs stamped on the inside."

"So, what are you?" Nicole Detweiller asked me.

"Yeah," Megan Jankovic chimed in. "What are you? If Jason and me are Serbian, and Nicole is Polish, German, Irish, and one-sixteenth Indian, what are you?"

"Jewish," I muttered, looking down at my desk.

"You're Jewish?" Jason asked, his blank peasant eyes blinking with confusion. "Yeah, I guess I can see that. I mean, you have brown hair."

Nicole was getting impatient. "But what *are* you?"

"Jewish," my mother said, when I went to her later for help.

I sighed hoarsely, as if I were being strangled. "But where were we from? Like, originally?"

"Israel," my mother said innocently.

"No!" Of all the things that pissed me off about my mother, this brand of willful misunderstanding was top of the list. "Like your mother, and Bubbe."

"My mother was born in Lithuania," my mother said, "and my father was from Latvia."

"Great!" Now we were getting somewhere. "We're Lithuanian and Latvian, like Chris Pupka's family. His sister Shannon won the Little Miss Baltic pageant they have down at the Polka Hall. She spun plates on her chin while playing 'I Want to Know What Love Is' on the accordion, and her mother made her a sequined unitard in the colors of the Lithuanian flag. Maybe next year I could enter! If I won, I'd get a crown and five hundred dollars worth of gift certificates to Arby's and become an emblem of Baltic heritage and pride for the entire state of Nebraska."

"If my parents were alive to hear you say that," said my mother, "they'd be spinning in their graves."

"If your parents were alive," I said, "they wouldn't have graves to spin in."

"Nobody likes a smart-ass," my mother replied. "If my parents hadn't left when they did they'd be lying in a mass grave in some forest in Belarus with the rest of my extended family, and not because they were *Lithuanian*."

"Maybe my talent for the pageant could be acting out that scene I like from *The Ten Commandments*," I said. "The one where the nurse reveals Moses' true identity. *Torn from the hem of a Levite's robe*," I intoned solemnly, holding up an imaginary wad of crumpled fabric, "*Moses' swaddling cloth*. I can do all the parts. And that way I'd be honoring both heritages equally."

"The dead Jews are turning," my mother chanted, "spinning in that frozen pit. Murdered cousins, uncles, aunts. *THE EARTH SHAKES WITH THEIR SHAME!*"

The rest of my family responded similarly to this line of questioning. My father gaped at me with open horror as though I'd just asked him to measure me for a diaphragm. My grandmother, when I asked if her family was from Poland or Russia, looked blank until inspiration struck and she exclaimed, "Prussia!" which, obviously, is in Germany, and suggested that if I was so interested in dredging up the painful past, we should pay a visit to Bubbe, my senile ninety-seven-year-old great-grandmother, who was currently awaiting the comforting hand of death in the Rose Blumkin Home for the Jewish Aged. Bubbe responded to my questions about the land of her birth with a spittle-flecked "*feh*" and instructed me to change the hand towels, as the ones currently hanging on the rack in the bathroom were smeared with human shit. I hoped at least it was hers.

"Poor Bubbe," my grandmother said sadly, as we deposited the offending towels in a biohazard waste bag. In the other room Bubbe hissed racial epithets in Yiddish at a rerun of *The Cosby Show*. "When she was young, she was a great beauty. She and your great-grandpa Max made such a handsome couple. God, he was a doll! With that English accent? Believe me, all the girls were after him."

"Wait," I said. "Your father had an English accent?"

"Well, sure!" my grandmother said. "He lived in England from the time he was a little boy, and came to America as a young man already. Oh, he was a dream. That accent! That beautiful English accent, just like a movie star." She looked down at her hands. "Dammit. I got some of Bubbe's poop on my tennis bracelet. Where the hell is that nurse?"

And that, to make a short story long, is how I became an ancestral subject of Her Majesty. From then on, whenever I was asked, I would tell all the eager little Christians in my study hall that "my mother's family is from various places in Eastern Europe, and on my dad's side we're mostly English." And now, in the merciless hands of Amy Finnegan, it had come back to bite me in the ass.

"I'm not really English," I said. My mouth was dry.

"You're a liar." Amy gave her hair a final flip. "We can still be best friends, I guess. But you better be really nice to me, since the Irish suffered so horribly at your hands. I don't think any group of people in the world has suffered as much as the Irish."

I muttered, "I can think of one."

It wasn't solely the naïve ancestor worship of Dwight and his lovely wife Cathy that day in Vienna that had brought the question of identity to the forefront of my mind. A millennium of religious war, political and military nationalism, cultural jingoism, imperialism, and straight-up genocide had turned Europe into a continent of amateur ethnographers. Americans, with our soupy accents and mismatched, made-up names, provided a rare opportunity for them to try to pick out a distinct type from our muddled faces, from the melting pot turned flesh. For people like my countrymen at the next table, this tendency was a fascinating affirmation of a shared heritage and common genetic destiny. For people like me, who traditionally had something to hide, it was deeply, deeply creepy.

In the space of just a few weeks, I had become something of an expert at deflecting this line of questioning.

"Shukert. What kind of a name is that?"

"A last name," I would reply.

"Rachel," another person would say. "Why would your parents give such a name as Rachel?"

"Biblical names were very popular in America in the 1980s," I answered. "There are a lot of Sarahs and Rebeccas too."

"You have a look almost of the East," a sharp-faced woman in a bar hissed softly. Her accent made it sound almost romantic—the *s* in "East" softly sibilant, like a sudden whisper of wind ruffling the robes of a desert caravan. "You are not a Nordic type at all. There is something almost . . . Asiatic about you."

I shrugged insouciantly. "The Mongols raped a lot of people. If you'll excuse me, I've got yaks to milk." And so on. I deflected, drew away from, and danced around it, using the traditional weaponry of my people—irony, intellect, an overdeveloped sense of danger. But one night as I went across the street from the Kummer to get my customary beer and *Käsekrainer*, I let my guard down.

We were coming to the end of our stay in Vienna, and over the past weeks, I had developed a kind of grudging fondness for the monosyllabic, grease-spattered sausage man. I was the only customer that night (the skinheads presumably still working up an appetite defacing Holocaust memorials and harassing Turkish dry cleaners) and when he began to speak to me in a very passable English, I was delighted. We talked about many things—my impressions of Vienna, my play, my country.

"I just love the people in New York," I enthused. "People from all over the world, speaking all different languages, living side by side."

"You find this is a good thing?" the sausage man said. "This mixing of peoples?"

"Of course," I said. "It's what America is all about."

"And this war your president has now started in Iraq," the sausage man said. "You think this is a good thing too?"

"No!" I cried. "Of course not! But Bush is not America. He didn't even really win the election. You'll see. He'll be out of there in no time." I took a sip of my beer. "But what you really should have seen was how . . . well, you know, 9/11?" The man nodded, with marked impatience. "You should have seen the way the entire city—the entire country, really—just kind of pulled together. People would just come up to you on the streets and, like, hug you. I know things are kind of fucked up now, but I just can't help but feel like maybe that's *it*. That's the future, you know?"

"And you?" said the man. "What is your background?"

I downed the rest of my beer. "What do you think my background is?" I asked.

He shrugged. "I don't want to insult you."

I let that pass. "Well," I lied haughtily, "some of my family is actually from Austria. Some of them may have even lived in Vienna at one point."

He snorted. "In the Second District, maybe. But not anymore." The man began to laugh.

"Why?" I asked, laughing along. "What's the Second District?"

Still laughing, he gave me a look that chilled my blood. "The Jewish district."

Snappy Comebacks to Loaded Questions

Loaded questions: They're not just for anti-Semites anymore! Just being an American abroad means you may be subjected to all kinds of prejudicial inquiry about the inner workings of our great nation. Sure, you're going to tell everyone at home all about how much better things are in Europe, but that doesn't mean you can't stand up for yourself and your country while you're there.

They ask: Why are Americans so fat?

What they want you to say: Because we're big greedy pigs obsessed with gobbling up more than our fair share of all the world's resources.

What you'll probably say: Well, there are a lot of factors, like our fast food culture and the breakdown of family meals, and the fact that so few American cities are pedestrian friendly, and poverty has a lot to do with it too . . . (trail off embarrassedly, wondering if they're actually talking about you).

What you should say: They aren't fat. They are world-class athletes who are part of a top-secret program by the government to at last seize international sumo wrestling supremacy from Japan.

They ask: Are Americans religious because they are stupid, or just ignorant?

What they want you to say: Both! How did you know?

What you'll probably say: Well, Americans have always had a deeply Puritanical streak bequeathed to us by our founders, although the methodical stirring up of cultural resentment for political purposes began in earnest on a mass level during the Reagan administration . . . (*yawn*).

What you should say: Americans aren't religious. They're just saying that to avoid sex with you.

They ask: Why do Americans cruelly refuse to provide public health care for all?

What they want you to say: Because Americans are terrible, venal people with no regard for human life.

What you'll probably say: Because our deeply dehumanizing free-market culture worships profit before all and because many of the authors of legislation designed to correct this are wholly owned subsidiaries of the private insurance industry.

What you should say: Because we're following through with the eugenics program you guys were too chickenshit to finish.

They ask: Do you not find that America is a very racist society?

What they want you to say: Yes. Unlike the traditional haven of tolerance that is Central Europe, America is full of hatred and every day I weep with shame.

What you'll probably say: Well, the legacy of slavery is certainly damaging, and there remains a certain amount of institutional racism, but class remains the true divider in American society.

What you should say: Talk to me when you've got your own black president.

Berthold and I had been seeing each other fairly regularly over the past weeks. While I had sex with him just one more time, mostly out of politeness (to my pleasant surprise, he finished in time for me to get back to my hotel room to watch *Cheers* dubbed into Turkish), I still enjoyed his company. He was solicitous and fatherly, making sure I ate and bringing me little gifts—old sepia-toned postcards, a toy elephant made from wooden beads and elastic string—and when he wasn't working, he took me to art museums where he provided me with a running commentary on the lives of the great Austrian painters.

"First, he burns all his papers and nearly all of his paintings,"

Berthold murmured in my ear as we stood in front of one of Richard Gerstl's hazy landscapes, viscous daubs of green and gray melting into a mountainside made blurry with despair. "Then he hangs himself in front of the mirror in his studio. And while he stares at himself dying, with his last strength, he takes up his knife and he stabs himself, deep in his heart." To make sure I had understood, Berthold mimed the wretched last moments of Richard Gerstl with great relish, popping out his eyes and palpating his tongue as he jerked his imaginary blade violently over his chest. "This is an artist. Not like Schiele, a little boy with his sad prostitutes. Schiele dies of a cold. Pfah."

Later, we might go for a walk in the Prater, the large park on the outskirts of the city, which was where all the most fashionable perverts of the nineteenth century used to lurk behind the chestnut trees, looking for unsuspecting ladies' maids from the provinces to whom they could expose themselves. Berthold would buy me a balloon or an ice cream cone, and to further complete my infantilization, we would pause in a café, where I would gleefully order a babyish beverage like a chocolate milk or an Almdudler, a sort of Austrian soda pop given to nursery school children that tasted like apple juice mixed with ginger ale. Berthold would reach across the table and pat my hand distractedly while he futzed around with his lighter and his tobacco and his gin and tonic. I looked young for my age, and with the way he smoked and drank, he looked old for his, and I imagined that the people who smiled at us as they walked past took us for a father and daughter. An estranged pair, perhaps, an irresponsible daddy startled to realize that his little girl has somehow transformed into the grown woman sitting before him, nearly as old as the women he brings back to his loft from parties and gallery openings, our halting conversation not born from a language divide but from the bittersweet effort of getting to know each other again.

I suspected Berthold knew I was, shall we say, not of the Master Race, but he never brought it up, just as I never brought up just who his father might have been arresting when he began his career in law enforcement in the very early '40s. It didn't seem fair to force someone to confront their family's Nazi past until you'd been dating for at least six weeks, and as I did hear him openly express disgust for Jorg Haider, the leader of the ultra right-wing Austrian Freedom Party (and alleged Nazi sympathizer), on at least two occasions, I figured that was good enough. Still, I was relieved when I told him about the incident with the sausage man and he seemed genuinely appalled. "Some people in Vienna," he muttered with disgust. "Some people . . ."

We were having our coffee in the Naschmarkt, the labyrinthine, never-ending souk of cafés and food stalls where the Viennese buy dried apricots, spices, coffee, fruit, and other comestibles. I loved it most for its name, quite literally "Nosh Market." I liked to wander through and imagine that my grandparents, two of the most committed noshers the world has ever known, were there in the stalls, their dentures expelling a frothy blizzard of half-chewed pistachio and sugared prune as they harangued the vendors about where they got their chicken from, a limping, screaming testament to the triumphant survival of the Jewish people. Take that, Hitler.

"This man," Berthold was shaking his head angrily. "This man has no right to say this to you."

"Whatever," I said. "I mean, I know he didn't mean it as a compliment, but really, all he said is that I look Jewish."

"No." Berthold placed his hand over mine and gazed deeply into my eyes. "No. You are beautiful."

It's possible to be beautiful *and* Jewish, I wanted to say.

"You do not seem Jewish," Berthold continued. "Please not to worry. Some people in Vienna are still full of hate."

• • •

On Sunday mornings there was a huge flea market in the empty field just past the Naschmarkt. It was known as the biggest and best in all of Central Europe. I had begged Berthold (a compulsive collector of late 1960s suburban housewares) to go with me, but at first he refused, having recently spent close to four hundred euros on a set of Naugahyde ice-cube trays with a coordinating bucket and sworn off the flea market for good. But since it was my last day in Vienna and our last afternoon together (I had a dinner with the cast and crew that night), he agreed to make an exception, provided I held his wallet and didn't let him out of my sight.

Not that it did any good. The minute we arrived at the flea market, Berthold immediately jerked his arm from mine, running to a table laden with mid-century Tupperware like a starving man to the Sizzler buffet, the wad of bills he had secreted in his cigarette pack already in his hand. I didn't call after him. If he needed a mustard-yellow salad spinner that badly, who was I to tell him no? After all, I had dreams of my own.

It was another beautiful day. Spread before me as far as the eye could see, the detritus of Europe glittered, a vast museum of the unexceptional: faded biscuit tins and bits of old glass, picture frames and atomizers and eyeless dolls with matted hair and parted lips. The sun hid the chips and scratches with dancing spots of light, lending the stacks of painted china and the rows of dusty old clocks an eager new sheen, like bedraggled puppies putting on a valiant show for prospective parents at the pound.

I have a game I play at flea markets. I tell myself that somewhere in the vast array of abject crap is one perfect object, a talisman, a thing of essential rightness that has traveled through time and space to reach me. Some *thing* for which I have unknowingly searched my whole life, and if I can just be wise and patient and

worthy enough to find it, it will be the key to everything: to fulfill-
ment, to salvation, maybe even to immortality. To choose unwisely,
however, will lead to ruin and despair.

My game is a cross between that scene in *Indiana Jones and the
Last Crusade*, when the guy who played General Veers in *The Empire
Strikes Back* picks the wrong cup and his eyeballs explode, and a
really good sale at Bloomingdale's.

"Is it you?" I palpated my hand over a crystal paperweight
embedded with the gilded skull of a mouse, cooing like Miss Jane
Pittman to a newborn. "Are you the One?"

"This is a very rare antique from France," said the bearded man
behind the table. "The cost is three hundred forty-five euros."

I snatched my hand away.

It seemed most of the items for sale in the inner stalls were out
of my price range, but the outermost edge of the market was lined
with makeshift stands bearing merchandise of a decidedly less rar-
efied nature: broken toys, scraps of greasy clothing hanging haphazardly against a length of wire fence. I went to investigate, and a
large man carrying a stack of cardboard boxes brushed roughly past
me, nearly knocking me to the ground. I grabbed the edge of the
nearest table for balance, and suddenly I saw it.

It was at the bottom of a half-empty carton, tucked carelessly
inside a creased plastic sleeve like an old comic book. The cloth
was badly discolored, and its frayed edges had started to fold up on
themselves, but there was no mistaking it for what it was. A yellow
Star of David bearing a single word in faded black: *Jude*.

When I was a very small child, long before I had heard the words
"panic attack," I used to tell my mother that my "tummy was beating." I'm not sure she ever knew what I meant, but to me it seemed
the best way to describe the terrible feeling of descent, of dread,
as though I had mistakenly swallowed my pulsating heart. Now, I

actually thought my heart might force its way out of my body and land on the grass with a bloody squelch. A memory flashed through my mind of a recurring dream from my early childhood. My father and I were in the desert, prisoners on a forced march led by cruel men. The men wore turbans and belts of ammunition slung across their chests. When I faltered, sick and hungry, the leader of the men seized me by the neck and told my father he was going to kill me. After I was dead, he said, he and his henchmen planned to cut out my heart, tattoo it with a decorative design, and sell it in the marketplace. In the dream he had gestured toward a wagon, where dozens of other human hearts bearing inked drawings of eagles, dragons, and arrows were being sold by a couple of handsome blond boys wearing footie pajamas printed with airplanes (I was four). Every time I had the nightmare I woke up screaming, and my mother, wanting to comfort me, would ask me to tell her about the dream. I never did. To speak it aloud seemed to make it real. Besides, even then I knew how uniquely disturbing the images were, and I didn't want her to think I was crazy.

The woman behind the card table pounced. Nattering aggressively in an unfamiliar language, she seized the star from the carton and pressed it hard into my palm. The plastic sleeve fell open, and I could feel the coarse cloth against my skin.

"No," I cried reflexively, and yanked my hand away, knocking a small metal vase and a ceramic ashtray to the ground. The woman began to scream at me, waving the plastic-covered star in my face in an accusatory salute. Suddenly, I heard a man's voice behind me, shouting angrily in German. Berthold had come to my rescue.

"Where have you been?" I whispered frantically, as he and the woman exchanged heated words. The woman changed her tone and held up the star cajolingly, gesturing toward me. Berthold grabbed my elbow and jerked me away, an act made somewhat less masculine by the fact that he was carrying a shopping bag full of table linens and an enormous lamp shaped like an elephant.

"That woman . . ." I stammered.

He sniffed. "That woman was a Gypsy. Who knows how she gets what she is selling."

"But the star . . ."

"You don't want that," he said.

"But I do," I said softly. "It was there for me to find."

"Forget about it!" he shouted. "It's not nice! It's not something to buy!"

The harshness of his voice seemed to startle us both, because he immediately plastered his face with an artificial smile. "I have bought some wonderful books, books from when I was a child. Come! We'll have lunch and I'll show you."

"I'm not hungry," I said.

We said our good-byes later that afternoon, when he dropped me off at my hotel, kissing me on the forehead like a child. I promised to keep in touch, but I knew I wouldn't—we both knew.

"Will this be *Fräulein's* final meeting with the older gentleman?" *Herr* Winkler inquired when I asked for the key to my room.

"I'm afraid so," I said. "I'll think of him fondly, but I am sure I will never speak to him again."

"Perhaps that is as it should be," said the Fonz. "After all, *Fräulein* must have so many other clients who require her attention."

I smiled my sweetest smile. "*Herr* Winkler," I said, "you are a real fucking prick."

Dinner that evening was a festive occasion. Everyone dressed up, and our director had arranged for lots of wine. I hadn't spent much time with the company socially since getting involved with Berthold, and I was surprised at the relief I felt being with this smiling group of loud Americans, laughing and joking and ridiculing the country whose virtues they had piously extolled while sober.

"Can you not just get a fucking cup of coffee without it being a whole fucking production?" Connor howled. "These people invented psychoanalysis, can the concept of a fucking to-go cup be that difficult to comprehend?"

"Bullshit. These people didn't invent psychoanalysis," hooted Kevin, my coreligionist stage manager. "They got rid of the people who invented psychoanalysis. What did the Austrians ever invent? Yodeling?"

"Ski jumping?" offered Caroline, an actress.

"Sausage-making!" cried Connor gleefully.

"Facism!" I yelled.

"Oh, *nein, Fräulein*," Kevin answered in a high-pitched voice nearly identical to the supercilious Winkler. "You are confusing us perhaps vit zee Germans. Ve Austrians are nothing like zee Germans. Ve love music and opera and ve are far, far more anti-Semitic."

The table roared with laughter. More wine was brought to us. We had gone through several bottles when the director finally arrived, giggling to himself and brandishing a slim green booklet with unbridled glee.

"Look!" he exclaimed, rushing to his seat at the head of the table. He thrust the booklet in the face of Kevin, who was nearest. It was a passport. Stamped under the photograph, undiminished with age, was a huge, black, official-looking swastika.

"Well," Kevin deadpanned. "That's a Nazi passport all right."

"Pass it around!" cried the director.

We obeyed, murmuring appreciatively, fingering the swastika with admiration.

"I went to the flea market today," the director said, "and there was a man selling all kinds of old papers—magazines, periodicals, things like that—and he had this entire box of passports. All from the war, and all stamped just like this. An entire box of Nazi passports! Naturally, I wanted to take all of them"—this in the wistful tone of someone who has just visited a Third World orphanage—"but I finally chose this one because the bearer"—he snatched the passport out of Connor's hands and pointed to the small photograph in the corner—"just looked so perfectly Aryan." He sighed happily. "It's the greatest object I've ever owned."

Our entrées arrived, and we dug in, trying to soak up some of the booze before the first-round hangovers set in. Our director bounced around the table, seemingly too excited to eat. I was drunkenly negotiating the bones from my trout when I felt him standing close beside me. I lunged for my wine.

"So? What do you think of my Nazi passport?" he asked me.

I thought of the thing that I had seen in the market today, and how strangely ashamed I felt now. Compared to his gleeful brandishment of his evil relic, my reaction seemed so sentimental, so histrionic, like a weeping fifteen-year-old girl, hysterical over the rejection of some boy she won't remember in six months. I had been that hysterical girl, more times than I cared to recall. There's that line in *The Breakfast Club* about how when you grow up, your heart dies. Fucking right, and thank God it does. How else could we bear to put one foot in front of the other on this narrow road called Life, forever slouching toward the unimaginable oblivion, accompanied by and large by total shitheads? The most we can ask for is to be able to gaze out at the abyss and laugh. "I'm not impressed," I said.

"Oh no?"

"No," I said. "You should have held out for a yellow Star of David. Now *that* would have been something to list on your customs form."

He stared at me appraisingly for a long moment, and then he laughed. A strange, mirthless bark of a laugh, but a laugh nonetheless. "Well," he said. "I guess you told me. I'd better go eat my lamb chop before it gets cold."

I said, "There's nothing in the world worse than cold lamb."

Five

WHAT ARE YOU, SOME KIND OF REFUGEE?

Zurich. I am sure there are many fascinating and unique things about Zurich; unfortunately, they are things that I proved too stupid, lazy, and oblivious to notice.

Instead, I will tell you a Swiss joke. It is the only Swiss joke I know. It is very probable that it is the only Swiss joke that exists. This joke was told to me by an unsmiling mortgage broker in the only country-and-western bar in Zurich. I had plunked a few Swiss francs in the jukebox, planning to get drunk listening to Conway Twitty and think about my feelings, when the mortgage broker approached me. The reason I knew he was a mortgage broker was because he gave me his business card before he even sat down. Presumably, this was his preferred manner of introducing himself to young ladies, in order to ensure they didn't expect much in the way of conversation. I told him politely that I wasn't planning to negotiate a deal on any property at that time. He said he just wanted to chat.

"How are you finding Zurich?" he asked me.

"I'm finding it expensive," I said.

He looked grave. "You are not enjoying your holiday?"

"I'm not on holiday. I'm working."

"Ah!" He rubbed his hands together vigorously. "Already, we speak about your work!"

"Please," I said. "Let's not."

"Well, we must speak of something," he said. "Otherwise the project of our conversation will not find very much success." He unhinged his jaw like a boa constrictor and expelled a staccato rasp of pained laughter. From the jukebox, Conway Twitty was singing about taking my virginity, slowly and tenderly. Closing my eyes for a moment, I imagined the scratch of the warm-smelling hay, the plunk of Conway's turquoise-studded belt buckle on the truck bed as he dropped his pants and lowered his Stetson-for-Men-drenched body to mine. When I opened them again, the man was still there, his face bleary and eager. I didn't have the heart to brush him aside. "Why don't you tell me a joke?" I said.

He obliged. "A man dies and is sent to purgatory before the final judgment is made upon his soul. He stays in purgatory for a long time, wondering whether he will be sent to heaven or to hell. Finally, he says to one of the angels: 'Excuse me! Can you tell me what heaven is like?' The angel says: 'In heaven, the policemen are all British, the engineers are German, the administrators are Swiss, the cooks are French, and the lovers are Italian.' The dead man asks: 'Then what is hell like?' The angel says: 'In hell, the policemen are German, the engineers are French, the administrators are Italian, the cooks are British, and the lovers are Swiss.'"

When the joke had finished, he asked me if I would like to go to his apartment to make sex with him. I declined.

"I have money," he said.

"Oh no," I said. "No, no, no, no. There's been some kind of misunderstanding." Misunderstanding, my ass. If only Conway Twitty were here and not popping my dream cherry on the side of the highway about ten miles down from Huntsville, he'd be pulling his belt out of his pants and getting ready to teach somebody's neutral behind a good old American lesson right about now.

The man held up his hands in apology. "I am sorry," he said. "You are alone at the bar, naturally I just assumed . . ."

"I'm not a prostitute," I replied tersely. "I'm just a borderline alcoholic."

The Swiss: Europe's Perverts?

A CRITICAL ESSAY

> "He was shy, a little withdrawn, but not real bizarre.
> Kept to himself, he never bothered anyone."

Does this sound familiar? It's how a next-door neighbor described Jeffrey Dahmer after his convictions on multiple counts of murder and cannibalism.

Make a couple of minor changes to the pronouns, and it sounds like she could have been talking about Switzerland.

What do we *really* know about the Swiss?

They are secretive, with their high-tech bank vaults and finicky extradition laws. They are meticulous, bringing to their manufactured projects an attention to detail that would not be unfamiliar to someone who might spend years obsessing over a certain make of shoe buckle or amassing antique leg irons for the perfect replica medieval dungeon concealed behind the wall unit in his basement.

German-speaking peoples are without equal in the generation of sexual deviants: In Germany one finds people who like to wear bags of pee around their necks and the cannibal who trolled the Internet, looking for willing victims. The Austrians are also no slouches in the pervert department, giving the world Josef Fritzl (the guy who kept his daughter in the dungeon for twenty-four years) and Adolf Hitler. But the Swiss may be a special case. They are what ethnographers and racists call a "blended" people, combining the Gothic creepiness of the Germans with the lusty self-indulgence of the Italians, the sexual inventiveness of the French with the superior goat-rearing skills of the Romansh. They haven't had any wars or other upheavals to occupy their time or energy for five hundred years, and as I have mentioned before, the country's unflinching commitment to perfect neutrality indicates a moral compass that is curious at best. One can only imagine what they might get up to over there.

Luckily, you don't have to, because I've already imagined it for you! For example:

- **The Exploding Fondue:** A group of men participate in a circle jerk, ejaculating into an orange Le Creuset enamelware fondue pot. This continues until the pot is full, at which time they take turns dipping their respective penises into the pot and allowing their comrades to lick off the semen. For best results, this maneuver should be performed only in the year 1974.
- **The Swiss Miss:** A man spreads on each testicle a light coating of marshmallow, followed by a dusting of cocoa powder. He then dandles his garnished scrotum over the open mouth of his partner, leaving him/her with a sweet cocoa mustache reminiscent of childhood.
- **The Geneva Convention:** Before intimacy commences, all partners mutually agree on safe words, equipment, and physical, emotional, and moral boundaries; they then proceed to ignore them completely for the duration of sexual contact.
- **The Vanilla Zellweger*** (BDSM only): The dominant partner scrunches

---

* According to Wikipedia, Academy Award–winner Renée Zellweger is of Swiss heritage.

face in adorable pucker and speaks in baby voice until submissive partner runs screaming from the room in agony.

- **The Chocolate Zellweger:** Same as above, except scrunching/baby talk is performed by submissive partner through dominant partner's asshole.

Interactive Activity: Invent Your Own Swiss-Themed Sex Acts!

Here are some ideas to get you started:

The Flaming Cuckoo

The Hungry Heidi

The Roger Federer

The Yodeler's Surprise

The Angry Watchmaker

The Dada Gangbang

Kraft Korner!

MAKE YOUR OWN SWISS ARMY BALL GAG!

Step 1: Get a ball gag. These can be easily obtained in specialty shops or on the Internet. Before you buy, make sure it fits properly: the ball gag should be large enough to make speech impossible, but not so big as to suffocate you. Minor discomfort is optimum.

Step 2: Paint the ball of the gag red, using as many coats as are necessary for a vivid, even tone. Let dry.

Step 3: When the background is dry, decorate the center of the ball with a square white cross, as seen on the Swiss flag. You can use white paint, white paint pen, or even white-out. For best results, make sure you place the cross on the outward facing side, or the acids in your saliva will eventually render it illegible.

Step 4: Enjoy with someone special!

• • •

Life as we know it is a series of random circumstances. From the very beginning, the odds of the universe are so stacked against any of us even being born. What if your grandmother had died in childhood? What if your father had never met your mother? What if your mom hadn't lied about being on the Pill? What if your dad hadn't pretended to be allergic to latex? And once the genetic signature of your unsheathed father was hurtling down the meaty corridors of your mendaciously contracepted mother, what are the chances of that particular sperm colliding with that particular egg to eventually become the current incarnation of you? Everyone on Earth today could easily have been an entirely different person. We each could be much worse off than we are, or maddeningly, we could have turned out much, much better.

I don't want to waste too much time on this idea, which is obviously familiar to anyone with even a glancing knowledge of the human reproductive system or the joys of *Cannibis sativa*. But let me just say this: Once one has successfully managed to be born, one must *exist*, and existence is basically also a never-ending series of coincidences. Most of these amount to nothing and are quickly forgotten, missed opportunities we never even knew we had. But a very few change the course of our lives forever. It is about these coincidences that novels are written and movies are made. In them we see the hand of God, of karma, of fate. When we recount them to friends and lovers, we smile bemusedly, and say that these things were "meant to be," implying that some all-powerful force had bothered to formulate for each one of us a kind of existential itinerary designed to show us the best time possible during our stay on Earth, like a really omniscient travel agent. Angry male playwright David Mamet had a different idea; he once said that everyone gets the same number of breaks, but that the secret to success lies in being ready for them when they come. Mamet was talking about showbiz, but I think the idea applies to other things. What he failed to mention, however, was that these breaks might come in mysterious forms, only to be recognized for what they are in the hindsight of time.

Many years later, I can say with total certainty that meeting Mattijs van Kampen was one of the great breaks of my life.

Just before Halloween, only a week or so after we had started rehearsals, my friend Evelyn dragged me to a party in Brooklyn. I had plenty of reasons for not wanting to go—I was tired, I was broke, I was developing a urinary tract infection, there was a strange lump at the base of my skull that I felt certain was the outer edge of an advanced glioblastoma that would soon rob me of my speech and end my life—but Evelyn wasn't taking no for an answer.

"I know you're still depressed about breaking up with Sam," she said. "But you have to move on."

"I have to *move*," I said. "This place is like a museum to him. This kitchen is the kitchen where I made sushi for Sam on Valentine's Day. This futon is the futon where we had sex for the first time. This drain cleaner is the drain cleaner that Sam bought me for my birthday."

"He bought you drain cleaner for your birthday?"

"The drain was always clogged in my shower. He said it disgusted him." I sighed wistfully. "Now he won't even answer my phone calls."

"Yeah," Evelyn said, "but let's be honest. He didn't break up with you because he didn't *like* you or anything like that. He broke up with you because you cheated on him, and you were a terrible girlfriend. It's not like you were *rejected*. You gave him no choice."

I began to cry.

"Oh God," Evelyn said. "Not again."

"You're a lesbian," I sputtered, wiping my nose. "You're supposed to be sympathetic and wanting to talk about woman feelings all the *time*."

"I believe you have me mixed up with a gay man," Evelyn retorted. "Gay men are supposed to bring over ice cream and tell you how thin you look and show you where to get tested for STDs. Lesbians give tough love and tell you what to put in the cat's food to keep it from shedding."

"Wow," I said. "My mother is a lesbian."

"Cut the shit," said Evelyn. "Savannah's out of town and I want to have some fucking fun. I've got to work until about midnight, and then I'll swing by your place in Brooklyn and pick you up. You'll have fun. There will be guys there."

"Straight guys?"

"Straight guys. And gay girls. Maybe it's time to branch out," Evelyn said. "And by the way, that thing on your neck is a *lymph node*. Everybody has them. Stop thinking you're so damn special."

The party was a furtive, chaotic affair in the furthest reaches of industrial Brooklyn, held in a freezing warehouse that had once stored air-conditioning belts and greasy canisters of motor oil. Its former denizens—squat, powerful men with names like Ernest and Whitey who had never once weighed the merits of Brown's MFA program against Columbia's—were ghosts now, replaced by a crowd of self-impressed youngsters crammed together on the cracked concrete floor, suctioning cheap vodka from thin plastic straws and adjusting their summer scarves. At the back of the room was an assortment of musical detritus (a disassembled drum kit, a black stack of giant amplifiers) that had been commandeered by a group of young men in full clown makeup. Despite the autumn chill, several of the young clowns had taken off all their clothing, and stood naked and unashamed atop the speakers, pelting each other violently with handfuls of bingo markers, as the delighted crowd spurred them on.

"This was supposed to be a fund-raiser." Evelyn raised her voice against the noise. "I guess we missed the show."

Someone started up some loud music, and one of the clowns flung himself off the highest speaker, testicles flapping impressively with the velocity of his descent. His back met painfully with the cement, and I cheered with the rest when he jumped back up again and staggered over to the corner to vomit.

"I'm getting a drink," Evelyn shouted, and quickly disappeared into the crush around the makeshift bar. I was bobbing foolishly along to the music, surveying the crowd, when I felt a large hand close over my wrist and pull me toward the group of people dancing in the middle of the room. Too startled to resist, I was soon moving wildly in the very center of the floor. My mysterious partner was a blur; I glimpsed a shock of yellow hair, the colored sleeve of a shirt, but it wasn't until we staggered to the bar, sweaty and too tired to go on, that I got a good look at him. He was a tall, raw-boned man in his late twenties, dressed in a button-down shirt tucked haphazardly into a pair of snug corduroy pants. He was also completely shitfaced.

"What would you like to drink?" he said, pronouncing each syllable with elaborate care.

I asked for vodka on the rocks. He ordered the drinks and produced a large wad of bills, which he began to handle with puzzlement, as though they had been planted in his pocket by some mysterious benefactor; he struggled for a moment or two until I plucked a ten and two ones out of his hand and thrust them toward the impatient bartender.

"Thank you," said my new friend. "That was very nice."

I thought I detected an accent, but as we know, I've made that mistake before. "Where are you from?" I shouted.

He smiled. "I am from Amsterdam."

"Really?" I said.

"You know Amsterdam?"

"Yes," I said. "I spent a summer there when I was in college. Studying acting."

"At de Theaterschool van Amsterdam?"

"It was a big brick building, the Lindengracht. With those big doors, like a slaughterhouse."

The man nodded, smiling broadly. "It is the same! I also went to there! Now I am a theater director!"

His name was Mattijs, which is Dutch for Matthew. He was twenty-seven years old, had just finished his graduate degree, and was now spending several months in New York doing a few internships with some theater companies before returning to Holland to begin his career in earnest. I told him about the play I was in with the famous director and he was duly impressed.

"You've heard of him in Holland?" I asked.

"We know of many things," he said, "even though we are a small country. We are tiny, but we are brave. Did you know when the Germans invaded, our army had no planes. We had no tanks. We had not even very many guns."

"What did you have?" I asked.

"Bicycles," Mattijs said. "We are facing down the Germans with an army of bicycles. And when they have conquered us, the Germans have taken in revenge the bicycles from everybody. Now, when our national team is playing the Germans in the football, the Dutch fans will scream at them, 'Give us back our bicycles!'"

"Are you a sports fan?" I asked.

"No." He blinked, bewilderedly. "I am a theater director."

We exchanged phone numbers before I went home, and the next day, he left me three voice messages. Used to the malignant but tantalizing indifference of broke and questionably coiffed child-men in Williamsburg, I found his enthusiasm off-putting, but he continued to call me until I finally agreed to meet him for a drink one night after rehearsal. As I was still fragile post-breakup, I was a little bit anxious about our appointment, that is until Mattijs invited me to come to his apartment later and have dinner with him and his boyfriend, Jeroen, an aspiring filmmaker who was doing a yearlong film course at NYU, and it all made sense.

"Oh my God, of course!" I exclaimed. "I'll bring the ice cream."

I soon was a regular at Mattijs and Jeroen's Upper East Side apartment, which was populated by a rotating cast of international roommates: Carina the Dutch Actress, Mariska the Dutch Journalism Major, Hermann the German Plastic Surgeon, and Barbara the Prematurely Middle-Aged Canadian Bulimic. Mattijs and Jeroen loved to sing, and we would often make the rounds of New York's many piano bars, serenading each other until the wee hours of the morning. In between raucously melancholy performances of "And So It Goes" and "I Know Him So Well," Mattijs planned grand theatrical projects for us. "You will come to Holland, and I will make you a star!" he would proclaim and, flush with the rising euro, order another round for the house.

We were all stranded in New York over the holidays, so we spent them together at my place, along with Connor and BJ, who were also trapped. That was the Christmas when BJ, without telling me, put the extra chicken back in the oven, where it remained for two weeks until the methane buildup made it explode, imbuing my kitchen with a haunting odor of death that no amount of oven cleaner could assuage; but that night, as we marched through the silent streets of Greenpoint, singing Christmas carols in the fresh-fallen snow, the world seemed close to perfect. In May, when Jeroen completed his film course and he and Mattijs adjourned back to Amsterdam, I was filled with a sadness I couldn't quite name.

"I already miss you guys so much," I had said to Jeroen when he called to tell me they'd arrived safe and sound. "I feel like when my parents dropped me off at college for the first time. I just don't know what to do with myself."

"Oh, darling," Jeroen laughed. "We miss you too. If you get too lonely, you can always come to stay with us in Amsterdam."

Now, with the tour ending, I had no idea what was next for me. By virtue of my total lack of prospects stateside, I'd already decided I wasn't going home anytime soon. Some of the other cast members were planning to stay behind and travel around for a few weeks. I guessed I could do that. But I didn't relish the idea of being on my own (they hadn't invited me to travel with them), and with the exchange rate getting worse all the time, even a couple of weeks in the big capitals like Paris or Rome would completely erode the money I had managed to save. My weakening dollars would go further if I strayed off the beaten path, into the euro-free zones of the former Communist states, but I was dissuaded by a horrible vision of myself stranded in Moldova or such, begging my mother to wire a plane ticket to the American embassy while a mob of illiterate, Jew-hating peasants pelted me with cow manure and decaying potatoes. Wherever I went, I wanted it to be a place with dentists, widely available Diet Coke, and a native population that could keep its anti-Semitism contained at a genteel cocktail-party level. Besides, I wanted to find a place I could stay for a while, maybe get to know some people, and have a little bit of a life. I wanted people to be happy to see me. I wanted a place where, even for a little while, I could belong.

•　•　•

"Of course you can come!" Jeroen shouted when I finally managed to reach him from the pay phone in the train station. "We will be so excited to see you!"

"Really?" I squeaked, overcome with gratitude. "You don't mind that I'm just inviting myself to come and live with you for an unspecified period of time?"

"Sweetie, it's fab-oo-lous. You can stay as long as you like. Here, Mattijs wants also speak to you. He is coming to the telephone now."

"Darling!" Mattijs's cheerful voice came bubbling stridently over the extension. "How are you? Have you been good? Have you had many love affairs on your European vacation?"

"Actually, I have," I said proudly. "I participated in two acts of full sexual intercourse with an Austrian photographer old enough to be my father."

Mattijs chuckled. "Very good."

"I think his father might have worked with the Gestapo."

"Have you mentioned that to your mother yet?" he asked. Jeroen and Mattijs had met my mother when she came to New York for a visit one weekend, and she seemed to have made quite an impression.

"No," I said. "But I'm looking forward to it."

Jeroen said, "Wait until you get here. We want to listen on the extension."

We made plans. I would go and live with Mattijs and Jeroen in Amsterdam for an unspecified length of time, which was made possible (and even vaguely legal) by virtue of my unstamped passport. I would probably run out of money in about a month, even living rent-free, but the boys had a plan for that too: I would receive a weekly salary for performing in a play, a bilingual production of *Lunch*, by the British playwright Steven Berkoff, which they hoped to mount as the debut work of their newly formed theater company.

We would go into rehearsals as soon as the grant from the government came through.

"We haven't filed all the paperwork yet," said Mattijs, "but now that we know for sure you are coming we will download the proper forms and prepare them at once. I do not think it will be too difficult."

"You really think that'll happen?" I said.

"Of course!" Mattijs sounded indignant, as though I had asked him if he was a biological male, or if his apartment had a functioning toilet (full disclosure: I have learned the hard way that neither of these are things you should take for granted). "It is a good project. Why would they not?"

"I don't know," I said. "In the States, getting the government to give money for theater is like convincing your health insurance to pay for cosmetic anal bleaching. It could happen in theory, but the circumstances are almost impossible to imagine."

"*Ja*," said Jeroen, "but having your anus bleached costs only something like 40 or 45 euros. I can't imagine that anyone who needs it done would not be able to pay for it himself."

"You're right," I said. "And the people who need it done can probably write it off as a business expense."

"There's another procedure that is possible for the anus," Mattijs said thoughtfully. "It's very expensive. They are performing it all with very high-tech lasers. I don't know if it's possible to get a government subsidy for it, but I imagine so."

"Great," I said. "I'll be on the next train."

I waited until I was in the railway station in Frankfurt, about to board my connecting train, before I called my mother collect and informed her that, starting tomorrow, I would be living in Amsterdam.

"You're what?" she shrieked, after she had accepted the charges. "You can't!"

"I understand your surprise," I said calmly. "But I thought you should know it's something I've decided to do."

"You can't just stay in Europe forever!" she ranted. "What are you, some kind of refugee? You'll be deported! The immigration people will kidnap you in the middle of the night and send you back in shackles! Your credit will be ruined and you'll never get health insurance. You'll go straight to jail, or worse!"

I assured her that as long as I resisted joining a terrorist cell, this was highly unlikely.

"What do you think you're going to do for money?" she asked vehemently, switching tack. "How are you going to support yourself?"

"How do I support myself in New York?"

"Oh no," she said. "No, no, no. If you think I'm going to schlep to Western Union and wire you money every two weeks, you are out of your fucking mind."

I said I had enough money to get by for a while, and besides, I would be working.

She scoffed. "In Amsterdam? Feh. I don't even want to think about it."

Coldly, I informed her that I didn't appreciate her insinuation, and that I had been invited to star in a multinational theatrical production by one of Amsterdam's most promising young theater companies.

"And this is something they're going to actually pay you money for?" she asked.

"In Europe they give value to the arts," I replied in my snootiest voice.

She sighed mightily. "Will you have an address? Will I be able to mail you things?"

One of my mother's favorite pastimes is to send me large manila envelopes containing scraps of information that she feels need to be brought to my attention: notices culled from the local newspaper reporting that my high school boyfriend has once again been imprisoned for car theft; excerpts from the rabbi's latest sermon torn from the synagogue bulletin; photocopied magazine articles detailing gruesome diseases for which she believes I might be at risk. Just a few months earlier, she had sent me a birthday card in which she tucked a pamphlet about the horrors of cervical cancer. On the card itself, underneath a printed couplet telling me how pleased she was to have me as a daughter and wishing me a special day, my mother had written her own message in her round, girlish handwriting: "Remember—having multiple sexual partners significantly increases your immediate risk of developing cancer of the cervix. Please consider." I tried to tell myself that this was the kind of thing I would miss when she was dead.

"What do you need to send me?" I was half afraid to hear the answer.

"Well," she said, "your old friend David Kaplan is playing Cornelius Hackl over at the Playhouse and got a very nice write-up in the *World-Herald*. And I have an article I saved for you from *Science Times*, about the long-term effects of gonorrhea on the reproductive system. If it's not treated, the disease builds up scar tissue in the fallopian tubes and can make you sterile."

"Good," I said. "One less thing to worry about."

She sighed again. "It also increases your susceptibility to HIV infection."

It was my turn to sigh, which I did impressively. My mother may be the odds-on favorite in Freestyle Kvetching at the Martyrdom Olympics, but I am a lock for the silver, at least. "For the last time, Mother, I am not, nor have I ever been, a prostitute."

"Well," she muttered darkly. "If you change your mind, you're certainly going to the right place."

An announcement crackled over the loudspeaker, telling me in German that it was time to board. I said good-bye, promising to e-mail her my new address and phone number at the earliest opportunity, and lugged my heavy suitcases to the platform, tugging my skirt down self-consciously as I walked. That made two people who had mistaken me for a prostitute in the past week.

"Excuse Please, How Much?"

WHEN SOMEONE MISTAKES YOU FOR A PROSTITUTE

Being mistaken for a prostitute is a rite of passage for practically any young woman, effeminate man, or male-to-female transsexual who is traveling abroad. Still, you may be confused as to how to respond. Your first instinct may be to answer the Hypothetical John (or HJ) by screaming obscenities in his face or by attacking him physically. While cathartic, such a response can lead to unfortunate complications, such as heavy fines, prison time, or even death, all of which can really ruin your vacation. Here is a guide to safely navigating unwanted attentions with dignity and grace.

Step 1: Think. Have you ever considered prostitution as a career choice? Have you sold your body for money or drugs before and do you feel physically and emotionally capable of doing so again? Have you long harbored an erotic fantasy about having sex for money and feel like this might be a good time to finally indulge it? Are you completely and utterly broke, or just desperate for a decent meal?

If you have answered in the affirmative to more than one of these questions, turn immediately to page 151 ("Are You About to Be Sex-Trafficked?") If you are only desperate for a decent meal, gastronomic prostitution might be the right choice for you (see box opposite).

If you have answered each question in the negative, continue reading.

If the person who thinks you are a hooker is your mother, seek immediate counseling.

Step 2: Be clear. It is possible you may have misunderstood what the HJ was trying to say to you. A simple inquiry into the matter can save you both a world of embarrassment. Be direct. In loud, clear English, stripped of coyness or euphemism, ask the HJ if he believes you are indeed a professional sexer. You may need to substitute the English word for "whore" with its equivalent in the HJ's language. See glossary below.

Prostitute (English)

Hoer (Dutch)

Hure (German)

Puta (Spanish)

Putain (French)

Prostituta (Italian; another term is *puttana*, but this is more commonly used to indicate an enthusiastic amateur)

Meretriz (Portuguese)

Prostytutka (Polish)

Step 3: Be gracious. Once you have established, beyond the shadow of a doubt, that the HJ is indeed offering you X amount of money in exchange for your participation in an undetermined sex act, let him know how flattered you are by his attention. After all, if he has taken you for a professional, he must think you are objectively attractive enough to get paid for it.

Step 4: Let him down easy. Even perverts and degenerates feel the sting of rejection. Politely but firmly explain to the HJ that he has made a mistake. (Ask the bartender or another patron to translate if necessary.)

Step 5: Leave immediately. Leave your drink and go. It's not worth lingering: The HJ might get the idea that you'll change your mind. If the HJ seems angry or menacing, ask a buddy or another patron to see you out.

Step 6: Let it out. A strong emotional reaction to this experience is common, perhaps even healthy. Once you are safely outside and are sure you have not been followed, feel free to weep and/or laugh hysterically. Fend off disapproving glares from Northern Europeans unaccustomed to such displays by screaming: *"YOU WANT A PIECE OF THIS ASS TOO, COCKSUCKER?"* They will quickly mistake you for a psychotic, whom nobody wants to pay for sex with.

Gastronomic Prostitution

IS IT RIGHT FOR YOU?

You are eager to sample Europe's rich food culture but haven't a cent to your name. Consider an arrangement known as gastronomic prostitution, in which one accepts a date with a man or woman one has absolutely no intention of sleeping with in exchange for a nice meal. Such a transaction requires some skill; one must manage to extricate oneself from the implication of sexual obligation early in the evening, while remaining charming and flirtatious enough to take one's companion for all he/she is worth. Gastronomic prostitution is not recommended for those without considerable dating experience, or if the person you are dining with has already mistaken you for an actual prostitute. Again, before accepting a date from any stranger, please consult the guidelines on page 151.

Mattijs was waiting for me at Amsterdam Centraal Station, where he was wedged in between two banks of automat windows displaying wrinkled gray sausages and crumbly deep-fried objects of indeterminate provenance. I waved at him bashfully, suddenly feeling a bit shy. He shoved the rest of a fried thing he was eating in his mouth and with a muffled squeal ran toward me, catching me in a hug so hard it lifted me several inches off the ground.

"Finally, you are here!" he exclaimed, spraying fine crumbs of greasy breading in my hair as he kissed me on both cheeks three times in the Dutch way. "I thought you would never arrive!"

I told him that my train had stopped in Frankfurt and had been delayed for more than an hour during a surprise check at the German border when three young Somalian men were found to be traveling on expired passports.

"The German customs police handcuffed them together and marched them single file off the train while everybody watched."

Mattijs sniffed disgustedly. "That's from your government, darling. Haven't you heard? We are now fighting the global war on terror."

It seemed unnecessary to mention that I had been completely convinced the three men, who had spent the journey whispering together and glaring tensely around the car, were up to no good, or that, before their arrest, I had spent quite a long time barricaded in the sewage-scented bathroom, bracing myself for the inevitable explosion, until the furious knocking of an angry woman with two damp, screaming children had shamed me out. "Where's Jeroen?"

Mattijs smiled. "Jeroen is at the apartment, preparing a few things. We go there now."

I suggested we take a cab, but Mattijs insisted on loading my two tremendous suitcases onto one of the blue and white aboveground trams waiting outside the gingerbread façade of the station. "A cab is very expensive," he said, "and you have wasted so much money already." The tram careened through the cobblestoned streets, narrowly missing flocks of bicyclists and pedestrians, its jointed floor shifting alarmingly when it made sharp turns, like a trick walkway in a carnival funhouse. I held on to the handle of my suitcase for dear life until Mattijs pressed the yellow strip beside the window and the tram skidded to a halt. We dragged my suitcases about seven blocks before reaching his apartment building, where it was then necessary to lug them up six flights of stairs. There was an elevator in the building, Mattijs told me, but the only person who was allowed to use it was a woman called Helga who lived on the top floor and had received a special key from the government. Helga was dying of cancer.

"That's what she says, anyway," said Mattijs. "She's been dying of cancer for twenty years. Yet somehow she summons the strength to telephone the police anytime you try to play music after eight o'clock." He glanced up toward the ceiling anxiously. "It is my belief she has a cancer of the soul."

Jeroen was waiting for us on the landing, a huge smile plastered across his face. His hair was longer than I remembered it, and an even whiter blond. "Sweetie, you're here! Welcome, welcome, welcome!" He greeted me with an intimate variation of the Dutch three kisses, pecking me once on each cheek and once on the lips, and ushered us inside. Mattijs dragged my suitcases into the living room, where a white futon was already unfolded and made up for me. Beside it was a low glass coffee table upon which someone had placed a vase of pink and white hydrangea.

"Hydrangeas are my favorite flower," I said.

"I know!" Jeroen said happily. "I remembered you telling me about the summer you spent in France, when it grew wild everywhere on the cliffs, so I went to the market and bought some for you. It is okay?"

"It is beautiful," I said, pressing my face against the petals.

On the long table in the kitchen, Jeroen had arranged a little spread of things he knew I liked. There was a large bottle of Diet Coke, a bowl of gummy candies, several packets of instant tomato soup with dehydrated croutons. He had even made a special trip to the American shop and bought three boxes of Kraft macaroni and cheese and a tub of creamy Jif peanut butter. "Is it the right kind?" Jeroen asked worriedly, peering at the red lid. "I could not remember if it was this one or the Skippy that you like best. I just want you to feel at home."

The last time I was in Amsterdam, I had stayed in a student housing facility. My room was bare, with a concrete floor, and I had a suitemate named Faroud, a cocaine-addicted Tunisian who seemed to think that I had been contracted as his personal maid. Faroud would burst into my room to berate me, loudly and often, if he felt I had failed to replace the hand soap or to properly clean the bathroom we shared. When he found a used tampon applicator I had wrapped in several layers of paper towels and buried at the bottom of the wastebasket (the weak flush in the water-saving toilet couldn't process them), he called the Amsterdam student housing authority, telling them I was an "unclean pig" who should be "sent back to where I came from." Several of the other residents neglected to store their food properly in the communal kitchen, and one night when I ventured inside for a late snack, I found the cupboards and counters swarming with rats. But the gothic pièce de résistance was when I padded sleepily into the elevator one morning on my way to class and found myself ankle-deep in human waste. An underground water main had burst, filling the lobby with raw sewage. It took the building's management more than a week and the intervention of the head of my university program to clean it all up. In the meantime, we were all advised to invest in some sturdy rubber boots.

I wrapped my arms around Jeroen, hoping he wouldn't see the tears in my eyes. "Thank you," I said. "I do."

Six

THERE ARE NO LAWS FOR THE FISH

Amsterdam doesn't change. You can go years, even centuries, without setting foot in the place and return to find everything precisely as you left it, an immaculate shrine, like the untouched bedroom of a long-dead child. You enter a building through a three-hundred-year-old door, gleaming with fresh lacquer, and glance upward to see a crooked little chimney with the year 1634 still scratched cleanly in the clay; you gaze out at the canal, at the fleet of wooden sailboats clipping calmly through the water, and you wonder for a moment if the modern world has been nothing more than a dream, a frenzied parade of ideologies and massacres and useless things for sale, passing vividly and blood-soaked through the mind's nocturnal eye and forgotten at the first light of dawn.

But look a little deeper and the march of time is evident. The outdoor markets are no longer filled with apple-cheeked milkmaids and bewhiskered herring merchants bellowing lewd songs over the percussive thud of the cleaver, but with harried-looking women in hijabs shepherding small tribes of dark-eyed children through the crowded stalls of fish and flowers and fruit. The streets are lined with kebab shops and tanned, glistening men with leather trousers slung low on their hips. Turn a corner, and the skunky pungency of marijuana masks the scent of rain and sewage that veils the air. The half-bared breasts of an Eastern bloc teenager are pressed against the windowpane of a breathtaking seventeenth-century building, as a group of bleary-eyed youths in LSU caps dare one another to lick the glass over her pierced nipple.

There are elderly people on the street: old men drinking small glasses of warm beer in unfashionable cafés, shriveled women painstakingly negotiating their wheeled baskets of shopping over the uneven cobblestones. They still look sharp, despite their age. Not for them the glittery sweatshirts; the soft pants the color of melted ice-cream; the whimsical, childish raiments that make Granny and Gramps look like a pair of hideous balding babies left in the bathwater for a hundred years. The elders of Amsterdam are dressed in plain skirts and pants with zippers, neat cardigans and wool neckties. Some shuffle along stiff-backed, others with the waddling gait of a worried toddler, and you can just infer the outline of an orthopedic corset or a sodden adult diaper lurking beneath the tasteful armor of tweed and wool. The inside may be rotting, but outside all is dignity; quiet, unbending dignity. The old people are like the buildings that way.

Mattijs and Jeroen lived in a neighborhood called de Pijp, which means "the Pipe," which is also slang for "the Penis." Their apartment building was the newest on their block, with an entrance of brick and steel and a mechanized door that opened automatically when you pressed a button on the doorjamb. This convenience was the doing of the unseen Helga, who seemed to have devoted her final days to intimidating the housing authority into remaking the building to her specifications. The tireless campaigns she conducted from her deathbed had so far resulted in the elevator, the remodeling of the staircases to include landings wide enough to accommodate a wheelchair, stretcher, or coffin, and the systematic stripping away of the original moldings, the wrought-iron railings, and with them (according to Mattijs and Jeroen) any character or charm the building might have once possessed. Now it had a distinctly clinical air; when you walked inside you couldn't help but feel like someone was about to ask you for your insurance number. The building's lone concession to beauty was an enormous sunflower, well over eight feet high, growing out of the pavement and secured to the drainpipe with bits of green twine to keep the stem from breaking. The sunflower had twice won a special prize for being the tallest in the neighborhood, and the residents of the building regarded it with the same communal affection accorded a beloved old tree or a laundry room cat. Naturally, Mattijs felt it was only a matter of time before Helga managed to destroy it too.

"Just watch," he said darkly. "One day she will stumble over it and play as if she has broken her knee. Or maybe she will decide it blocks the light from her window. Then the housing authority comes and tears it from the ground. Everything this woman touches, she kills. I don't believe she really has the cancer. I believe she is immortal, like the cockroaches. She takes her life force from the things she destroys."

Still, the apartment was by far the nicest place I had lived since I left my parents' house, with plenty of light and glass doors leading to small balconies where one could drink coffee or barbecue meat for dinner, if Helga didn't complain about the carcinogenic properties of wafting smoke. (Mattijs took this as further proof of her malingering: "If she already has cancer," he would say, "what difference does it make?") The boys used the second bedroom as an office, so the living room became mine, and I quickly devised a routine to make it work. Every morning I stripped the futon, folded it up, and replaced the cushions I had tossed on the floor the night before. My books and laptop were stashed under the coffee table, and I bought a portable clothing rack and a plastic chest of drawers from a discount store, turning an empty nook behind the piano into a kind of closet that I kept covered with an old white curtain during the day. I am a hoarder by nature, a family trait. You couldn't open a closet in my grandmother's house without fear of being crushed to death by an avalanche of wrapping paper, yarn, or enough unsent greeting cards to encompass the birthdays, graduations, Christmases, and Passovers of fifteen lifetimes. My father could easily spend a half hour searching for a working felt-tip pen from the sea of old markers that spread across his drafting table. I had kept every piece of written correspondence I had ever received, and held on to ill-fitting, inappropriate pieces of clothing for years, because I had worn them when something important happened. Now, for the first time in my life, I had relatively few possessions. My mountains of junk and embarrassing secrets were at my parents' house, in storage, or gone with the wind. The living room could easily be made rid of me. In less than a minute, it was as though I had never even been there at all.

After I finished tidying up, I'd get dressed and draw back the big sliding door to the kitchen, where Jeroen and Mattijs were eating breakfast. Their morning meal was simple and unvarying, consisting of plain slices of untoasted bread, spread with a thin layer of butter and topped with a single slice of sharp-tasting yellow cheese or slick, translucent mystery meat, or a thick layer of *hagelslag*, a kind of soft chocolate sprinkles dispensed from a square carton with a cardboard spout. Jeroen ate with great care and attention, dissecting his food with a knife and fork and emitting hoarse groans of appreciation with each bite, but Mattijs narcotically inserted wads of greasy bread into his mouth while bathed in the hazy glow of the television that hung from a cradle near the ceiling, which appeared to run an endless loop of the opening shot of *The Sound of Music*. Every morning, I waited for the camera to zoom in on Julie Andrews in her weird little strapless apron, spinning in brisk Aryan ecstasy. But Julie Andrews never came.

Mattijs poured about half a cup of chocolate sprinkles directly into his palm and began to ladle them up aggressively with his tongue. I pointed at the TV screen with my spoon. "What are you watching?"

"Snow," he grunted. "I am watching the snow."

Setting down his knife and fork carefully on either side of his plate, Jeroen said, "It is a very special program. You see, they have set up all these television cameras and all these kinds of things for to show how much snow there is now in the mountains."

"I thought Holland was flat," I said.

Jeroen picked his fork back up and caught another tiny square of buttered bread in the tines of his fork as he chuckled merrily. "No, no. Of course you are right. Holland is flat, like a . . . a . . . what is something that is flat?"

"A young girl's chest," I said helpfully. "A cardiogram of a dead person. The world, before Columbus discovered otherwise. My hair."

"A pancake," Mattijs offered.

"Yes," said Jeroen, "a pancake. Holland is flat like a pancake. The TV shows Austria, Switzerland, places like that. It is done in order for people to be able to plan their ski holidays."

"I am a licensed ski instructor," Mattijs said loudly. Sprinkles tumbled from his lips and landed in his coffee cup, where they dissolved into a watery brown froth.

"But it's still summer," I said blankly.

"Yes," Jeroen said, "but the snow must be built up over time in order to enjoy excellent skiing conditions, and people already now are reserving their packages. Otherwise, it's not possible to get the best price."

"A ski holiday is very expensive!" bellowed Mattijs. The plates on the table rattled gently. "It is necessary to prepare or for most people it cannot be afforded!"

"This is why they have such a special program." Jeroen patted my hand soothingly. "So it can be made possible. As you know, the program is on all the day long. All day, every day."

I said, "Are you trying to tell me that in this country, where premium cable service consists of only eleven stations, there is an entire television channel solely devoted to monitoring the snowfall of the Austrian and Swiss Alps?"

"No!" Mattijs was indignant. "They also show the Alps of France!"

"That's great," I said. "I guess that's the difference between our two cultures, how Europeans are able to slow down and appreciate the little things. From now on I'm going to take my time and get the most out of life. I'm going to go in the living room and watch the paint-drying channel. Unless you think I'd prefer another one where you watch glaciers melt."

"Excuse me," said Mattijs, "but was it not on Christmas at your house when we are watching the television channel where all day it is only one shot of the fireplace?"

"The Yule log," I snapped, "is special. Every American is entitled to spend Christmas beside the metaphysical concept of a roaring fire."

Mattijs scoffed. "Oh really? Who says?"

"The law," I said, like a five-year-old. "The law says."

"And the program where two old fat men sit in a boat for hours trying to catch a fish? The law says also this?"

"Mattijs, don't be ridiculous." Jeroen downed the last dregs of his coffee and began to clear up the plates and cups. "There are no laws for the fish."

Where the Fuck Am I?

A GUIDE TO DUTCH STREET NAMES

Amsterdam can be an impossible place to navigate. This is confusing because the Dutch are the greatest urban planners in the world, but this can just be added to the list of inherent contradictions in the national character. (See page 199 for the "Topics for Discussion.")

First of all, the streets in Amsterdam are oriented around a ring, as opposed to a grid. While this may be all very well and good for morally equivocating, sexually ambiguous Europeans, a red-blooded, patriotic American used to honest, concrete concepts like "east" and "west," "north" and "south," "good" and "evil," "with us" and "against us" will have a hard time, particularly as said American will almost certainly be stoned out of his or her mind.

The nice thing about circular streets is that you'll always get where you're going eventually; the hard part is going the right way around. It can make the difference between a journey of five minutes or one or two hours. (At least you'll be stoned, which takes the edge off, until it starts to rain and you wish you were dead.)

The only truly foolproof way to get anywhere is ask a native for directions, which they are usually happy to provide. But this too poses a difficulty, because the names of Dutch streets are, to a native English speaker, completely impenetrable. Like German, Dutch uses compound nouns, and a street name can easily have more than twenty letters, which, I'm sure you'll agree, is completely fucking ridiculous. While embedded in the street names are clues as to their nature and positioning—*straat* for "street," *gracht* for "canal," *eerste* for "first," *tweede* for "second," etc.—unraveling their mysteries would require one to actually learn to speak Dutch. I considered doing this, but a four-week language course proved prohibitively expensive and essentially useless, and I already have a degree in experimental theater, thank you very much.

Therefore, the best solution is simply to pronounce the unpronounceable by substituting the unfamiliar words with familiar English look-alikes. The results are informative and often amusing.

Example: Reguliersdwarsstraat

Reguliersdwarsstraat is the main drag of Amsterdam's gay area (which basically encompasses the entire city except for the Muslim neighborhoods). It is often referred to as "Rue de Vaséline" by locals. However, in the place-name argot of Rachel Shukert's The Grand Tour™, it becomes Regular Dwarf Street.

You see? *Reguliers*, a difficult word involving several epiglottal stops and no small amount of phlegm, becomes the eminently manageable word "regular." Is there anything more comforting than the word "regular," with its pleasant symmetry, its happy promise of placid intestinal activity? *Dwars*, meaning "side," as in a side street, becomes the charming little noun "dwarf." Like Santa's workshop! I'll take that rocking horse in orange, Snowball! And finally, *straat* is anglicized simply to "street." Reguliersdwarsstraat = Regular Dwarf Street. Easy as pie.

Of course, as this is a dwarf street, there must also be just a plain old Regular Street, which there is! Reguliersstraat.

I think you've got the hang of it. Here are some more samples to get you started. Remember, be creative, and don't be afraid to sound stupid! Everyone thinks you are anyhow, so you've got nothing to lose.

Leliestraat	Lily's Street
Leliedwarsstraat	Lily's a Dwarf Street
Laurierstraat	Laurie's Street
Laurierdwarsstraat	Laurie's a Dwarf Street
Eerste Laurierdwarsstraat	Errr, Laurie's a Dwarf Street?
Weteringplantsoen	Watering Plants, Son
Nieuwezijds Voorburgwal	New Side for Burgers, Y'all!
Oudezijds Achterburgwal	Old-Time Actor Burgles All
Warmoesstraat	Hot Mess Street (an apt description)
Kamperfoelieweg	Camper Following
Kolpinstraat	Klonopin Street
Rustenburgerstraat	John Ratzenberger Street
Huidenstraat	Houses Street
Meerhuizenstraat	More Houses Street
Korte Meerhuizenstraat	Even More Houses Street
Funke Kupperstraat	Fucking Couples Street
Pettenstraat	Petting Street
Pienemanstraat	Penis Man Street
Uranusstraat	Your Anus Street

After breakfast, Jeroen and Mattijs would disappear into their office to make phone calls and pore over the mysterious piles of paperwork I was told had something to do with securing the funding for our play. I liked to linger alone over my coffee for a few minutes, writing in my journal or going over the folding laminated street map Jeroen had given me before I timidly ventured outside on my daily rounds. The apartment was near the Albert Cuyp Markt, a permanent outdoor market that went on for several blocks, and every day I walked through its entirety, buying a packet of olives or a couple of sour pickles to munch on as I ambled past the plastic tubs of poppies and periwinkle, the huge round cheeses that emitted a waxy glow like the rays of an alien sun, the silvery prawns and fat herrings staring glassily from beds of finely crushed ice. I especially liked the sweet stall, where wedged between mounds of dried apricots and shards of creamy nougat were several trays of three-dimensional chocolate penises in a variety of sizes and shapes. Some of the penises were milk chocolate with a white chocolate glans; others had white shafts, the tips coated a troubling deep brown. The penises stood erect, curving forward eagerly on the haunches formed by their molded scrotums, the smaller ones arranged carefully in front, an eager choir preparing to burst into song. Once I saw a frazzled-looking young mother snatch up one of the larger penises and thrust it roughly in the mouth of her wailing toddler. The child's sobs subsided immediately, and I thought of the skinheads with the *Käsekrainer* in Vienna. This, again, was the difference between peoples. The Austrians needed a shape, a symbol, a bun. The Dutch were frank, uncomplicated. In Holland, a sausage was just a sausage, because a penis was just a penis, something one could mold in chocolate and use to shut up a kid.

It occurred to me that if my acting career failed (a possibility that seemed more likely with each passing minute) I could instead travel the world, taking artistic photographs of sexually suggestive foodstuffs. I would record the consumption of reindeer testicles among the Sami people of northern Finland and traverse the Amazonian jungle on the trail of a mythical fruit that oozed a clumpy red fluid and was fed to native boys as part of an initiation ritual; I would compose a penetrating (if you'll pardon the pun) essay accounting for the popularity of the misleadingly named ladyfingers at the kiddush following a ritual Jewish circumcision. I would then amass all this material into a glossy, expensively produced coffee-table book, which would sell a million copies and make me rich beyond my wildest dreams.

It tells you something about me that, in case my acting career proved a failure, my only contingency plan was to publish an international bestseller. I'm sure that you are already aware of this. I just want you to know that I know it too.

In truth, with each passing day, more and more of my time was devoted to my fantasy life, which had always been rich but was quickly becoming all-consuming. When I had first arrived in Amsterdam, I considered joining one of the language classes organized by various government agencies and community centers to help recent immigrants integrate into Dutch society. I fantasized that the experience would be very much like *Dear John*, the 1980s sitcom starring Judd Hirsch as a recently divorced man deeply involved with his support group. I invented a colorful cast of characters. There would be a smooth-talking British playboy, a friendly Australian lady-pothead, a couple of Italians in billowing patterned shirts who would shout dramatically and inexplicably burst into tears and were also gay boyfriends, and a heavily veiled Muslim woman who would shock and delight us with explicit references to her rich and varied sex life. We would meet in a brightly lit classroom decorated with inspirational posters of kittens and with disembodied hands holding flowers, and presiding over us would be our teacher, a lovably humorless Dutchman called Marcel who wore funny glasses and could never find a girlfriend. His ineptitude with the opposite sex (and his subsequent crippling loneliness) would be a source of great mirth for our class, but we would do what we could to help. Fatima, the veiled Muslim woman, would give him tips about esoteric sexual maneuvers with evocative names—the Flatulent Pita, the Hamid Karzai—which she claimed were commonplace in her country and expertly administered by her never-seen husband, a successful real estate broker called Jamal. At the mention of such exotic perversions, Marcel's funny glasses would steam up (a running gag), and he would have to wipe them with the end of his tie. Trevor, the suave English playboy, would be constantly setting Marcel up on disastrous dates with women Trevor had recently discarded, until halfway through season three, when Marcel told him he was in love with me. As Trevor and I often expressed our simmering sexual tension through insults and various plots to humiliate each other, he would agree to help Marcel woo me, that is, until Trevor realized the depth of his own feelings for me. This would lead to weeks of addictive will-they-or-won't-they buildup until spring sweeps, when Trevor and I would accidentally be locked overnight in the Anne Frank House during a blizzard. Certain we were about to die, we would then breathlessly fall into each other's arms and make tender yet animalistic love to each other on the floor of the Secret Annex. When this was revealed to the class, in the next episode, everyone would feign horror—everyone, that is, except for Fatima, who would calmly assert that the Holocaust was a Zionist hoax and then mention a new bedroom move that Jamal had invented, which he called "the Chocolate Treblinka," and we would officially become a controversial, boundary-pushing comedy. In the season finale, Trevor and I would become engaged, but in a new twist on an old classic, we would leave *each other* at the altar—I being overwhelmed at the thought of becoming the Countess of Shropshire and having to deal with his snobbish, casually anti-Semitic mother; he feeling unready to give up his playboy ways. Trevor would then leave the show for a couple of seasons to pursue film projects, but we would be reunited in the series finale, when Marcel would marry Sheila the Australian lady-pothead after accidentally impregnating her during a time-travel episode set in the floating hotel in Amsterdam harbor. Their wedding would also be the first and only time we would ever see the mysterious Jamal, who would be played by Adam Sandler.

My show seemed so real to me that I even composed a set of dummy lyrics for a theme song, which was to be sung to the tune of the theme from *Dear John*:

> Amsterdam (doo doo doo doo doo doo)
> Amsterdam (doo doo doo doo doo)
> Don't know where the hell I am, Amsterdam
> Amsterdam (doo doo doo doo doo doo)
> Not Siam (doo doo doo doo doo doo)
> Paris, France, or Vietnam
> Amsterdam

Where Everybody Knows Your Name

COPING WITH LONELINESS THROUGH THE POWER OF TELEVISION

Constant loneliness is the greatest struggle for anyone attempting to spend some serious time abroad, worse even than bewilderment, poverty, and the constant temptation to sell one's body for money (presumably alleviating said poverty). No matter how adept one is at striking up conversations with strangers, the solitude cannot be kept at bay for long. Its triggers are everywhere. One might observe the easy camaraderie of a group of friends in a café, chattering away giddily in a language of which one has no comprehension, and come to the sinking realization that the little corner of the world one has come to think of as one's own is nothing in the greater scheme of things. The vast majority of people in the world have no knowledge of you, nor do they care to. They will go through their entire lives quite happily without the faintest clue that you exist.

When children are lonely, they invent imaginary friends to talk to. Adults such as myself invent imaginary television shows to keep the howling dogs of alienation at bay. Nobody is lonely in a sitcom. The characters show up at bars, diners, or sporting events, and everyone they know is already there. I often think that all I have ever wanted in life is a group of people to stand with on a soundstage, in front of a Christmas tree, while we chant in unison, "Happy holidays from NBC."

The ascendancy of my age group in popular culture is already waning, and future generations will find the best antidote to loneliness is to bring along a camera crew and a team of reality television producers. But in my imaginary world the sitcom is still dominant. The possibilities for your own imaginary Amsterdam-set sitcom are endless, but should you need some pitches to get you started, I have thoughtfully provided a few options. And to my friends who work in TV development: If you read only one page of this book, please let it be this one.

Adolf's Family. A hilarious hybrid of *Everybody Loves Raymond* and *The Diary of Anne Frank*, *Adolf's Family* is a heartwarming half-hour comedy about two Jewish families hiding together from the Nazis in war-torn Amsterdam: the Finkelsteins, a genteel couple with a petulant, prissy teenage daughter (Michelle Trachtenberg), and the Leventhals, bawdy borscht-belt types with a sex-obsessed teenage son (Christopher Mintz-Plasse). The show gets its name from family patriarchs Adolf Finkelstein (Robby Benson) and Adolf Leventhal (Jason Alexander), as well as their namesake, the controversial leader whose policies brought this misfit bunch together! Also in hiding is Franz (Sebastian Stan), a melancholic cousin of the Leventhals, who is like Anthony from *Blossom*, and is a sometime rival for the Finkelstein girl's nascent affections. Michael Richards (*Seinfeld*) plays the wacky neighbor who is always dropping by unannounced, bearing food and news from the outside, although his wild antics cause more than one hilarious scrape with the Gestapo. When the show reaches its inevitable fourth-season ratings drop, the producers bring in a couple of adorable, smart-mouthed African American orphans (Jaden and Willow Smith) found wandering the streets after their parents have been sent to Westerbork!

Sex and the Alley. In this sexy and sophisticated comedy, four sassy female friends search for love in the big city while working as prostitutes in adjoining windows in Amsterdam's red-light district: Saskia (Kirstie Alley), the fiercely independent old pro who dreams of someday saving up enough money to open her own brothel; Masha (Vanessa Hudgens), a wide-eyed young BDSM specialist from Belarus who still believes that one of her (mostly Swiss) clients will turn out to be her "Richard Gere" and take her away to live happily ever after; Hilda (Michelle Rodriguez), a hardened, no-nonsense lesbian who has turned to sex work to support her string of vulnerable, smack-addict girlfriends, and finally Kjirsten (Ginnifer Goodwin), a lovably neurotic sex blogger who has a dysfunctional on-again, off-again relationship with her pimp/lover, a worldly Belgian porn mogul the girls call Mijnheer Groote (which is Dutch for Mr. Big).

Bulb Men. A hard-hitting, lavishly art-directed drama about a group of rival tulip merchants in 1637, just before the bulb bubble bursts, *Bulb Men* is the story of Diederijk Draager (Dylan McDermott), a successful bulb salesman betting everything he's got on the introduction of the exotic hyacinth to the wildly speculative bulb market as he struggles with his identity; his troubled marriage to Beetje (Erika Christensen), the daughter of a wealthy burgomaster from the Utrecht suburbs; his multiple affairs with artists' models, servant girls, and wealthy Jewesses; and his struggle to find his place in an incrementally changing world. Costarring Mandy

Patinkin as Baruch Spinoza, a kindly Jewish watchmaker with whom Diederijk strikes up an unlikely, intellectually stimulating friendship, and who performs a variety of period music during the show's frequent and artistic dream sequences.

It didn't take long for Mattijs and Jeroen to destroy my sitcom dreams. "This is not possible. The fees for such a class will be far, far too expensive."

"I thought they were government subsidized," I said meekly.

"Yes, if you are an asylum seeker. But for you, it will not be possible. Besides, it is not necessary to learn Dutch. We are only a tiny country. Everybody here knows how to speak English. Better to save your money for food and other things."

It would have been easier to tell them to count their own damn money had I not been living rent-free on their couch. So instead of having an enriching cultural experience that would have made me an infinitely better global citizen, I saw *Legally Blonde 2: Red, White, and Blonde* in the theater eleven times. When I was little, I used to imagine that Sally Field was my real mother (a fantasy totally informed by the movie *Soapdish*) and after the first three or four viewings, I started to audibly weep when Congresswoman Rudd (played by Field) killed Bruiser's Bill on the floor of the House. Some might have taken this as a sign of how much I missed my real mother. *Some* might.

In the early evening, after the movies, I would stop by an Internet café to check e-mails and scan the headlines of the *New York Times* before I headed back to the apartment, where Jeroen and Mattijs were emerging from their office after a long, hard day of yelling at each other. Mattijs would light the first of several evening cigarettes and begin to fry various patties and tubes of unidentified meat products. Jeroen handed around tiny glasses of warm white wine, and as Mattijs cooked, the two of us would settle down at the kitchen table to watch *Are You Being Served?* on Nederlands 3. This was the part of the day I liked best, not only because it pleasingly mirrored a recurring scene from a novel I liked very much, *The Extra Man* by Jonathan Ames, but because it was often the first time since breakfast that I'd had any meaningful contact with another human being. Watching *Are You Being Served?* with my friends made me feel like myself again, and it gave me a chance to be useful, as Jeroen needed my help to understand some of the more sophisticated double entendres.

"I understand why it is humorous for Mrs. Slocombe's pussy to become sodden and need to be dried out in front of the fire," he said, knitting his pale eyebrows, "but why is there this horny smile on the face of Mr. Lucas when Miss Brahms says she will have him on the carpet?"

I explained that in English, the verb "to have" could mean a variety of things: for example, to eat, to receive as a guest, or to possess, sexually or otherwise. "Ah!" Jeroen would exclaim. "That is completely ridiculous! I believe *Are You Being Served?* may be the best television comedy I have ever seen!" I agreed.

As the credits rolled, Mattijs would serve us our meat shapes and instruct us to "*eet smakelijk*," which translates literally to "eat tasty," the homely Dutch equivalent of bon appétit.

"You must buy a bicycle," Jeroen said to me, meticulously cutting a morsel of cube steak and placing it on his tongue as though it were a dollop of Iranian caviar. "As soon as possible. It is really the very best way to get around the city."

Mattijs slipped an ice chip into his wine. "Why must she buy one? After all, she is able to borrow one of ours."

Jeroen clucked. "Oh no. Ours are far too big for Rachel to ride."

"There!" I exclaimed. "You did it! You made a double entendre!"

"I did!" Jeroen looked delighted. "Far too big for Rachel to ride! I understand!"

Mattijs shrugged. "How is Rachel going to buy a bicycle? She has no money."

"Well, I'll be getting paid soon, won't I?" I said hopefully. "For the show?"

Mattijs ignored me, ticking out his points on his fingers. "Even a secondhand bicycle is maybe one hundred euro. One hundred fifty including the lock." He rounded on me fiercely. "You must buy a good lock. This is not the place to look for a bargain. Otherwise the junkies will steal it from you immediately."

I nodded wisely. "My old boyfriend had a junkie living with him for a while in Brooklyn. His roommate met him on the street and invited him to come stay. His name was Jasper. He was English. He said he used to be the road manager for Oasis, but I think that was a lie."

Jeroen nodded wisely. "Of course. Americans will believe anything an English person says."

"Sam and I were having problems," I continued, "and Jasper decided he had a crush on me." Actually, Jasper had said to Sam's roommate that he was hoping to catch me on the rebound, as that was when "a bird like that will shag anything that fucking moves." "One day, when I come into the apartment, he takes out this shopping bag and tells me that he got me a present. I open the bag, and inside it is a skirt I had left there. He had actually gone into Sam's room, stolen my skirt, and then given it back to me as a gift."

"Whatever did you do?" asked Jeroen with wonder. "Did you tell him it already belongs to you?"

"I didn't want to offend him," I said. "And anyway, I was lucky to get it back. Just a few days later, he disappeared with three guitars, a DVD player, and the toaster oven. Nobody ever saw him again."

"So then you understand," Mattijs said sternly, "that junkies are not to be trusted. Whatever you do, you must not buy a bicycle from a junkie. Because then you will know it is stolen, and that is really bad. No matter how hard you wish for a bicycle, and no matter how cheap he is offering it to you, you must not buy it."

"No—" I began.

"*No matter how good a bargain it is, you must not buy it.* Even if he offers it up for ten euros. Even if he offers it up for five!"

Jeroen patted my arm as Mattijs lit a fresh cigarette off the one that was still going. "It would just be . . . very bad karma," said Jeroen. "To buy a stolen bicycle."

"I understand," I said. "I saw *The Bicycle Thief.*"

A few days later, Jeroen said he had a surprise for me.

"Are we starting rehearsals tomorrow?" I cried, overjoyed. "Do I need to open a bank account?"

"No," said Jeroen, "something else."

Suddenly it hit me. "Oh my God! I can't believe it! You found me a bicycle!" His face fell. "Just kidding," I said quickly. "What's the surprise?"

Jeroen asked, "Do you remember Mariska? She is living with us for a while in New York?"

I did remember Mariska—a bubbly, round-faced girl usually dressed in athletic apparel. We had had several conversations about baked goods, particularly muffins. Muffins fascinated Mariska. "If you could have only one kind of muffin for the rest of your life," she said to me one afternoon, "which would you choose?"

I answered truthfully. "I'd have a bagel."

After that, we hadn't had much to talk about.

"I ran into Mariska on the university campus the other day," Jeroen continued. "I told her you were here and that I was very sorry that you were having to spend so much time alone, and she said of course she would be happy to see you. So today, you will meet with her for lunch at the university café and have a nice visit together. It is all arranged."

I could hardly say no. He knew I didn't have anything else to do.

Lunch was surprisingly pleasant. It was a beautiful day, and Mariska and I sat outside at a table overlooking the canal. In the dazzle of the sunshine, the water almost looked clean, and happy tourists with cameras around their necks waved to us from the big cruise barges as they lumbered past. On her own turf, Mariska was comfortable and cozy, and we chatted easily about the things we had in common, namely, Jeroen and Mattijs.

"How about their fights?" I laughed, motioning to the waiter for another glass of wine. "It's the worst when they get drunk. The screaming goes on all night sometimes. I wish I could understand what they're saying."

"No, you don't." Mariska rolled her eyes.

"Why?" I leaned in conspiratorially. "Is it filthy?"

"No," said Mariska. "It is always just Mattijs picking over every little thing. Jeroen, why didn't you tell me this? Jeroen, why didn't you tell me that? Why are you looking over there, Jeroen? Jeroen, why didn't you telephone? Always, always Mattijs is on his case about something. I saw Mattijs in the market a while back"—now she leaned in—"and he is really losing his hair now. Also, don't you think he is getting a bit fat? I found his pants were much too tight."

I suddenly remembered how back in New York Jeroen had worried that Mariska was becoming obsessed with him, after he had drunkenly confessed to her that, as a teenager, he had twice slept with a female tattoo artist twenty years his senior. Once sober, he realized his error. "I should never have told her I've been with a woman," he said to me gloomily. "Now she will think there is hope for her."

"Mattijs is slim-hipped and youthful," I said loyally, "and I think that he and Jeroen mostly argue as a prelude to hot sex. Which they have every single day." Mariska stared across the water and wiped her nose roughly with her napkin.

"It's inspiring to be around them," I continued. "It makes me believe in love." It was with some surprise that I realized this was actually true.

"I have to go back to class," said Mariska apologetically, after we had paid the check, "but if you bring your bicycle around I will ride with you part of the way to your apartment. So you won't get lost."

"It's so nice of you to offer," I said, "but I don't have a bicycle."

"Why? Are you afraid to ride in the city?"

"No," I said. "I love to ride. I just can't afford one."

"What do you mean? You want to buy a brand-new bicycle?"

"A used one would be fine," I said. "But Mattijs said even that would cost at least a hundred euros. A hundred fifty with the lock."

"And of course you must get a good lock," said Mariska, "or it will immediately be stolen."

"I just don't have the money to spare right now." I looked sadly down at my feet, listening to the whirring creaks and jangling bells as other riders whizzed by. I felt like Pee-wee Herman, slumped on the park bench just after his precious red bicycle is stolen. Everyone had a bike but me. "I'll get one once we start rehearsals for the play, and I start getting paid."

Mariska's gaze had settled on a gaunt, gray-skinned man in stonewashed jeans and a filthy hoodie who slouched against the railing of the bridge, one pale hand draped over the handlebars of a battered black bicycle. Under the weight of her stare, he flicked his eyes up from under the lip of his hood to meet hers.

"Do you know that guy?" I asked, shyly.

Mariska breezed past me and approached the man, gesturing vaguely to the bicycle. They exchanged a few brief words, and with a brisk nod, she trotted back over to me.

"It's a girl's bike," she said. "It seems like it's in pretty good shape. Ten euros, he says. You want it?"

"Mariska!" I said. "Isn't that guy a junkie?"

She shrugged. "Since when are you such a judge of people?"

"But that bike is stolen!"

"So, maybe it's stolen." Mariska reached into her purse for her cigarettes. "If you don't buy it, it will still be stolen. He's not going to give it back." She lit up.

"Mattijs said not to buy a bike from a junkie. He said it's the worst thing you can do."

"Mattijs!" Mariska expelled the name, along with an angry cloud of smoke. "What does Mattijs know of suffering? Nothing! The worst thing? Worse than rape? Worse than killing?" She waved her hand in the direction of the Jonas Daniel Meijerplein, where there stood a bronze statue of a burly man commemorating the Dutch workers who went on strike for two days in 1941 to protest the beginning of the deportation of the Jews. "Worse than war?" she said.

"Didn't you ever see *The Bicycle Thief*?" I muttered weakly.

There is absolutely nothing like riding a bicycle in Amsterdam. Speeding along the perfect bike paths, outpacing the traffic a million to one. Plowing across the square, parting the flocks of skittish pigeons like Moses with the Red Sea, pedaling furiously up an incline before you breathlessly let go and soar over the cobblestoned slope. I've only been skiing twice in my life. Both times I've fallen down and hurt myself and had to be rescued by condescending border collies with an unbecoming interest in my frozen private parts, but at the end of a ride in Amsterdam, I feel the way other people look at the end of a ski run: red-cheeked, thrilled, laughing, and alive. I rode for hours, circling the canals, tottering my way through and between the *Amsterdammertjes* (as the Dutch call the short pillars that guard the sidewalk from the street like fat little dildo-shaped sentries), hurtling around the trails in the Vondelpark and leaving great clouds of dust in my wake. By the time I glided, sunburned and windblown, against the curb in front of our building, it was nearly dinnertime. Mattijs was standing on the sidewalk, carefully pouring a bottle of water through a funnel at the base of the sunflower.

"I was getting worried," he said when he saw me.

"I'm sorry," I said. "I should have called."

"Not about you," he said. "About the *zonnebloem*. It hasn't rained in almost two days."

"It's a wild sunflower," I said. "I think it'll be fine."

He narrowed his eyes. "Where did you get the bicycle?"

I said, "It was a very good deal."

Mattijs plucked the funnel back out of the ground and brushed off the dirt. "And which shop did you buy it in?"

Living in a foreign country robs you of your ability to lie. The bits of general knowledge one requires to compose a believable fabrication under duress are simply not there. Just look at Amanda Knox. Gritting my teeth, I said, "It was Mariska's idea. She made me do it."

Mattijs scratched his head diffidently. "You'd better bring it in the lobby if you don't have a lock."

He opened the door and held it open for me with his foot. I

wheeled the bike inside, set it carefully against the wall. "Thank you for being cool about this. After everything you said about buying bikes from junkies, I thought you would go crazy on me."

"Why should I?" said Mattijs. "It's no concern of mine."

I said, "I'm glad you feel that way."

"You have done something terrible," Mattijs continued. "Why then should I scold you or get angry? You are the one who is going to suffer. You'll see."

Seven

IT TASTES SO GOOD

It is a truth universally acknowledged that a single woman who spends a lot of time alone is going to find herself on the receiving end of all sorts of attention from strange, often sinister, men. This is ground we've covered before, but it bears repeating, particularly as regards the following narrative.

The real conundrum lies not with the obvious perverts: the fellow who exposed himself to me on the tram, the grinning drunks in the red-light district who lie supine in the street for an unobstructed view of my crotch as I ride by. Such men are repulsive and hateful and something no woman should have to deal with, but they are also easy enough to ignore. Far more confounding are the men who, while clearly creepy, manage to wear down your defenses through unbridled chutzpah. The English word for chutzpah is "nerve," but that anemic little monosyllable is to the heady blend of obnoxiousness, anxiety, and bravado exhibited by such a person as a stolen kiss is to a full-throttle gangbang. These men aren't rapists, at least not in the classical sense. In their minds, "no" doesn't translate immediately to "yes." "No" means "maybe" or "I need to know more about you" or "while I find you physically repugnant, I might be persuaded to hold it in my hand for a little while if it means you'll finally leave."

While many young women, no matter how capable, fall prey to such individuals at some point in their lives, the young woman living abroad finds herself uniquely vulnerable to such offensive machinations due to linguistic barriers, a disinclination to be rude, and an ambition to live up to her own invented image of herself as a free spirit who is up for anything. To my deep shame, I was no exception. Thus far, I had been convinced to allow an aggressively dull financier to tongue my neck at a bar, despite his strong resemblance in looks and manner to Howard the Duck; I accepted a complimentary "back correction" in the Leidsestraat from a man in violet parachute pants during which he grazed both of my breasts (in my defense, he did claim to be a Reiki master, which is like a doctor for people who don't eat animal protein or wear clothing with zippers). Like I've always said: Love is wonderful, but bad sex is a story. And I sensed there might be quite a good scoop waiting for me in the unusual earthling a few tables away, staring at me intently, and making a soft growling noise in the back of his throat, like a tiger.

As I was bored, anxious to begin work, and trying to save money, I had begun to write in cafés to pass the time. Given my background in theater, it seemed to make sense to write a play. I didn't have any expectations of it ever being produced, but it gave me something to do, and with no phone, no friends aside from Mattijs and Jeroen, and no real responsibilities, the work was soon well underway. My previous literary attempts had been labored little expectorations, painful but necessary, like a visit to the periodontist, but now I found I actually looked forward to spending time in the little world I was creating, in the company of my new fictional friends. If necessity is the mother of invention, boredom and loneliness are the obstetricians of literature.

The strange man and his sex growls, however, were not helping my concentration. I raised my head, inadvertently meeting his eyes, and he got up from his table and walked over to me.

"*Chi state aspettando?*" he said, angling his torso insouciantly against the wall. He had a very round face that reminded me of Bod, the hydrocephalic British cartoon character who used to appear on Nickelodeon in the '80s, but he had nice shoulders and I didn't hate what he was wearing: a plain white V-neck T-shirt with a small hole in the shoulder and faded blue jeans. A variety of objects that appeared to be bladder stones hung from rough leather thongs around his neck. In America, these clearly are the amulets of a powerful douchebaggery but, like purses and man-sandals, are the kind of thing you sometimes have to overlook on a European male. Pushed back to a rakish angle on his head was a vintage-looking porkpie hat. This was another bad sign, but I wasn't quite old enough to know that yet.

"I can't understand a word you just said," I replied.

"Oh, *scusi, scusi*," he said, making a little bow. "You are an English. So sorry. You are so beautiful, I think for sure you are *italiana*."

I wanted to roll my eyes, but I have a disease where being told I am pretty causes my brain to secrete a chemical that temporarily paralyzes neuron function. (Luckily, I've since found a cure for this affliction. It's called "aging.")

"Actually, I'm an American," I simpered.

"An American," he repeated. "But of course then your family must be Italian." To this, I gave a noncommittal little grunt, because I am a self-loathing New York Jew.

"You are a writer?" he said, leaning forward to peek at my open notebook. I lunged forward, covering my work with my hands.

"It's okay," he said. "Me also, I am writer. All the day, I am writing the stories, the plays, the poetry. My name is Ivan, a Russian name, because my mother, she name me after Turgenev. You know Turgenev."

"Yes."

"Most of all I love Boccaccio. You know also of him?"

I said I had read most of the *Decameron*, a statement that would be perfectly true if the *Decameron* were forty pages long. Clutching his heart with both hands, he sneered. "But you have not read it in Italian. You must read it in Italian, or is like you have never read it at all."

I believe this aspersion on my ability to fully appreciate the profundity of Boccaccio is what practitioners of *The Game* would consider a "neg." And it worked, just like it's supposed to. Say what you will about those guys (and believe me, I have), they do, in a horrible way, sort of know what they're talking about. I guess even a potential campus shooter with satanic facial hair, a leopard-print cowboy hat, and a boiling abyss of rage toward women is right twice a day. I wanted this stranger to think I was smart again, and obviously the best way to do that was to follow him to his table while he told me what was wrong with me. Also, his table had a bottle of prosecco on it that I didn't pay for, so who's stupid now?

Ivan was not alone. At his table was another man who had been hidden from my view by a large planter of fake geraniums.

Ivan said, "This is Enzo."

Enzo had used some sort of powerful ointment to slick back his shoulder-length black hair to the nape of his neck, where it erupted into a club of tight curls, like middle-period Joan Crawford. His cheekbones were of the sort not seen outside a Versace ad or a male escort service, and he wore a shirt of skintight mesh that bore an unholy combination of rhinestones, religious imagery, and tie-dye, like the wallpaper of the gayest church in hell. Beneath his clothes, his muscles bulged; his bicep easily matched the circumference of one of my thighs.

"Nice to meet you, Enzo," I said.

Ivan said, "Enzo doesn't speak English."

I said, "Is Enzo a writer too?"

Ivan quickly translated for Enzo, and they both had a good laugh. "No," said Ivan, wiping his eyes. "Enzo is not doing the writing. Enzo is . . . how do you say it? Enzo studies to be a dentist."

"A dentist?" I was sure I had misunderstood.

"*Sì,*" said Ivan. "A dentist. Is for the teeth." He tapped impatiently with his fingernails on one of his incisors. "Enzo say you have very nice teeth," Ivan said. "Big." Enzo was staring directly at my breasts.

I'm done here, I thought. I drained my glass and set it hard on the table. "I have to go."

"One minute," said Ivan. "This weekend, we have a big dinner. My friend Angelo, he make all of the pasta for the Italian restaurants of Amsterdam. This weekend, he make ravioli, we have big dinner party for many, many friends. We drink, we eat, we dance. Please, say you will come."

This is how people get sex-trafficked, I thought suddenly. They compliment your teeth/breasts, they promise you ravioli, and the next thing you know you're chained to a mattress while a mobster with a picture of Stalin tattooed on his chest shoves a curling iron up your ass and tells you he loves you.

"I don't think that's a good idea," I said.

Ivan pulled a pen from his pocket and scribbled a number on the blank side of a paper beer mat. "Call me if you change your mind."

Jeroen was on the balcony when I got home, grilling pork sausages in a roasting pan he had filled with charcoal and wedged under the drying rack for the laundry.

"Wonderful news!" he exclaimed. "Helga is gone into the

hospital to have part of her stomach removed! At last we are able to barbeque!"

I said, "And our underpants will have that authentic mesquite flavor!"

Jeroen told me to go make a salad. I went into the kitchen, where Mattijs was selecting the least stale rolls from a white paper bag and placing them inside a napkin-lined basket, a cigarette dangling from his lips. Hastily, I sliced a tomato and a cucumber and dumped a bag of prepackaged lettuce into a glass bowl.

"I met a couple of guys today," I said, as we settled down to eat. "Italians."

Mattijs dropped his cigarette into the puddle of salad dressing he was using as an ashtray, where it dissolved with an oily sizzle. "What did they want?"

"What do you think?" smirked Jeroen, slicing firmly into his sausage.

"How was your day?" I asked.

"Not bad," Jeroen answered for both of them. "We spoke to the artistic committee today, about the money for the play."

"And?"

He shrugged. "They need us to file a few more forms."

To mask my disappointment, I grabbed a roll and shoved it into my mouth. It was stale but, if I chewed hard, not inedible.

Mattijs made a face. "I hate these kind of phone calls. Every time I must speak to a kind of official person, I feel like I have done something naughty and now I am being called into the office of the principal."

I started to tell him that I could relate, having been called into the principal's office on account of unchecked naughtiness many times, when I suddenly realized there was something very wrong with my mouth. Instinctively, my tongue flew to the back of my jaw to find my molar was gone. In the place where it used to be was a gruesome stump, hollow and dry, like a dead thing.

"Oh my God," I said. "Oh my God."

"Or like a dream," Mattijs pressed on, "where you go before your entire class to give a speech, then realize you are completely naked. Also in the dream I am often peeing on myself. I don't know what this means."

I shoved both my hands inside my mouth.

Jeroen looked up from his sausage. "Are you all right, sweetie?"

"My tooth!" I cried. "My tooth!"

Jeroen said, "Darling, I can't understand you. Take your fingers out of your mouth."

"My tooth! It's gone! I ate my tooth!"

"It's not possible," Mattijs said. "How could you have eaten your tooth?"

"It was a cap!" The profound horror of what had just happened began to dawn on me. "It's been loose for ages, but I could never afford to get it fixed, so I would just sort of jam it back into place!" Frantically, I shredded my dinner roll, dismantled my untouched sausage, plunged my hands into the salad bowl, scattering lettuce leaves and bits of vegetables over the balcony. "It's gone. I must have swallowed it. Oh God," I wailed. "Oh God. What am I going to do?"

Jeroen was already on his feet. "I'm going to call my mother." Wordlessly, Mattijs lit a cigarette and handed it to me. The smoke stung the tender socket around the dead stump, but I sucked deeply anyway.

"I remember when I had my wisdom teeth removed," Mattijs said suddenly. "A piece of onion became stuck in the empty space. It was weeks before I could get to see the dentist, and by that time it had fused together with my gum. It finally was necessary for a surgeon to cut it out with a scalpel." He shuddered. "Even now if I eat an onion I think of it always."

Jeroen returned, phone in hand. "Did you talk to her?" I asked.

"*Ja*, she says it will not be possible to visit a public dentist for maybe one to two months. But she also says that if you do not have it fixed soon, you will get an infection that will spread to your brain, and then you will die. So to wait this long, it is also not possible."

"It is not possible." This is something the Dutch love to say. It's not possible to take out the trash except on alternating Tuesdays, no matter how bad it smells. It's not possible to obtain medication for lactose intolerance or clinical depression, as it is not possible that either exists. It's not possible to see a dentist in time for your brain not to cave in on itself like a rotten bell pepper.

"What *is* possible?" I asked.

"You will have to see a private dentist," Jeroen said, "and my mother says that it is going to be very expensive."

"How expensive?"

Jeroen winced as though to avoid a blow. "Very, very, very expensive."

The last emergency dental procedure I required had immediately followed my high school graduation ceremony. My family and I were eating celebratory sundaes at Petrow's Grill and Soda Fountain, when I was felled by a sudden, searing pain in my jaw. While my friends were out doing keg stands and having clumsy, instantly regretted sexual encounters with people they hoped never to see again, I was splayed on the floor of the basement with an ice pack pressed to my jaw, screaming in agony. The emergency root canal had left me with the cap that now made its stately promenade through the recesses of my digestive system and, including a special fee for "expedited service," had come to $3,800. That was *with* insurance. During the *Clinton* administration.

I said, "I think it's time for me to call *my* mother." The boys crowded around me as I dialed.

"Hello?" said a peeved-sounding voice on the other end.

"Mommy?" I wailed. "Oh, Mommy, it's so good to hear your voice!"

"Oh," she said flatly. "It's you."

"Yes, it's me. Mommy, I'm in big trouble."

"Oh God," my mother gasped. "What happened? What did you do?"

I told her the whole story: the swallowed cap, the macabre stump, the evils of socialized medicine. "I'm going to have to find a private dentist and it's going to be very, very, very expensive," I said. "I need you to wire me some money right away."

My mother laughed a horrible laugh. "I'm in Hawaii."

"You're what?"

"I'm in Hawaii. In Kauai. Even if I wanted to rush right out and send you thousands of dollars, I wouldn't have a clue where to go."

"Let me talk to Daddy," I demanded. My father, psychotic hypochondriac that he is, would understand the seriousness of the situation. My father would not allow his oldest daughter to succumb to acute encephalitis in a foreign land.

"He's on his bike," snapped my mother. "I'm following in the car."

"What *time* is it there?"

"About seven. He likes to get an early start. He'll get tired in a few hours, and then we'll have lunch before he rides back to the hotel. Then it'll be time for dinner."

"Sounds romantic," I said. "I'm glad you're having such an enriching trip."

"People who live in glass houses," said my mother, "shouldn't be assholes."

"That doesn't even make any sense."

My mother sighed. "Find a goddamn dentist and put it on your credit card. We'll deal with it later."

Mattijs was shaking his head violently from side to side, like a lunatic trying to shake away the demons. "What?" I mouthed, putting my hand over the receiver.

"You cannot put your medical bills on a credit card in Holland," he said in a stage whisper. "The system is not set up for it."

"Mattijs said the dentist won't take a credit card here," I said.

"You're fucking kidding me," said my mother.

"What am I going to do?"

My mother said, "I don't suppose you'd consider . . . waiting for it to . . . you know, to pass?"

"No," I said firmly. "Absolutely not."

"Well, then I guess you're shit out of luck," my mother said, "if you'll pardon the pun. What the—GODDAMMIT!"

"What?" I said.

"Your father just stopped at a traffic light and I almost hit him." In the background I could hear my father cursing violently at a familiarly hysterical pitch. "ALL RIGHT, MARTY, I SEE YOU!"

"Mom? Mommy? Are you still there?"

"What? Yes. I'm here—*ALL RIGHT, MARTY*, GIVE IT A GODDAMN REST! Listen," she said sharply, back to me. "I can't deal with this right now. Your father is out of his FUCK-ING mind, I've got heartburn that would kill a horse from all this goddamn pineapple, and I've had to pee for the last hour and a half. I'm pulling over somewhere before I wet my pants in the rental car."

"But what am I supposed to do?" I wailed.

"How the hell should I know? FUCK! I just missed the entrance to that McDonald's. Fuckity fuckity fuck. Good-bye."

Horrified, I turned to face my friends. "Now what?"

"I'm afraid you will just have to pay a huge amount of money," Jeroen said sympathetically, "unless you happen yourself to know a dentist who can help."

"As a matter of fact," I said, "I think I do."

_____

Are You About to Be Sex-Trafficked?

A CHECKLIST*

❏ Have you been approached with an offer of work as a fashion model, despite the fact that you are four foot ten and more than forty pounds overweight?

❏ Have your companions jokingly asked to see your passport and refused to hand it back?

_____

* Sex trafficking and sexual slavery are terrible, terrible things that happen, terribly, to millions of people worldwide. It is very serious. This book means in no way to demean the plight of the millions of women and children consigned to horrific existences through no fault of their own. This book is, however, a work of sometimes tasteless "comedy," for which it apologizes in advance. Please be forewarned: This checklist in no way comprises a realistic set of criteria for identifying actual sex traffickers. Rachel Shukert, HarperCollins, and its subsidiaries can in no way be held responsible for any harm that might come to someone seriously attempting to use this checklist for its stated purpose. In fact, anyone who uses this checklist for its stated purpose is a fucking idiot, and no one can be held responsible for them in any capacity, unless they have been consigned to the care of the state on the grounds of truly supernatural stupidity. They pose a danger to themselves and the world and should not be permitted to bear children or run for political office.

❏ Has anyone asked for the address of where you are staying and, once given an answer, followed up by asking if your father is or was a special operative in the CIA?

❏ Have your companions displayed a working knowledge of early twentieth-century modernist artistic movements? Have you spent the last half hour discussing the allegorical significance of Castorp in *The Magic Mountain* by Thomas Mann? If so, you are probably safe, as the only sex traffickers who read Thomas Mann exist in novels written by men who attended extremely expensive prep schools and attempt to humanize their essentially sociopathic characters with endearing characteristics such as a love for prewar German literature in order to facilitate long chapters of psychologically revealing text explaining to us that we all have the capacity for evil.

❏ Have you asked your companions what they do for a living, and have they replied that they are "big-time showbiz agents," "director from film, very good for you," or "vagina inspectors"?

❏ If you have decided to take heroin or other drugs, have you made sure your companion has taken some first, *using the same bag*?

❏ Have you overheard anyone say anything like: "Excellent. The sheik will be pleased with her?"

Years ago, in Omaha, I knew an old man named Jackie. An elderly hipster in dark glasses and a scruffy goatee, Jackie hung around the same secondhand bookstore that I did, and he told me stories from his fascinating past as a musician in New York in the '50s. His band had toured all over the world to much acclaim before succumbing to the usual cautionary woes, and Jackie had returned to Omaha, where he managed to make a decent living repairing refrigerators, ovens, and other household appliances. He didn't seem altogether dissatisfied with the way things had turned out, but there was more than a hint of wistfulness in his stories, and I had a sense that he was encouraging me to go for it, to live bigger, if wiser, than he had. But when I received my acceptance letter from college and proudly told Jackie that I was moving to New York, he simply grunted and turned back to the shelves, pretending to be absorbed in a dog-eared biography of Arnold Schoenberg. Feeling hurt, I asked what the problem was. He removed his dark glasses, something he rarely did, as he was self-conscious about the milky cataract that he couldn't afford to have removed. His good right eye bored directly into mine.

"New York City is a tornado," he said, "and just like a tornado, it's going to snatch you up if you put yourself in its path. Some of the people it snatches up get caught in the tornado and pulled down inside it, and they become real New Yorkers. And others get caught on the outside, and the tornado lifts them up into the sky, until it spits them out, back down to earth." Jackie's cataract was milky and iridescent. It reminded me of a moonstone ring my sister had given me for my birthday. I had worn it every day until I accidentally slammed it against the corner of my desk. The moonstone cracked in half, and I never wore it again. "Now, whether you get caught on the inside or the outside of the tornado," Jackie continued, "is a matter of chance. But the problem is that sometimes it takes ten, twenty years to figure out which side you're on. You think you're on the inside, but you ain't. And in the meantime, the tornado has lifted you up higher and higher, and when it spits you out, you've got a long ways to fall."

He paused expectantly, but I didn't know what to say. I was eighteen years old. A single year seemed like an eternity. I couldn't even imagine how it would feel to be twenty. Smiling faintly, Jackie replaced his dark glasses. "I'm just going to tell you one more thing," he said. "Whenever anybody invites you anywhere, you remember this: You got no idea what's going on behind that door. Could be anything. Could be something good, or it could be something a nice kid like you got no business being part of. But *you ain't got no idea.* You remember that"—Jackie nodded somewhere off into the distance—"and maybe you'll be all right."

For better or for worse, the New York City I moved to in 1998 was in the process of being converted to a 22.7-square-mile Bed Bath & Beyond, and Jackie's advice had proved largely unnecessary. Now, as I stood in front of the hulking door of the address Ivan had given me over the telephone, his words came back to me. I wondered if I should flee. But a sharp pain coursed through my gum and up my jaw, and I brought my fist down heavily against the door, again and again, as though I could beat it into submission.

I heard footsteps and held my breath, prepared for anything. The door swung open, revealing a small dark man dressed in white and covered from head to toe in an even dusting of flour, as though he were about to be sautéed for a giant's supper. He raked his narrow black eyes over me without interest and spoke quickly and angrily in Italian. From the shadows, Ivan's face appeared over one of the man's powdery shoulders.

"Bellissima!" Ivan cried.

He lunged for me, planting several noisy kisses on my cheeks before crushing me against his chest in a rib-cracking embrace and wedging his pelvis carefully next to mine, in order to give our clothed genitals a proper chance to get acquainted. When he finally released me, the floury man was retreating into the dark recesses of the building, a gritty cloud following in his wake.

"All day long," Ivan said, clasping my head in his hands, "as I think I will see you tonight, my heart is pounding, pounding, like in the tale of Poe. I am a writer! But now, at last, *bellissima*, you are here!" He rained another volley of kisses on my face, my eyelids, my hair. I screwed up my face and turned my head like a little kid deflecting the unwelcome saliva of an ancient aunt.

"Was that the ravioli guy?"

"*Sì, sì*, is Angelo. I am supposed to answer the door, but I am bringing in the tables and I cannot hear."

"He seemed so angry."

"*Pah*. He is angry to leave his sauce, he curses at us," Ivan said. "Angelo has no lover," he added, by way of explanation. "He has only his pasta."

I wanted to make it very clear to him that we were not lovers, that any acts I might feel compelled to engage in for the sake of my infected molar had nothing to do with love, but he was already ushering me inside the basement, where several people sat at a long table drinking red wine. Ivan introduced me. There was Marco, who with his tiny black beard and large hoop earring appeared to be taking a night off from his job as the bride auctioneer in the Pirates of the Caribbean ride. Marco had paired his white jeans with an orange paisley shirt unbuttoned to the navel, and as he leaned forward to kiss me, once on each cheek and once on the mouth, I could feel that the shirt was made of washable silk, like the colorful blouses the boys at Hebrew school used to wear to Bar Mitzvah parties.

"Are you a dentist too?" I asked.

Ivan quickly translated my question for Marco, who threw his head back, laughing, and kissed me sloppily on the nostril, which was creative. His tongue flicked the corner of my mouth as the heavy gold crucifix he wore around his neck thudded passionately against my clavicle.

"*Bellissima*," said Marco. "*Ti amo, ti amo!*"

Beside Marco was a wraithlike couple clothed in narrow black, their elegant heads emerging from clouds of cigarette smoke and tangled skeins of slim silk scarves. "This is Alessandra," Ivan said, pointing his chin toward the female of the pair. "Alessandra is now the woman of Todd," he whispered in my ear. "But once she was my lover."

Even if he hadn't told me, I would have known from the way she jumped up too eagerly to greet me, her kohl-rimmed eyes widening with ersatz friendliness as she embraced me. "It's so nice to meet you! Ivan has told us so much about you."

"I didn't know Ivan knew so much about me."

"Oh, he does. He's an excellent judge of character. We're so excited that you're here!" Her English was perfect. "This is my boyfriend, Todd."

"What's up?" said the male wraith, leaning forward to shake my hand. As he poked his face out of the shadow, I saw that his eyes were also heavily made up.

"Are you American?" I asked.

Todd hissed dismissively. "I don't know."

"What do you mean, you don't know?"

"Well," he said, rolling the word in his mouth like a spoonful of soup too hot to swallow, "I was born in Orlando. I went to high school there. But I've moved around so much since I've been modeling and everything that I don't really consider myself anything anymore."

"Oh, really?" I said. "You're allowed to do that?" I felt the same scorn I did for people who say things like, "Well, my parents are Jewish, but I'm nothing." Bullshit. If you're Jewish to Hitler, you're Jewish to me.

Todd launched a cloud of cigarette smoke in my face and crossed his arms over his skinny chest as Alessandra gazed at him adoringly. "We are all the sum of our own creation," he said.

Ivan pulled me aside, under the pretext of hugging and kiss-

ing me some more, before I could respond. "Todd is a secret homosexual," he murmured, as he thrust his tongue into my ear
canal. "Alessandra soon will tire of him. She will look again for a
real man."

I jerked away, running the tip of my own tongue over the dead
stump of my tooth. "Where's Enzo?" I asked. "Isn't he coming tonight?"

"*Sì, sì.* He is with Fabrizio, his brother," Ivan said. "Together
they are gathering more wine."

"Two," Marco said, grinning, holding up two thick fingers upon
which a pair of gold rings flashed. "They are twin." It was the first
time he had betrayed any sign of understanding a word any of us
had said.

Enzo and Fabrizio were, in fact, identical twins, although Fabrizio had distinguished himself from his brother by means of a large
diamond earring and a cropped leather vest, which he wore over his
bare chest. His left bicep was also tattooed with a flattering likeness
of Jesus, grimacing under a crown of very convincing thorns.

"It's very lifelike," I said politely, as Fabrizio urged me to trace
Jesus' anguished mouth with my forefingers. "You can almost feel
the scourging."

Fabrizio evidently took this as a compliment, seizing my index
finger and swirling it around inside his mouth. I looked to Ivan for
help, but he just smiled, swinging an arm around my waist. "Come,"
he said. "Drink some wine. The other guests will soon arrive."

Every once in a while, you find yourself at a party that feels like
what you pictured as a child when you imagined what adulthood
must be like: dark, semi-secret, filled with beautiful people from
all walks of life. New acquaintances and old friends laughed and
joked, welcoming each other with wide, wine-stained smiles, and

the food, as promised, was divine: long loaves of crusty bread torn into fat wedges and dipped in golden pools of olive oil slicked with sweet vinegar, platters of gnocchi and pillows of ravioli in every imaginable sauce: brown butter and sage, rosy cream, crushed piquant tomato studded with vivid basil and slivers of sausage. In one corner, Fabrizio was making bicep-Jesus dance for a pair of well-dressed Swedes, in another Enzo was grinding his pelvis to the delight of a table of German backpackers. The Italians had roamed the streets looking for talent, I thought, casting the perfect party. Ivan nestled next to me, sopping up the sauce from my plate with a chunk of bread and placing it against my tongue. The flavor filled my mouth and he buried his face against the nape of my neck, covering my hairline with damp kisses. I didn't mind anymore. I was beyond caring. There's a time and a place for self-determination, and a great party full of shirtless Italians where nobody speaks English is not one of them. Sometimes, you just have to drown your hypercritical, personal-space-needing persona in a giant glass of Chianti. Why wait until you're dead to take a vacation from yourself? Why not try to get out sometimes while you're still alive?

After the feasting, we danced to Brazilian bossa nova until the crowd started to thin and the party moved to the living room upstairs. Marco and the twins disappeared. I was crouched on the floor, locked in conversation about the anachronism of the Electoral College with the still avowedly not-American Todd (whose North Florida accent was back in full force), when Ivan curled up beside me. "You are too beautiful," he muttered thickly. "I can no longer control myself. Please. We must go now to the bed."

I couldn't pretend I didn't know this was coming. But Ivan had started to grow on me. If I had to sleep with any of them, it would be him. He'd read Turgenev. And this had to be an important step on the road back to dental health: "I fuck-a your friend, now fix-a my crown!" I rose and followed him up a flight of Dutch steps, the kind so steep that, depending on your level of intoxication, you sometimes have to climb on your hands and knees. Just before we reached the top, we were stopped by an anguished shriek. Alessandra stood at the foot of the stairs, screaming and crying as though she would die.

"She says, I am in her blood, she is in my blood, I will never be free of her," Ivan said disgustedly. He roared something back. "I tell her she is in my blood like a disease, like the AIDS," he explained.

Mentioning AIDS before casual sex is like saying "bomb" on a plane. But before I could flee down the steps and into the night, Alessandra dissolved into tears and threw herself across the stairs, shouting and pointing at me between great hiccuping intakes of breath.

"Ah," Ivan groaned. "Now she curses you."

"What?" What did I have to do with this? I was but a stranger in this land, doing what I had to to keep my brain from exploding. (I'm pretty sure that's the title of a country song, by the way.) "What's she saying?"

Ivan shushed me in order to make out the words of Alessandra's frenzied tirade. "You are a whore . . . you should be raped by dogs . . . you should never give birth to a child . . . no, you should have a child, and the child should be a monster. Is very typical," he finished. Alessandra lay crumpled on the floor, a lumpen, beautiful puddle convulsing with sobs.

"Maybe we should forget the sex," I said hopefully (used here properly, to mean "in a hopeful manner"). I may have been willing to go through with this, but as prostitutes and married people know, willing and eager are two very different things. "She seems really upset."

"No, no, no," commanded Ivan. "She is dead to me. I do not love her anymore. Now it is you I love. I love only you."

"Give me a fucking break," I started to say, but Ivan had already whisked me into a bedroom, romantically furnished with several piles of dirty clothes and a bare mattress lying directly on the floor.

"AAAAAHHHHHH!!!" Out of nowhere, a hulking apparition had leapt from behind the door, tackled me onto the bed. It was Marco, resplendently nude apart from his neck chains and a mesh zebra-print G-string. *"Bellissima!"* he shrieked and pinned me flat on my back between his walnut-colored thighs.

"What the *FUCK!*" I screamed, beating his shoulders with my handbag, but Ivan, also suddenly minus his shirt and pants, was atop me as well, rhythmically thrusting his tongue in and out of my mouth in a manner I assumed was meant to remind me of intercourse. On the downstairs end, Marco, quick as a shot, had jerked my panties roughly to one side, threatening to cut off circulation to my upper thigh, and begun to lap enthusiastically at my pubic hair. I made the horrible mistake of looking down. With his pink tongue darting out of his scrubby black beard, it looked like another vagina was licking my vagina, like one of those pictures within a picture within a picture, the kind that go on forever and eventually drive you insane.

"No!" I cried, clutching his head in my hands and forcing it away. "Stop it!"

"DO NOT BE ASHAMED, *BELLISSIMA*!" Marco bellowed. "IT-A TASTES-A SO GOOD!"

"THAT'S NOT WHAT I MEANT!"

Ivan stroked my hair, covering my face with conciliatory little kisses. This was date rape at its most romantic. "Is okay, *cara mia*. I love you. I love you."

"NO MEANS NO!" I shouted. "I am not going to have sex with you! *Definitely* not with both of you!"

"No, no, no, of course not," Ivan murmured sweetly. "We will not have the sex. We will just *make the love*." And with that important clarification, he resumed his ferocious tongue thrusts, while the befuddled Marco returned happily to his post between my legs. *I'm being date-raped*, I thought, *I'm being fully threesome date-raped*. Then Marco's insistent tongue hit his target, and in spite of myself, I gasped. This was a catastrophe. Can you still prosecute if they make you come?

"Yes," I said to myself, firmly. "Yes, you can."

"Yes, yes," muttered Ivan. "You beginning to relax." He grabbed my hand and forced it on his penis. I felt something strange under my fingers, something that wasn't supposed to be there. When my sister was little, she contracted ringworm from a cat named Potato. For weeks, her scalp was laced with scaly, yellowish streaks that made me recoil from her whenever she came near me. It appeared that something similar had happened to Ivan's dick. A raised, worm-shaped tendril was snaking over the head and creepily circling the shaft. That did it. I wanted my tooth fixed, but not enough to get raped and get ringworm in my pussy. This bullshit ended *now*.

"GET OFF OF ME!" I shouted, sitting up so abruptly that I clocked Ivan in the face with the top of my head. He winced in pain. *Good*, I thought.

"*Cara*, what is wrong?" Ivan pleaded. "You don't like us?"

"NO!" I yelled. "I don't! I just wanted to see a fucking dentist!"

Marco glanced up from his labors, his face falling under its coating of slimy goo. Ivan looked equally hurt. "But, *bellissima*," he said, "I love you so much. I wish to love-make with you all through the night."

"Look at this," I said, switching on the lamp beside the bed, and pulling back my lip to reveal the dead stump.

"Oh no!" Ivan was on his feet, pulling on his pants. "*Cara!* Why you not say something? We get Enzo. Enzo! Enzo!" He ran into the hallway. Marco, still in his zebra thong, patted my hand comfortingly. "Enzo!" Ivan pounded on a closed door on the other side of the landing. "Enzo!"

From the other side of the door came a cry of outrage, which Ivan countered with his own entreaties. At the foot of the stairs, Alessandra still lay, fully clothed and snoring peacefully. Marco continued to pat my hand. "Is okay," he murmured kindly. "I sorry. Is okay."

"Thank you," I said. Despite the fact that he had sort of tried to tongue-rape me, I felt fond of him. If we had all been clearer about our motives from the start, maybe none of this would have happened. It was a good lesson for the future. "I accept your apology."

Enzo emerged at last, scowling and fully nude. On his stomach, just a few inches above the crest of his massive erection, I noticed his name was tattooed in swirling gothic letters. E-N-Z-O. I wondered who was down there that might need a reminder.

Ivan spoke rapidly, gesturing toward me, and Enzo, looking irritated, grabbed my jaw and forced open my mouth to peer inside. Ivan stepped up to translate.

"He say you lose your tooth."

"Mrrmmmpphh," I replied. "Aaaahh nnrhoooo."

"Is okay," said Marco, his zebra-printed genitals warmly grazing my thigh. "Is okay."

Ivan said, "He say you will need to put a new . . . how do you say it . . . like the hat on the head of a king."

"Krrnnwwn," I said.

"*Sì, sì*, crown. On the top." Ivan pointed to his own magnificent gold-topped molar. "Also," he continued, "Enzo think around it is a little bit . . . sick. *Contagiato.* You will need the medicine."

Enzo tapped the stump with his finger. I wrenched my face away from his grip, my face clenching with pain.

"Can he fix it?" I asked. "I mean, obviously not right this second"—I gestured to Enzo's penis, which, despite his examination of my oozing gum, remained miraculously erect—"but sometime soon? Tomorrow, maybe?"

They conferred. "He say he has not yet learned to make such a procedure," Ivan informed me regretfully. "And he cannot make for you the letter for the medicine. If you want, he will make for you a time to see a true dentist. But, he must tell you that it will be very, very expensive. And now he must return to the German girl and his brother. They are waiting for him to finish in making the sex."

Ivan and Marco retreated back to their bedroom. Through the narrow window of the hallway, I could tell that it would soon be light. Sore and defeated in more ways than one, I crawled under a clothing rack where, unmolested, I could wait for the dawn.

When I staggered into the apartment, hungover and exhausted, Jeroen was waiting for me.

"You're alive!" he exclaimed, throwing his arms around me.

I said, "My faith in humanity has been sorely tested."

Jeroen laughed. He sounded unhinged. I cringed as his cackle reverberated through the inflamed cavern of my skull. "How many cups of coffee have you had?" I asked.

"Five. I feel fabulous. And I have some good news."

"What?"

"Well," he said, savoring the moment in his gentle, infuriating way, "I have spoken to my mother, and it seems she has been able to find you an appointment with a dentist."

"Really?"

"It is this afternoon. My mother was very lucky—she is a friend of the dentist's sister—and as it turned out, there was a cancellation, so she was able to book the appointment for you. He is really one of the best dentists in Amsterdam. It will be like you are going to the dentist on Park Avenue. The only thing is that it is going to be—"

"Very, very expensive. I know."

Jeroen pursed his lips. "Well, it is up to you. But the appointment is yours if you want it."

That afternoon, I grimly rode my bicycle to the dentist's office. I had withdrawn every cent from both my checking accounts, and also brought along my passport, my computer, and a few bits of jewelry that I hoped I might be able to use as collateral, should it come to that. Maybe they'd let me work out some kind of payment plan, or perhaps I could work off my debt cleaning toilets or disposing of biohazardous waste.

The office was filled with oriental rugs and tasteful artwork. A courteous receptionist checked me in, told me that they had been expecting me, and I spent a relaxing few minutes watching the koi play in an enormous wall tank and listening to Queen on the hi-fi before the dentist appeared and showed me into the examining room. Back in the States, my childhood dentist plastered his few remaining hairs over his scalp with what appeared to be saliva and wore eyeglasses with tinted ocher shades, like a forest ranger or a child molester, but this dentist, dressed in white jeans and a snug white Lacoste polo that showed off his tan, appeared to have stepped directly from the pages of a cologne ad. Despite my ordeal of the night before, I couldn't help but feel a little bit turned on as he gently positioned my head against the foam doughnut at the end of the bench. I was aching and sexually traumatized, but I was still human. Maybe this was why I was paying extra. Maybe ugly dentists cost less.

The dentist worked quickly and silently, injecting my sore gum with Novocain and expertly fitting a temporary crown over the stump. He scribbled out a prescription for antibiotics on a yellow pad and then took me outside to deal with the bill.

"Okay," he said, "I must prepare you. Obviously you don't have the national insurance, so I have to say it's going to be a little bit expensive."

"I know." I fingered the wad of bills in my pocket mournfully in a lovingly tactile farewell. "Just tell me what it is."

He sucked the air between his sculpted cheeks in an apologetic hiss and looked down for a moment before he could meet my eye. "It is eighty-two euros."

I said, "You are fucking kidding me."

"I know," he said sympathetically, "but at least you will not have to pay for the medicine! You must only take the prescription to any pharmacy and they will give it to you for free."

"You are fucking kidding me," I said again.

The cap in my mouth felt foreign, cool, and smooth. I could have covered the dentist's face in kisses and called him *bellisimo*. But that would just be creepy.

Eight

THEY GIVE ME CHICKEN, BUT STILL I AM A STRANGER

On the blustery winds of October came the great misfortune. A one-two punch of deeply awful luck:

1. The request for funding was denied. There would be no play.
2. My purse and everything in it was stolen.

I should have seen it coming. Despite Mattijs and Jeroen's assurances that the Dutch government handed out funding for the arts like subprime mortgages in an Orlando suburb, the idea that it would be prepared to hand over in excess of eighty thousand euros on six weeks' notice to a fledgling company with no production history had been a tad optimistic. Nor had it been terribly savvy of me to leave my bag, which contained my credit cards, my checkbook, and what remained of my ready cash, unattended at an outdoor party in the red-light district. Jeroen had warned me for weeks about stealthy pickpockets who crawled underneath tables in dimly lit restaurants and other public places, stealing everything they could lay their hands on and occasionally molesting the private parts of ladies who couldn't keep their legs closed while they ate, but I had dismissed this as an urban legend, like the people who claim they woke up in a bathtub full of ice cubes with "Congratulations! Your kidney is now on its way to Ecuador!" scrawled in eyeliner on their shower curtain. (I bet they took out their kidneys themelves. Some people will do anything for attention.)

Jeroen at least made a show of sympathy, but Mattijs was intractable. He had been raised a Catholic and had a rather more inflexible sense of retribution than his irreligious companion. "This is what happens when you buy a stolen bicycle," he said, with no small hint of satisfaction. "An eye for an eye, a tooth for a tooth, a bag for a bike."

Jeroen tried to smile. "What will you do now?"

"I don't know," I said. "I can't go home. I can't even book a plane ticket without a credit card."

"Maybe your parents can make you one," Mattijs said hopefully.

"No!" I said, startled at the vehemence of my response. "I'm not going home. And I don't want my parents to know anything about this. I'm sick and tired of asking them for help."

Deep down, I had always known this day must come. You can run from reality, but you can't escape it. It just hangs back, biding its time, mocking you, until the horrible moment when it bursts forward in a kinetic jolt of speed, leaving you with no way to catch up. Eventually, you have to accept that you're outclassed. There was a throb in my voice as I said the words I had hoped never to utter as long as I lived. "I guess I'll have to get a job."

Some people wax rhapsodic about the nature of work, the sense of purpose derived from honest labor, the satisfaction of receiving one's hard-earned pay. There is a name for these people: retirees. I, on the other hand, have always felt it was more than a coincidence that "job" as in "occupation" was spelled the same way as "Job" as in "Book of." To my mind, both were synonyms for crushing despair.

My terrible work experiences started early. In high school, I worked on the weekends as a barista at a strip mall coffee shop in Omaha called Casey Joe's. I had noticed the "Help Wanted" sign in the window one afternoon while I was picking up the dry cleaning and, sick of asking my parents for money every weekend (although as yet ignorant of how this would become the major theme in my life), went in to fill out an application. The shop was owned by a man named Spider, who appeared to be in his late thirties, with thick red hair that he wore piled on top of his head in a Wilma Flintstone chignon and forearms covered in intricate spiderweb tattoos. When I wondered aloud if he got the tattoos because of his name, or if he had gotten his name because of the tattoos, he gazed down at his arms in wonderment as though he had never seen them before. "Nobody's ever asked me that before," he marveled. "That's a far-out question, man. Can you start right now?"

Spider gave me his personal phone number in case any-thing went wrong, but I was only permitted to use it between the hours of three and five p.m., which I think were the only hours of the day during which he was awake. Otherwise, I was on my own, although I came to realize this was really better for business, as Spider tended to put some patrons off. Apart from his tattooed arms and fiery bouffant, his wardrobe appeared to consist solely of a University of Kansas T-shirt with the sleeves torn off at the shoulders and two alternating sets of pants: one made out of a rough, multicolored Guatemalan fabric that looked like the woven mat my mother had put by the door in the mudroom; the other a pair of black chef's pants with a col-orful habanero-pepper motif, which he wore on more formal occasions, like when he visited the bank to dispute the terms of his small business loan. Still, it wasn't the style of Spider's clothing that was the problem so much as its condition. He had stopped using deodorants, shampoos, laundry detergents, and other commercially produced personal care products years ago, he told me, because the chemicals utilized in their manufacture interfered with the body's natural ability to cleanse itself.

"I had some pants that could stand up on their own," he said wistfully. "That was the shit. Those pants could stand up and tell you what they'd *seen*, man. Then my bitch ex-girlfriend threw them out. That fucking cunt just did not understand the rich pageant that is life, you know?"

Despite his aversion to soap and water, Spider did avail himself of the odor-masking properties of essential oils, particularly patchouli oil, which he splashed liberally over his person as part of his regular toilette. This aroma, combined with the ripe scent of stale marijuana (not to mention the other, more intimate smells) that clung to him, formed a pungent cloud that lingered in the shop long after he had gone, making it somewhat difficult for me to push on my increasingly scarce customers the assortment of vegan quiches and muffins in the glass case beside the counter. Nobody wanted to eat after they met Spider, especially after I mentioned, as instructed, that all baked goods had been lovingly prepared on the premises by the proprietor himself.

I had worked at Casey Joe's for about two months, until Spider asked me to come in after school one day, saying we needed to talk. It had come to his attention that I was frequently absent from the front of the store during my shift. I refrained from telling him that for the past three weeks, the only customer I had seen was my mother, who graciously stopped in during her morning walk and would gamely stay to keep me company, ordering coffees until her hands started to shake. Nor did I mention that my frequent absences from the counter were because I had to run next door to the 7-Eleven to buy milk, sugar, and other supplies Spider had neglected to replenish, which I would pay for out of my tip jar (and since there were no tips, out of my wallet).

"But that's not the real problem," Spider continued. "The real beef we have is this." He drew a CD from behind his back and dangled it in front of my face. It was the original Broadway soundtrack to *Sweeney Todd*, which I had accidentally left in the CD player after my shift on Sunday. *Sweeney Todd*, it seemed, was offensive to vegans.

"Look, man," said Spider. "Casey Joe's isn't just, like, another fuckin' coffee place. Casey Joe's is an experience. And that experience extends to the music, man."

I looked down at the floor, fixing my gaze on one of Spider's fungal toenails. As usual, and in flagrant defiance of the health code, he was barefoot. "I hrrmm the Grfful Durr," I murmured.

He leaned in close. The stench was overwhelming. I willed myself not to faint. "What? What did you say?"

"I said, I hate the Grateful Dead."

Spider shook his head. "I don't think this is going to work out."

In college, I was briefly employed in a vintage clothing and memorabilia shop run by an irascible cabal of paranoid senior citizens, until I was fired for making a customer cry when she asked me how old I was and I told her. After graduation, I tried my hand at office work and was dismissed from two temp agencies in quick succession: from the first for using the phone at my desk and from the second for downloading a video of the man with the world's largest testicles on an office computer. Now, with an employability level somewhere between a sex offender and a functional illiterate, I was seeking gainful employment in a foreign country where I didn't speak the language and didn't have a work visa. And as vice was regulated in Holland, without a visa, I couldn't even be a drug dealer or a sex worker.

There was only one place I could go.

Boom Chicago was an Amsterdam institution. Once a guerilla mission of three American college grads who wanted to bring Chicago-style improvisational comedy to the European masses, it now occupied a grand nineteenth-century edifice on the corner of the Leidseplein, the bright, bold lettering of its signage clashing queasily with its cornices of pale stone. Fully equipped with two bars, a restaurant, and a black-box theater seating three hundred, Boom Chicago was also an American embassy of sorts, a clubhouse for travelers grown weary of all that was Dutch. The Dutch have a concept called *gezelligheid*, or coziness, which they consider a mandatory precept for life. *Gezelligheid* is a single ginger biscuit served with coffee, a napping cat on a well-worn velvet cushion—the small, the tasteful, the perfectly made. Boom Chicago, blessedly, was none of these things. At Boom, you could order a giant hamburger with French fries, a huge plate of pasta smothered in meaty sauce. You could have foamy beer served ice-cold in a frosty pitcher, instead of flat and warm in a tiny glass. You could have ice cubes in your Coke and watch American comedians with reassuringly Semitic features perform skits about horny grandmas and farting space people and Dick Cheney. It is a mathematical rule in Holland that, no matter where you go, every fourth song you hear will always be by Phil Collins, but at Boom Chicago one was spared the spectacle of grown men interrupting themselves in mid-sentence to close their eyes and sing along phonetically to "In the Air Tonight." If you didn't look outside you could be in any comedy club in any mid-sized American city, and when I entered the building for the first time, it was with an odd mixture of relief and defeat, like stumbling into your filthy apartment half-drunk at dawn.

You didn't have to pretend to be Canadian at Boom Chicago.

Another Century in Paradise

PHIL COLLINS AND THE DUTCH: A SURVEY

The Law of Phil Collins

Given: In every bar, café, shop, or other public place in the Netherlands where background music is played, every fourth song will always be a song by Phil Collins.

"Phil Collins is a magnificent soul, he has touched the world through his music and continues to fight against world poverty . . . He is one of life's true heroes."   —Sir Bob Geldof, singer and humanitarian

"I've only ever bought one album for myself and it was *But Seriously* by Phil Collins, and if there's a better reason never to buy another album, then I'd like to hear it."   —David Mitchell, U.K. comedian
and Shukert crush object
(Ed. note: Mr. Mitchell has since admitted
to buying an additional album:
I Dreamed a Dream by Susan Boyle)

"I'll have the music, and then I just turn the microphone on, press play, record, and sing. And whatever comes out is the melody."
                  —Phil Collins, Emperor of the Netherlands

Sobering Statistics

9: Number of Phil Collins solo albums in existence, including the soundtracks to *Tarzan* and *Brother Bear*.

9: Number of Phil Collins number-one singles (U.S. and U.K. total).

10: The number of times one can hear "Against All Odds" in a single day without entertaining seriously suicidal thoughts.

11: The number of times one can hear same in one day without actually killing oneself.

12: The number of times I have personally heard "Land of Confusion" during a single evening in Amsterdam.

1: Number of psychotic episodes I have personally suffered caused by listening to same as terrifying flashback of the life-size Ronald Reagan puppet in the video reacted horribly with the psilocybin in the hallucinogenic mushrooms I had consumed earlier on same evening.

Prior to my arrival in Amsterdam, I had never harbored any particular animus toward Phil Collins. Sure, I jammed out to the rock saxophone in "Sussudio," or mouthed "Against All Odds" into a stick of deodorant if it came on the radio while I performed my morning toilette, just like anyone with two ears and a heart, but I had never given him much thought until the ubiquity of his music and his obvious importance in Dutch social life became impossible to ignore. I had, of course, seen people in America halt themselves mid-sentence in order to call attention to the brief but penultimate drum solo from "In the Air Tonight" (and I would just like to mention that I wrote this sentence before the film *The Hangover* came out, in which Mike Tyson does this very thing—it was funny because it's true), but in Amsterdam, the entire bar will go silent, faces shining with joyful anticipation, bicycle-toned buttocks poised at the edge of their seats, as listeners wait for that fevered cascade of cymbals to push them over the precipice to aural orgasm. Once, I watched in awe as a crowd of thuggish football fans from the provinces, dressed in regulation orange, tearfully and tenderly embraced each other as they sang along phoneti- cally to "Take Me Home." The strength of their combined voices flooded the night streets with song. Phil Collins to the Dutch is like Jerry Lewis to the French, David Hasselhoff to the Germans, Alan Alda to the Jews. He is not of them, but they have claimed him for their own.

I was determined to get to the bottom of this. Perhaps Phil Collins used to be a speed skater? Perhaps the raw emotion displayed in "One More Night" or the way he harrowingly channels the feelings of the homeless in "Another Day in Paradise" is subconsciously reminiscent of the traditional *smartlappen*, the rousing, tear-jerking ballads of Life's Great Pageant (often accompanied by accordion) cherished by Amster- dammers young and old? These hypotheses seemed unsatisfactory. As did the responses I received when I started asking questions. "What are you talking about?" one man said to me, in shock. "The whole world loves Phil Collins." I was not permitted a follow-up question. The drum solo from "In the Air Tonight" was coming up.

Why do the Dutch love Phil Collins so much? After months of inves- tigation, my answer is this: I have no fucking idea.

So instead, I have done what a lot of cultural critics do and just made up something crazy.

Philipus Davidus Carolus van Collins was born in 1541 in the Gelderland town of Arnhem, the only child of Boudewijn, a tallow harvester, and his wife, Saskia, an illiterate Belgian. He showed a talent for music early on, often singing songs of his own invention to the vats of tallow in his father's workshop, until one day, fate intervened. Philipus was slogging home through the peat bogs on the outskirts of the village after a long day of berry-picking, when he noticed a leak had sprung up in the mighty dike that held back the water from the town. Bravely, Philipus wedged his entire body inside the dike's cavity, feeling his life ebb away as the water filled his lungs. In a final act of desperation, he prayed to St. Willibrord, patron saint of the Low Countries. The village was saved, and St. Willibrord rewarded young Philipus with immortality, like Tuck Everlasting. Fearless and now unable to die, he set off to seek his fortune. He led the Dutch troops to victory in their battle for independence from Spain in 1568, ushering in the Dutch Golden Age. After amassing a mercantile fortune, he next popped up in 1640, when he apprenticed himself to the up-and-coming Rembrandt van Rijn, serving as a model for many of the artist's most famous works, such as *The Night Watch* and many of his portraits of Saskia. (Some art historians claim that Saskia van Uylenburgh was actually a disguised Philipus van Collins, and that the two men were in fact lovers.) Over time, Philipus van Collins became a party to almost every great event in Dutch history, a Zelig of the Low Countries. Sometime shortly after World War II (which was a hell of a time for everybody) Philipus decided that after four hundred years he could use a change of scenery and relocated to the U.K., where he lived quietly, until one day the Angel Gabriel in disguise as a man named Peter Gabriel approached him about starting a band.

And so the Dutch alone of all peoples know the true identity of the international pop star known as Phil Collins. And only the Dutch can understand the sublime mysteries of his plaintive song.

It was late afternoon when I arrived at Boom to look for work. The downstairs bar was not yet crowded. A couple of boys in knit caps sat hunched over a multicolored map, struggling to make sense of its baffling anatomy lesson, the curling arteries with unpronounceable names. A girl with glasses sat behind the glass window of the box office, methodically counting out a stack of white envelopes, while another, a pudgy moppet of no more than seventeen dressed in a regulation polo shirt and long apron, rushed up and down the stairs bearing trays of glassware fresh from the dishwasher. Neither of them seemed to notice me. Timidly, I approached the bar, where a dark-haired man in a black T-shirt stood idly flicking a wet rag against the wood.

"Excuse me . . ." I began.

"What can I get you?" The metallic Australian twang startled me, throwing me off script.

I cleared my throat. "I'm . . . um, looking for a job."

To my surprise, he gave me a sharp, knowing nod and brought his rag back down to the bar with a slap. "American?"

"Yes," I said hesitantly. "But I didn't vote for Bush."

"I don't give a shit," he said. "No visa?"

"No," I said.

"It wasn't a question." He turned away from me to straighten a bottle so that its label showed to its best advantage. "You have to speak to Kat. She handles the promoters."

Promoters? Not those wretched souls who accosted you desperately on the street in New York, swathed in layers of fleece and nylon, insisting that you liked comedy and they had just the show for you. "Um . . . well . . . I thought I could help with the box office, or maybe work at the bar . . ."

"No papers means promoter. She'll be here in about twenty minutes or so," the bartender said. "You can wait at the bar if you want. You can have something to drink, but it'll have to be a soft one. Otherwise you'll have to pay."

I thanked him and asked for a Diet Coke. It came in a big plastic glass with a lot of real ice cubes. Just this was nearly enough to bring me to my knees in gratitude.

Kat, the promotions head, arrived on schedule. The bartender shrugged loosely in my direction. Kat looked at me quizzically.

"New blood," he grunted. "American, finally."

"Oh! Oh, great! Just one second," Kat said to me with a smile. She disappeared up the stairs and returned in a moment, divested of her coat and carrying a large black binder emblazoned with the logo of the club. Kat was stunningly beautiful, tall and delicate with an Audrey Hepburn, gazelle-like loveliness, and radiated the kind of placid serenity common to people who have spent their entire lives being admired. Despite these obvious flaws, I liked her at once, and I soon confessed the whole sad story—the canceled play, the stolen wallet—that had brought me to this sorry state of affairs. Kat was sympathetic. "Well," she said, "if you want to promote for us, that's fine. We'd be happy to have you."

I fumbled with the zipper of my bag. "I have a résumé, if—"

She waved me away. "We have meetings every Thursday at five o'clock. Come this week, and you can get started right away."

To be a promoter at Boom Chicago one needed to be only three things: physically ambulatory, reasonably fluent in English, and willing to approach total strangers on the street. There were literally no other qualifications. Nothing else mattered—not work experience, nationality, criminal record, nor respect for other people's personal space. In fact, a lack of the latter was encouraged. It helped get the point across.

Our hours were assigned on a first-come, first-served basis; at the beginning of the week, each promoter signed up for shifts on the big paper calendar in the upstairs office. Each shift was three hours long and situated at a major tourist landmark—the Heineken Brewery, the Van Gogh Museum—where the promoter, bundled tightly against the chilling autumn gusts of the North Sea, would stand outside, keeping an ear open for English speakers. Americans, Brits, Australians, Canadians, South Africans, it didn't matter; once the target was identified, the promoter approached, engaging them in friendly conversation and offering a free guide to the city. The guides, thin booklets printed in color on flimsy newsprint, were published by Boom Chicago, with covers decorated with the club's logo and a "comedy" photograph: a burly bearded man in the starched white cap of a little Dutch girl gesturing gleefully toward a joint the size of a large cone of fries, an elderly woman holding an enormous black dildo to her lips. Disarmed by the common language and the seemingly magnanimous gesture, the tourists usually accepted these guides gratefully, confiding how desperate they were for a map, how tired they were, their plans for the evening. Some might tell you slightly more about their visit than you cared to know.

"She used some kind of antiseptic gel that gave me a terrible rash down there," a bluff fellow in a Miami Dolphins jersey told me, "you know, on my asshole. So I figured I better take it easy tonight. Just a little oral, maybe from one of them window girls. You don't happen to know how much that'll run me, do you?"

That was when the smart promoter moved in for the kill. Rather than waste your money on yet another dead-eyed blow job, she would say, why not enjoy a real American-style meal while watching the best—and only—English-language comedy show that Amsterdam had to offer? If you like *Saturday Night Live*, if you like *Whose Line Is It Anyway?* (for our British friends), then you'll *love* Boom Chicago. This was when the subject would move quickly away from you, as if they had suddenly noticed a stream of fresh urine trickling from your pant leg. The bolder ones might declare that they could never get enough dead-eyed blow jobs, thank you very much, but there were always a few, about one in seven, who expressed noncommittal interest, at which point the promoter would call their attention to the stamped coupon printed on the back of the booklet that would give them a hefty discount at the box office if they decided to come to the show.

Each promoter was assigned a rubber stamp, the kind an elementary school teacher might use at the top of a completed worksheet to indicate a job well done. Mine was a knife and fork intersecting each other in the form of an *X*, like a sign on the interstate indicating restaurants ahead. The stamp was how you got paid. Customers came to the show, presented their coupons at the box office, and the attendant made a note of the stamp: how many smiley faces, how many palm trees, how many top-hatted penguins. For each customer who presented her stamped booklet to the cashier, the promoter received three euro. Unless she had persuaded Kat into assigning her the final shift of the day, luring in customers directly outside the theater during the two hours before the show (for which she was granted an eighteen-euro flat fee), this was all she would receive. This was how the company got away with hiring foreigners with no work papers—technically, none of us were on the payroll. We were independent contractors or, on very bad weeks, volunteers. Likewise, the three-hour shift was only a suggestion, the maximum time you had before your replacement turned up. If in the first five minutes of work you felt confident that you had lured an Australian tour group or a herd of good-natured Canadians large enough to be worth your while, you were welcome to fuck off and spend the rest of the shift as you pleased.

After a shift, promoters were welcome at the bar, where they would be given a single glass of wine, beer, or well drink, free of charge. Boom Chicago also offered a family meal, a bountifully American plate of food with a vegetarian option, every day at five p.m., provided you had the foresight to inscribe your name on the sign-up sheet in the kitchen. Each meal cost two euros, to be deducted from one's weekly take, although whether the sweet-natured Kat, who was in charge of dispensing the wages, actually had the heart to do this was unclear.

Our weekly gatherings, at which we were presented with our earnings, had a feeling similar to an Alcoholics Anonymous meeting: the same underlying buzz of tension, the same cloud of cigarette smoke, the same furtive gang of misfits gnawing at their cuticles, their eyes darting around the circle with a mixture of worry and hope. We were an international bunch. Luke, a powerfully built Australian, fancied himself a bit of a ladies' man; every week he was full of fresh stories about his many and varied sexual conquests, the telling of which he seemed to regard as a sort of job interview, arguing his qualifications for an opening that would never exist. Carolina and Sebastiao were from Portugal, in love, and claimed to be vampires. Sebastiao spoke no English, which disqualified him from full promoterhood, but when Carolina had declared heatedly that only Sebastiao's presence could prevent her from feeding on the hapless humans displaying an interest in improv comedy, Kat permitted him to accompany her on her shifts, provided he refrained from wearing the red contact lenses that made him look like a cross between an albino rabbit and Dark Heart, the evil red-haired boy from the second Care Bears movie. The girl with the Raggedy Andy bob I had seen carrying trays of glasses up and down the steps was Hattie, a teenager from New Zealand who seemed to have stepped out of a Norman Rockwell painting until, that is, she opened her mouth.

"I took four E's last night," she declared cheerily, her pupils still dilated. "And then I met these guys on the street, and they said they had a boat moored in North Amsterdam, so I went back with them and we smoked some crystal and then they all had sex with me."

"Were they Italian?" I asked, concerned. "What did they make you do?"

Hattie looked thoughtful. "Actually, I think they were Turks. Whatever language they were speaking, it was weird. Lots of *k*'s.

Like this." She imitated their speech with a series of glottal clacks, like a farmhand subduing a troublesome chicken. "I didn't use a condom, but that doesn't matter since I'm already pregnant from Luke. You'll come with me to the abortion clinic, won't you? I'll buy you a falafel afterward. It'll be fun!"

I didn't know quite what to say to Hattie. I wasn't sure if she was looking to shock or to be comforted. If she was anything like me, it was probably a little bit of both. So I just did what I wished someone would do for me. I patted her shoulder and, in my best big sister voice, told her everything would be okay.

"I know *that*," she said, looking at me curiously. "This will be my fourth one. I just want someone to hang out with in the waiting room. The magazines are all in Dutch."

Sometimes I thought I could learn a lot from Hattie.

Of all the promoters, I first got to know Mattijs, who (out of deference to Mattijs the former) I always referred to as Beta Mattijs. Beta Mattijs was the only Dutch promoter at Boom Chicago. He spoke English with a flawless American accent, despite having never been to the States. He was just a savant of the ear, able to mimic any voice or accent down to the smallest pattern of speech. I had never heard anything like it. I knew he secretly dreamed of being an impressionist or a stand-up, but was held back by his fanatical devotion to the tenets of a highly restrictive form of punk rock, a rigorous code of ethics that seemed to shun any kind of virtuosity or material success. To Beta Mattijs's mind, hustling tourists in the street for pennies was punk rock. Delighting a paying audience with your pitch-perfect Liza Minnelli impression, tragically, was not. This made me sad.

Observing our rapport, Kat assigned him to accompany me on my first few shifts, to show me how it was done and to help me feel comfortable. To watch Beta Mattijs in action was a thing of beauty.

Fearlessly, he would approach a line of cranky, jet-lagged tourists, effortlessly veering back and forth between the five languages he spoke until he found the right one. He flirted, teased, cajoled. He gave directions, posed for pictures, accepted hugs. He always made the sale.

Now and then, I caught glimpses of the real actors in the office or smoking in the stairwell. They had all been imported from the great comedy factories of Chicago and L.A. and Ontario, and many made no bones about wanting to get back there as soon as possible, preferably with a writing gig on *SNL* or a recurring guest spot on *The Drew Carey Show*. I would stare at their product-rich hair, their big, straight American teeth and familiar American shoes and sometimes I wanted to scream: *I'm an upper-middle-class Jewish kid from the Midwest! I studied acting at NYU! I took tap! My Bat Mitzvah colors were hot pink and black! Don't lump me in with the Portuguese vampires and that guy from Romania with one hand! I'm one of you!* But they looked right through me and went back to talking to their agents on their sleek transatlantic cell phones.

There was only one promoter the actors acknowledged: Antonio, our de facto leader. Antonio was from Argentina and had been at Boom Chicago for as long as anyone could remember. In accordance with his seniority, Antonio didn't hustle the streets in the cold like the rest of us, but had the privilege of dropping great stacks of booklets, stamped with his personal emblem of the skull and crossbones, in the lobbies of all the major hotels. He would roll in at the very end of our weekly meetings—in his leather race-car driver's jacket and tight T-shirts emblazoned with characters from '70s television shows—to collect his Ziploc bag of cash, which inevitably dwarfed the rest. He hardly needed the money. It was said he had a wife, an older woman with a high-paying job in finance. Antonio was unmistakably a cool guy. I was terrified of him.

• • •

One afternoon, when I arrived to stamp brochures, Antonio was sitting alone at the bar. With some trepidation, I sat on the stool next to him, trying to look hip and international.

"Kat say you are from New York," Antonio said, without so much as a glance in my direction. It was the first time he had ever spoken to me. His accent was strong, but he enunciated every word, as though he expected me to have trouble understanding him. I wasn't sure if this was meant to be considerate, or mocking.

I stretched my lips into a hopeful grimace, like an infant with gas. "Yes," I said, "that's right."

Turning toward me, he nodded solemnly. "You were there for the blackout?" He was referring to the catastrophic power outage that August that had shut down New York City and much of the Northeast. I had been in Zurich at the time, although I had certainly heard the horror stories of people wandering penniless through the streets, unable to retrieve cash from ATMs; of the elderly and handicapped forced to drag themselves up fourteen flights of steps to their suffocating apartments; of packs of neighborhood children running wild over rooftops in the darkness.

"No," I said.

"I was there," said Antonio.

He told me the following story:

My wife, she is from New York. When we are married, I live there with her for one year. In August, I find on the Internet one very cheap ticket, and I decide that since she is working all the time I will go back for one visit to see some friends of mine.

From the first time I am flying into New York City, I love so much to look out from the window at the twinkling lights. This time I lift the shade up to look from my window, and immediately I can see that something is strange. The lights, they are not there. The plane lands, but we are not told to stand up and gather our baggages from the overhead. We are told nothing. For maybe three hours, we are in our seats, wondering what has happened. Is it one bomb? Is it one terrorist attack? All around me, people are trying to call their families on cell phones. One woman she is crying. "I have come for the funeral of my father," she is saying, "and I cannot get through." She spit on her phone in anger. Finally, the captain appears. I am afraid the other voyagers will throw at him their phones, like they are making one stoning. You know stoning, as in the films of Monty Python.

The captain say to us there is blackout. No electricity anywhere in New York. We are the last flight to land, he say; all other flights must go elsewhere. You know the Americans go crazy always. Even when it is something tiny what goes wrong, the Americans, it is like they are eating their own skin from their bodies. But at this time also the Dutch people are going crazy. I begin to be for really afraid.

We are on the plane for maybe two hours more. In the terminal, it is madness. It is like the scene from one movie about one war. As if we are refugees fleeing our village in terror. Everywhere, piles of baggages. People lie down on the floor and they do not get up again. I have no American money. The cash machine, she does not work. The phone, she does not work. Five, six hours I am sitting on the floor, listening to the screams of the children. Then, through the darkness, I see one bright light. Is reporters, from the television station.

"Will you give us one interview for the television," they say.

I am tired, I am dirty, I smell bad. "No," I say. "Get lost. I don't do a fucking interview."

They begin to walk away, taking with them the light. I cry

out, "Wait! I will do interview, if when you are finished you will drive with me into Brooklyn." They say okay.

He paused dramatically.

But my friend, she is not at home. I am so hungry, I think I am going to die. People pass by and they think I am one homeless person. My friend, she lives in a Spanish neighborhood. All around me, people speaking Spanish, having barbecue. They make fire in garbage cans. They cook everything from the refrigerators before it will go bad. The bodegas give out cases of beers, slices of cheese. I go up to one group I see. In Spanish I am explaining what has happened to me, that I am coming from Amsterdam and I do not know where is my friend. They invite me to eat with them. We cook chickens. We dance to Spanish music they are playing from one boom box. We are drunk, shouting in the streets. Is amazing.

Soon, is very dark. Nobody wants me to come home with them. They do not trust me in their dark homes with their children. They give me chicken, but still I am a stranger.

Finally, one man say, "Is okay, you will come home with me."

His apartment is very small, one room with one couch and one bed. Is totally black inside. He begin to light some candles in long glasses with one painting of the Virgin Mary on the side. He ask me do I want something to drink.

I say to him, "Look, man, thank you so much for this. I really appreciate you will let me stay here for tonight. And if you want ever to come to Amsterdam, you will be my guest."

The man smile, and he say, "I love to go to Amsterdam, but I am not permitted to leave the country."

I say, "Why?"

"Because," he say, "I am convicted felon. I am in prison for twelve years."

My flesh, it has goose bumps. I ask, "For what?"

"Murder," he says.

Then he come and sit very close beside me on the couch. He say, "Do you want to take a shower?"

I say I am tired and pretend immediately to fall to sleep. He get up from the couch. Very slowly he take off all his clothes, and finally, he go into the bathroom. I wonder if I should escape. But where I am to go? Outside there is no light. It is pitch black. Whatever I do, I am going to die.

A long time passes, and he come back. He wears only one small towel. Through my eyelid I can see him drop the towel to the floor. He stands naked over me. I don't dare to move. For maybe twenty minutes he stands like this.

I don't sleep one minute this night. All the time I am thinking terrible things. He will rape me. He will murder me. I wonder if it is better he rape me all night and leave me alive, or is better to be killed immediately but not raped. I stay like this until at last one crack of light comes through the window and I escape. I take my bags and sneak out like a thief into the dawn.

I think I cheat death that night. I think it was meant for me to be murdered. Now, everywhere I go in Amsterdam, I see one woman. She is dressed all in black clothes. Her hair is black. One day, she turn toward me. Her face is like a mask. My wife, she thinks I am crazy. She cannot see the woman. Nobody see her but me. The woman is death. She has come to find me. I will not escape forever.

Antonio was pale. He seized his half-full beer glass and poured the remaining contents down his throat. "This is the end of the story."

I was tempted to throw my arms around his neck. *You're not cool!* I wanted to cry in relief. *You're a crazy person!* Instead, I said, "Do you really believe that?"

Antonio mused, "When I go back to New York, I will make one documentary film. I will collect the stories of people in the black-out. Some people are raped. Other people maybe their brother was murdered. Maybe there will also be good things too. Maybe some people find their soul mate in the darkness. Could be like the documentary of Spielberg, when he films the stories of the survivors of the Holocaust. You know this documentary?"

"Oh, boy, do I," I said.

"My grandmother, she is one Jewess, born in Argentina," said Antonio. "But now she is baptized, she sits at home all day and sends her money to the 700 Club."

I told him that my Great-Aunt Rita, who in addition to being a Jewess was also a recluse and a midget, had upon her death left the overwhelming bulk of her assets directly to Jim Bakker. "She liked men who cry."

Antonio smiled for the first time. "Mattijs likes you," he said. "I think he hopes you will be his girlfriend. Do you like him also in this way?"

To be honest, it had crossed my mind. It probably wouldn't be any grand passion, but it would be nice to spend the night at his apartment sometimes and give Jeroen and Alpha Mattijs a little privacy. Maybe we would go to the country sometime, to the village where he grew up. I could meet his mother and learn how to milk a cow.

"I don't know," I said. "Maybe."

"And his earlobes? You do not mind this?" Beta Mattijs wore plugs in his earlobe, the kind that stretch the flesh and leave a gaping hole when removed. Normally, I found these terrifying, as they reminded me of the tags punched through the ears of cattle marked for death, for whom my classmates and I would weep during our annual field trip to the stockyards, but Beta Mattijs's plugs were small and tasteful.

"I don't know," I said again. "I think I can handle them."

Antonio nodded gravely. "Okay. But if you decide to do the sex with him, there is one thing I must tell you. Inside his penis, he wears one ring."

"What?"

"He wears one metal ring. Is pierced, through the foreskin. He has shown it to me one time, and I have taken a photograph. Look." Antonio produced a small digital camera. The viewfinder was small and the image slightly blurred, but I could make out a long tube of flesh with what looked like a miniature barbell thrust through the tip. Antonio gazed at the screen fondly. "I wish to make with this picture one art project. I will blow it up huge, the size of a wall. The title of the photograph will be *Il Mostro*. In Italian, this means the monster."

"Ah," I said. "Well. I think I would find that a bit of a challenge."

"Don't worry," said Antonio. "He knows is not for everyone. We will both still be the friends of you."

After a week or so of training, Beta Mattijs proudly told Kat I was ready to strike out on my own. My first solo shift was to be outside the Anne Frank House. As a small child, I received a picture book about Anne Frank and her family for Hanukkah one year, which, given my preoccupation with the Jews and Those Who Would Destroy Them, quickly became a favorite. Unlike other children's books about the Holocaust, which were illustrated with photographs of firing squads and mountains of naked, emaciated corpses, the Anne Frank book had dreamy watercolors depicting the Franks in an assortment of touching familial tableaux: celebrating birthdays, walking among the tulips, being held at gunpoint by the Gestapo on the sidewalk outside their hiding place. I had never been able to walk by the Anne Frank House without thinking of that picture: Anne in the foreground, a stricken expression on her watery face; Mrs. Van Daan, draped in fur; the creases and pools of the policemen's leather coats skillfully rendered in the milky paint. Now I stood outside on the same shadowy cobblestones clutching to my chest a stack of brochures featuring the picture of the old lady and the black dildo. I wondered why I'd never noticed before that she didn't have any teeth.

I spoke shyly to a group of college-age girls with dreadlocks. They grabbed the booklets from my hands and stuffed them into their backpacks before I had a chance to launch into the rest of my pitch. A group of French tourists asked me for directions to the train station, and an exuberantly stoned pair of boys from Cleveland exulted over how fucking awesome it was that I lived here.

"You must be fucking wasted all the time," said the youth, cackling with glee. "If it was me, I'd just fucking wake and bake every day, and then I'd go down to the fucking red-light, pay some bitch to fucking suck my dick, and then go into one of those coffee shops and just get *stoned* off my motherfucking ass all day long. You don't know how fucking lucky you are, dude. You are so fucking *lucky*."

I turned an anxious eye to the cluster of ominous clouds beginning to form in the sky. It was about to pour, and mama needed a sale. "That sounds so fun!" I said. "But you know what's even more fun? Comedy improv!"

The youth spat on the sidewalk and turned away.

Many people snubbed me completely. Others quickly plucked a booklet from my hands but turned away in distaste when I tried to start a conversation, like I was a beggar on the subway. They'd given me a quarter, so why the hell was I still talking? I shook off the rejection. Maybe if I stood by the exit, I'd have better luck.

There was a woman striding from the exit doors across the square beside the Westerkerk, her two teenage daughters in tow. From the leaden-footed entitlement of her gait, I could tell she was an American, maybe even a New Yorker. My grandmother liked to say that you could always tell an Arab by his shoes. I can always tell an American by the way they walk.

Desperate, I threw myself in my countrywoman's path. "Hi, there!" I exclaimed in my folksiest voice. "Whatcha doin'? Feel like seeing a comedy show tonight?"

The woman looked up at me with swollen eyes. Fresh mascara streaked her face like the silhouette of a mournful tree. "How dare you," she spat. "How *dare* you come up to us like this, after what we've just seen?"

"I'm sorry—" I began, but she was on a roll.

"My daughters and I"—here she flung her arms fiercely across the shoulders of the two mortified teenagers on either flank—"are Jews. Proud Jews. Now that probably doesn't mean much to you, but to us, it means something. You are standing on *sacred ground*. And for you to try to . . . to sell us something, here, of all places—well, it's disgusting. I am *disgusted*. You ought to be ashamed."

"I am," I said truthfully. I was mortified, although not quite for the reason she meant.

The daughters had fled, but their mother stood her ground. "Good," she said. "Then maybe you'll think about what you're doing the next time you decide to exploit a place of tragedy for *your personal gain*. Maybe you'll stop and think about what happened here." There was a fierce gleam in her eye as she taught me this

Very Important Lesson. I considered setting her straight, but I thought that would just make things worse. An insensitive Gentile is one thing, but another Jew? We could be here all night, and there was a watered-down vodka cranberry at Boom with my name on it.

"Well," said the woman. "Aren't you going to apologize? Don't you think it's terrible, what you're doing?"

"I think," I said, "in spite of everything, that people are really good at heart."

"Fuck you," said the Jewess, and left to join her daughters at the hot dog cart.

Nine

A MATTER OF PERSONAL PRIDE

"NO, NO, *NO!* You are so wrong!" Mattijs's face had crumpled in fury. A sudden flush of red rushed over his cheeks and forehead as twin jets of blue cigarette smoke erupted from his nostrils, forming an ominous halo over the downy rake of his knitted yellow eyebrows.

"You look funny." I giggled. Perhaps I could fight him with humor, like the Boom Chicago people said they were doing with the Bush administration. "You're like Donald Duck when he gets mad and turns into the devil."

"Fuck you!" Mattijs shouted. "*I* am not the monster!" A fresh cloud of smoke burst from his throat, hitting me directly in the face. Sputtering, I fled to the other side of the room.

Things at home had become a little tense. The canceling of the play, while not entirely unexpected, had put us all in a foul mood, and I sensed that Jeroen and Mattijs had begun to view my presence in the apartment not simply as a mere inconvenience but as a talking, walking symbol of the government's rejection of their art. I tried to share their disappointment, but I found it pretty hard to feel sorry for them as I dressed in fourteen layers of wool and prepared to stand outside in the freezing rain for several hours attempting to convince strangers who were (a) drunk, (b) weeping, or (c) under the influence of psychedelic drugs of their irresistible desire to watch overpriced sketch comedy. I was staying out late, trying to give us some space from each other (and enjoying the newfound social life that was the redeeming aspect of my job), but as I was required to wake with the household, I rarely operated on more than two or three hours of sleep and was almost always hungover, which had turned me into a terrible roommate. I had guiltily abandoned the fastidious neatness I had struggled mightily against my nature to maintain. I no longer bothered to fold up the futon every day. Dirty dishes collected on the coffee table until a scorching look from Jeroen sent me scurrying to the sink. It was the decline of my grade school desk all over again, except this time the desk belonged to someone else.

Our first major fight was over a small plastic bag of rubbish hanging from the doorknob in the living room. I tried to remain calm. "It's just there in case I need to throw something away in the night!" I screamed, in a calm manner. "It's not my fault that you're only allowed to take the trash out once every two weeks in this goddamn country!"

"I DON'T WANT TO HEAR YOUR EXCUSINGS!" Mattijs had shouted. "THERE IS NO EXCUSING FOR FILTH!"

"THE PRIORITIES OF THIS COUNTRY ARE FUCKED!" I screamed back. "YOU SELL KIDDIE PORN IN SUPER-MARKETS, BUT IF YOU PUT THE TRASH OUT ON THE WRONG FUCKING DAY THEY'LL SEND YOU TO PRISON!"

"THE KIDDIE PORN IS IN BELGIUM, YOU STUPID AMERICAN!" Mattijs bellowed.

That had made us both laugh hard enough to put it behind us, and besides, sweet Jeroen had managed to intervene before things escalated beyond repair. But this time, it seemed, I had gone too far.

I had been scheduled to promote at the Heineken Brewery that afternoon, a coveted post. The last time I was there I had managed to talk a huge stag party of red-cheeked Mancunians into coming to the show instead of spending their last night in town watching exhausted-looking women peel bananas with their labia, and made enough money to keep myself in tinned soup for almost two weeks. But this time, rain kept me home. Jeroen and Mattijs were out, teaching an acting class at a local high school, so I went into their office to use the computer. My e-mail was filled with depressing news from friends about how *great* everyone was: how so-and-so was assistant directing for Joe Mantello; how someone else had booked a recurring role on a prime-time drama. To cheer myself up, I decided to read about the war. I skimmed the headlines of the *New York Times.* On the home page was an article about Jerry Falwell, who had proclaimed from his pulpit that, while God was certainly on the side of life when it concerned the discarded embryos of white American Christians, he was avowedly pro-death when it came to fully born Iraqi civilians.

I chuckled. I had always gotten a kick out of Falwell; in 1989, I had even named my hamster after him. "This is my hamster, the Reverend Jerry Falwell," I would say to my parents' friends when they came over, and I would be rewarded with an uncomfortable laugh, my favorite kind. Suddenly, I was fighting back tears. What was the matter with me? Was I homesick? Did I miss my parents? Did I actually want to go *home*? Desperate for a distraction,

I hastily clicked the link to Jerry Falwell's website, which made me laugh out loud. The reverend had never exactly been what you might call a "hardbody," but in the vanity portrait that decorated his home page he looked like a molten blob of Crisco that someone had hurled against the mottled backdrop of my fourth-grade school picture. At the top of the screen was a link cheerily titled "Ask Jerry!" which led to a page with a place where one could write directly to the reverend himself. A wonderful joke occurred to me. I moved the cursor to the glowing white box in the center of the window.

Dear Your Honorable Reverend Falwell,
I am a good Christian woman who loves the Lord. Many months ago, I became friends with two friendly Dutchmen. Because of some ongoing personal problems, I thought a change of scenery would help me figure out some things, and they took me into their home in Amsterdam.
Dear Reverend, at the time I met these men, I thought they were good and respectable Gentiles like myself, but over time, I have realized that they are in fact homosexuals in love with each other. As I am sure you are aware, this is strongly condemned by the Bible. While I am not a homosexual myself, I am afraid that I am risking my immortal soul by being among them. Unfortunately, due to some personal problems, I am financially unable to return to my home at this juncture. Reverend Falwell, please tell me what to do. Or at the very least, send me enough money for a plane ticket. I am not a beggar, but as the Bible says, ask and you shall receive.

You are an inspiration to me and countless other born-
again Christian Gentile people like me.
Mrs. Cheryl Pot
Tulsa, OK

As I pressed SEND the phone rang: Antonio, calling to tell me that Luke the Australian was suspected of having succumbed to the advances of the Portuguese vampires. They had been seen leaving Boom together around 2:30 a.m. by Lester, the cheerful Yorkshireman who ran the sound booth, and today at dinner Luke was observed to have two visible bite marks on either side of his neck. In Antonio's forensic opinion, said bite marks could not have been made by the same person.

"One bite is very faint, with the very small tooths," said Antonio. "The bite of a woman. The other is bigger, more deep. I am for sure it is the bite of a man."

"How's Luke?"

Antonio thought for a moment. "Very quiet."

The key must have turned in the lock, but I didn't hear it. Nor did I remember that my sent message was still easily visible on the screen of their desktop until I heard the bellowing from the office.

Mattijs was livid. "You are so wrong in what you have done! This is our computer that we allow you to use! We bring you into our home, and this is how you repay us?"

I was about to shout back that it was just a joke when Jeroen staggered out of the office. His face was puffy and streaked with tears. A large bead of snot trembled sorrowfully on his philtrum like a fairy's tear.

"How could you write such a thing?" He sounded as though someone was choking him. "After all this time?" Mattijs flew to

Jeroen's side and stroked his neck as though he were a wounded puppy.

"It's not supposed to be me!" I cried. "It's Cheryl Pot, of Tulsa! A fictional Gentile! Not me!"

"It's not that you write this," hissed Mattijs. "It's that this computer is for our work. For you to disrespect our office, I cannot forgive you right now."

How could this be happening? "I didn't think you would get so angry. I was just being funny."

"Funny?" Mattijs hissed. "How is it funny to write such things on the Internet where they can never, *never* be erased?"

"I don't know," I said. "Just funny. Like a performance piece." When I was in university, claiming that something was a "performance piece" could get you out of almost anything. I had successfully pleaded the "performance piece defense" the time I got caught stealing a chicken caesar wrap from the snack bar on campus, and when I once went for nine days without taking a shower, that was a "performance piece" too. "This is an exercise to see what it's like to have people be repulsed by me," I had said, "not the result of being locked out of my apartment for a week and a half and having lost all personal pride."

"You know what I think?" Jeroen said. His voice was frigid. "I think that you don't think of anyone but yourself."

"I . . . that's not true," I stuttered.

"I think it is," said Jeroen. "And I think I don't want to see your face anymore right now."

"But . . ." I felt the tears beginning to well up in my throat. "I didn't mean . . ."

"Just go," said Jeroen.

"What?"

"I SAID, JUST GO!"

I had never heard Jeroen shout before. He had always been my ally, my protector against Mattijs's habitual irrationality. It was like seeing your father cry.

The Contradictory Nature of the Dutch National Character

TOPICS FOR DISCUSSION

"Holland is one of the queerest countries under the sun. It should be called Odd-land or Contrary-land, for in nearly everything it is different from other parts of the world."

—From *Hans Brinker, or The Silver Skates* by Mary Mapes Dodge

Perhaps it makes sense that a people living on land that by rights should be at the bottom of the ocean should have in their nature a proclivity toward contradiction. While the Netherlands certainly doesn't hold a monopoly on counterintuitive irrationality, the country has truly made it into an art form.

I know this might sound condescending, but I actually mean this as a huge compliment. Unlike some countries I could mention, Dutch irrationality doesn't start wars or execute children; at its most perplexing, it simply gives ungrateful expats weary of being unable to find a place to buy tampons after six p.m. something to bitch about. Or to bring up obnoxiously to their Dutch friends in the heat of the moment, biting the hand that feeds them and leaving said expat feeling lonelier, more self-loathing, and more vulnerable to terrible decision-making than ever before.

The following discussion topics are meant to spur lively debate among your coworkers, book club (*especially* your book club), prison pen pals, and even with yourself, should you suffer from multiple personality disorder, or spend a lot of time alone.

- In the Netherlands, marijuana, psychedelic drugs, and prostitution are all legal or at least tolerated. However, taking your trash out on the wrong day, failing to deliver glass bottles to the proper public collection site, and riding your bicycle at night without a headlight (causing danger to no one but yourself) can result in hefty fines and possible legal action. Does this attitude improve on quality of life or tear at the moral fabric of society?

- Having virtually invented the modern banking system in the seventeenth century, the Dutch are known for their financial acumen and success as financiers and tradesmen; however, they often seem opposed to businesses actually making money. Example 1: On one of the most popular man-made beaches just outside the city, a place designed to be a weekend leisure spot for well-heeled Amsterdammers, there is only one shop where one can buy snacks, drinks, and other provisions. It is not open on Saturday or Sunday. Example 2: I once got into a full-on verbal fight with the concession stand attendant at the movies when I wanted to buy the smaller popcorn that cost more, rather than the larger popcorn, which was proportionately cheaper, and therefore a better value. I tried to explain that I wanted less popcorn. He lectured me about money management. After twenty minutes, I shouted back that I didn't have the self-control to eat the same amount of popcorn if I had a larger box. To which he replied: "Then you are really just a pig." How does this differ from American-style capitalism?

- Things the Dutch find "possible": permanently reclaiming land from the sea, hoisting an entire house's worth of furniture through a fifth-story window on a length of rope, and building a lasting merchant empire in places as far flung as Indonesia from a country slightly less than twice the size of New Jersey. Things the Dutch find "not possible": Chinese food delivery, the existence of lactose intolerance, seasonal allergies, and clinical depression. Do you find these examples inspiring, or utterly insane? (Or, in the case of the "impossibilities," latently anti-Semitic?)

- The Dutch will eat a slice of bread and butter with a knife and fork, yet croquettes and other fried snacks that spurt terrifying geysers of scorching meat paste known to result in second-degree burns are eaten with bare hands while standing in the street. How does this illustrate the conflict between superego and id? Do you find any parallels with the psychosexual phenomenon of the Viennese *Käsekrainer*? How stoned and/or drunk would you have to be to consume a food item that will very likely cause you immediate physical harm?

- Despite having the most developed and available vibrator technology in the world, I have never slept with a Dutch guy who seemed to have the remotest idea as to where he might locate my clitoris. Do I just pick the wrong men?*

- In the Netherlands there is something called "eel pulling," a traditional pastime in which a live eel is hung from a rope over a canal. Participants standing in moving boats below attempt to yank the live eel off the rope, or to club it to death with a metal pipe. In 1886, a passing policeman cut the rope holding one such unfortunate eel and widespread riots ensued, leaving twenty-six dead and more than a hundred injured. The eel was left unharmed. (The above does not actually relate to the topic at hand; I just thought it would be a nice thing for you to know.)

---

* Actually, maybe don't answer that.

My bicycle was outside, but I was too shaken to ride. Wounded, I walked slowly down the Van Woustraat, but by the time I had crossed the small ugly park at the end of the road and veered past the shops and cafés of the Utrechtstraat, I was nearly running, propelled by fury. Yes, I was in the wrong. Yes, I had done something hurtful and stupid. But what was also hurtful was that my closest friends had purposefully misunderstood me, refused to acknowledge that I was trying my best. What was stupid was that I was stuck in this fucking country, freezing, starving, miserable. I was wasting the good years, the fearless years, when everything seems possible and, by virtue of belief, *is*; that brief, blessed convergence of youth, of beauty, of charmed foolishness, before the world gets small again; your dreams compressed by limitation and regret until they are nothing more than a half-forgotten frivolity, like a penny you put in one of those machines on the boardwalk at the beach. A cheap souvenir imprinted with the image of a place you scarcely remember. And what was I even doing this for? To find myself? How? Let's be honest: I wasn't exactly trekking the Himalayas or sailing into the heart of the Amazonian jungle here: I was working a shitty job and being randomly harassed by creepy men, two things I had been doing just fine at in New York, thank you very much. And what the hell did "finding myself" even mean? The entire concept was so callow, so indulgent, so disgustingly bourgeois. My mother was right. Who was I to think I was missing? Yet here I was, and I couldn't leave. I couldn't leave for the same reason people couldn't leave a marriage that had died long ago: because all this couldn't have been for nothing. This couldn't turn into just another of my missed opportunities, another experience from which I had managed to wring every drop of failure and mundanity, another self-pitying anecdote to recount over drinks in a depressing succession of increasingly dingy bars. I knew that life isn't like the movies. Plot devices don't just appear when you need them to. But someone, something, had to come next.

"Rachel!" The voice was faint, but clearly male. Had Jeroen changed his mind? Was I allowed to come home?

"Yo, Rachel! Over here!"

Sitting at a small table outside a nearby café was my old buddy Tommy. I hadn't seen him since we'd been drinking together before I went with the fake European all those months ago. Overjoyed, I flung myself into his outstretched arms, enveloping myself in the hazy fragrance of marijuana and original-scent Tide. "Where your head at, woman?" he muttered. "I called your name like a million times. Wait, are you *crying*?"

"What are you doing here?" I asked, wiping my eyes.

"Vacation," he said. "Visiting some peeps."

"Did you even know I was here?"

"I do now," Tommy said. "Sit down. Let's get you a drink."

Tommy was with a couple of other guys. One of them, a tall fellow with lank black hair and a heavy beard, was Tommy's friend Arthur, whom I knew slightly from New York. We nodded hello.

"Dude," Tommy said, putting his head in his hands. "This weed is kicking my weak ass. These fucking coffee shops are *serious*, yo. I am so tripped out right now."

"Too tripped out to introduce me to your friend?" said the other guy, who wasn't Arthur. He had a warm, raspy voice, and was grinning at me good-naturedly.

"Oh, dude, sorry," said Tommy. "This our boy Pete. Haven't you guys ever met?"

Like me, Pete was an American living in Amsterdam, having moved about a year ago from New York. Obviously, we had friends in common, although our paths had never crossed.

"Do you like it?" I asked. "If you've been here for a year already you must feel sort of . . . I don't know . . . at home, right?"

Pete was tearing his beer mat into tiny shreds, making a small, orderly pile on the slats of the café table. "Sometimes I just don't know," he said, suddenly shifting his gaze up to me. His blue eyes were very bright through their lattice of bloodshot veins. "Like what I'm *doing* here, you know? I wake up every morning and wonder if I'm wasting my life." I was startled by his sudden tone of intimacy. It had been a while since I'd been around other Americans. I had nearly forgotten our habit of sharing our psychological traumas with perfect strangers. Americans size each other up by how much we're willing to share. *"Hello, nice to meet you, I hate myself."* Europeans, on the other hand, walk around naked and give their children chocolate penises to suck, but public confession, not to mention self-flagellation, went out with the Crusades. They already know it's all just vanity in a tearful package.

Tommy was staring glassily at the canal, his slack jaw a grotto for mosquitoes. Beside him, Arthur had produced an X-Acto knife from one of the many functional pockets of his military-grade knapsack and was meticulously carving the Heineken symbol from the center of his own beer mat—carefully feeling the *H*, the *e*, the small red star that dotted the *i*. They both seemed to have forgotten we were there.

"I don't know what I'm doing here either," I said softly.

Pete smiled lazily. "Maybe you're finding yourself."

I scoffed. "Do I look like some kind of hippie?"

Pete sat back in his chair, searching my face. "You look like you know a lot of things."

"Fuck off."

"No, I like it. I like smart girls."

"That's very highbrow of you. Personally, I'm only attracted to sexual compulsives with bulging biceps and the barest rudiments of spoken language. You know. The autistic gym teacher type."

Pete held up his hands. "We don't have to talk if you don't want to. Have it your way."

"I'm sorry," I said. "I don't mean to be obnoxious. It's just been a bad day."

Arthur lifted his beer mat to his face, peering out from the ghostly Heineken-shaped hole with one eye. Tommy emitted a low gurgle of laughter as his head lolled lazily to one side. "Do you think it's cool if I piss in the canal?" he asked.

"It's a little early in the evening for that," said Pete. "Why don't you just go inside?"

Arthur rose eagerly. "I'll come with you."

Tommy scoffed. "What are we, chicks? You wanna stand in front of the mirror and tell each other how cute we look?"

"You didn't answer my question," said Pete, when they had gone.

"You didn't ask me one."

"Look," said Pete. "You could talk to me. I know what it's like. I'm probably the only other person who knows exactly what it's like. And I want to talk about it. I *need* to talk about it. Don't you? I mean, what the fuck?" He smiled, jutting his shoulders up and turning his palms to the gray sky. Inside me, something softened. He was awfully disarming, and now that I thought about it, awfully cute.

"I don't know," I said. "I guess I thought I'd come here for a while, just to have a change of pace. I thought I'd have an acting job, but it fell through."

"Why didn't you go back?"

"Because I'm a failure," I said, with a loose, desperate laugh. "I failed New York. I got stuck on the outside of the tornado."

"What tornado?"

Suddenly, I felt embarrassed. "Like, New York City's a tornado.

And some people get caught on the inside and make it all the way down—"

Pete interrupted, "And other people wind up getting spat out from the other side?"

"Something like that."

"But how do you know you're on the wrong side?" he asked seriously. "Maybe it's too early to tell."

"No," I said. "I used to think it was all random, which side you wound up on, but it's not. It's all money, and connections, and knowing how to work them. Some people are just born on the inside, and some people aren't."

"Is that what you think?"

"That's what I know," I said fervently. "But I didn't feel like sticking around just to prove my point. I didn't want everyone around to watch me fail."

Pete frowned. "Don't you think everybody is more worried about how they're doing than they are about you? Isn't that kind of self-absorbed?"

"Oh my god, yes," I exclaimed. "But like I always say, of course I'm self-absorbed. I'm awake." Pete laughed. "Please!" I said. "Don't let me torture you anymore with my tales of woe. I told you I was boring! Let's talk about you! What about you? Why are you here?"

Pete blinked hard. "I guess it was . . . you know . . . love."

"You've got a thing for tall, skinny blondes?" I said. "How unusual."

"Well, my girlfriend doesn't really look like that," Pete said. "That's why I moved over here. To be with my girlfriend. She's Dutch."

"Oh, right." Now it was my turn to shred a beer mat. "You have a girlfriend."

"We met in New York," he continued, "and we were there for the first few years, so when she wanted to move back here, I figured it was only fair."

I gathered the beer mat shreds into the shape of a heart. "Are you going to get married?"

"Well, we kind of are already," said Pete sheepishly. "I mean, we're not married, but we're, you know, domestic partners. From a legal standpoint, it's very similar here."

"Good," I said perkily. "Good for you. How long have you been together?"

"Almost six years."

"Six years. That's a long time."

He leaned forward intently in his chair, bringing his face uncomfortably close to mine. I felt my cheeks flush. "It is *such* a long time. I never thought it would be this long. And I've *never* cheated on my girlfriend . . . but six years. *Six years.* How do people do it?" It should have been a rhetorical question, but somehow I felt like he expected an answer. His hand lay flat on the table, very close to mine, and I could feel the air around it grow warm, as if his body were a radiator coursing with a fresh burst of steam.

"I don't know," I said helplessly. A small knot, like a pang of hunger, was beginning to form in my stomach. "Nobody ever wanted to go out with me that long."

"You know what I think?" Pete said throatily. "I think something major is going to happen to you here. Something big. You look . . . you look *lucky.* I'm, like, almost jealous of you. Here you are, all on your own. Anything could happen. Something that takes you totally by surprise."

"I hope not," I said. "In my experience, most surprises are bad."

"That's pretty pessimistic."

"It's logical," I said. "Good things are never really a surprise.

They're the things you fantasize about. You never daydream about terrible things happening. That's why they're always a shock."

He grinned. "I think you're wrong."

"And I think you're crazy."

"Nah," said Pete, still grinning. "I'm just a Pisces."

Before I had time to formulate an appropriate response to the enigmatic imbecility of this remark, Tommy had reappeared. Arthur trailed behind him, calmly sipping a fresh beer. "I'm starving," Tommy exclaimed, hoisting his T-shirt up and vigorously kneading a hand over his gently rounded belly. "This weed, dude. I need to fucking *chow*."

"I know a good place," said Pete, looking at me. "It's traditional Dutch, but good. Lace curtains, candles, you know."

"*Gezellig,*" I finished.

He smirked at me. "*Echt gezellig.* You got a *fiets*?"

"It's a few blocks away. We can go get it."

"Don't bother. You can ride on the back of mine."

"I don't ride on the back of anyone's *fiets*," I said. "It's a matter of personal pride."

There's a reason that Dutch cuisine has never really caught on in other parts of the world: it's basically a combination of the worst elements of British and German food, mixed up with kale and gravy, and then pureed.

"But if you smoke enough weed, anything tastes good," said Tommy, as he speared a piece of stringy meat from its perch on a pile of unidentifiable mashed tubers on the edge of his plate. "Maybe that's why they legalized it, so people would eat. You know, like how they give it to chemotherapy patients."

"Right," I said. "Or people with that wasting disease you get from AIDS."

"Dude," murmured Arthur. "It would *suck* to have AIDS."

After dinner, it seemed like a good time for some serious drinking and, eager to show off my knowledge of hidden Amsterdam, I wrangled the whole group over to the Habibi, a small bar off the Leidseplein that had become Antonio's new favorite. Antonio had recently been appointed captain of one of Boom Chicago's fleet of rickety tourist boats, and in preparation for his new life on the high seas, he had grown a beard, a gleaming spade-shaped thicket of black hair that reached halfway down his neck. "It makes me look more like a sailor," he said. It also made him look more like a terrorist and was garnering him some suspicious glances on the street, particularly if he was carrying a backpack or anything that looked sharp. The Habibi, however, which catered mostly to an after-hours clientele of Egyptian cab drivers, was free of such hostility. "Yesterday, one man ask me to his home for feast of Ramadan," Antonio said proudly. "What I do if he asks do I want to marry his daughter? Already I have one wife, but for these people it make no difference."

Abdullah the bartender greeted us as we settled at the bar, beside a nonoperational hookah the size of an emperor penguin. "You have new boyfriend?" he asked me, casting a narrowed eye in Pete's direction as he brought over a round of arak. "I like old boyfriend. He have nice beard."

"I like Antonio too," I said. "But he's not my boyfriend. He's married."

Abdullah frowned. "Very bad. Very bad you step out with married man. You know better than this."

I dropped a big handful of change in the tip jar, which to my relief cheered Abdullah up enough to drop the subject. If I needed a lecture on the traditional morals of the Levant, I could always call my mother.

It was at least four by the time we oozed out of the Habibi.

Arthur stumbled heavily against the bridge, sending several bicycles to the ground like a cascading row of dominos. Tommy looked ashen, gripping on to the railing next to him for dear life. Pete, surprisingly alert, shrugged apologetically. "It's really late."

"I know," I said. "I should go home."

"Do you think your roommates are still pissed off?"

My roommates. I had almost forgotten about our fight. "Jeroen and Mattijs are not just roommates," I added fiercely. "They're my best friends."

"Sure. But whatever they are, if things are tense, it's probably not the best idea to go home in the middle of the night and wake them up. My girlfriend's away, and I've already got these jokers staying with me." Pete gestured toward Tommy, who leaned over the edge of the bridge, unhinging his jaw like a feeding python as a graceful arc of vomit swooped from his mouth into the rippled murk of the canal. "You're welcome to crash at my place too, if you want."

I am a jealous person by nature, but the moment we crossed Pete's threshold I was gripped with an envy I had never experienced. It was nothing like the baffled covetousness I felt upon seeing a sprawling vacation house in Newport or the well-born undeserving at the Academy Awards. That was just aspirational nonsense. But this, *this* was the home I had dreamed of in my *realistic* fantasies. Not some Elle Décor Cote D'Azur compound with an infinity deck littered with India Hicks lounge chairs and the languid scions of deposed royal dynasties, but a perfect replica of what I had always believed I might actually have one day: the black-and-white tiled kitchen with hanging copper pans, the cozy L-shaped sofa, and especially, the man puttering around the kitchen with his mussed hair and frayed sweater, humming softly as he made our tea. There was something monstrous inside my chest, beating its claws against my rib cage in a horrible tattoo. *Why don't I have this? Why not me?*

Arthur and Tommy had collapsed on the sofa without a word the moment we came inside. They were both already sound asleep.

"We're the ones who should pass out," Pete said. "They're still on New York time." He handed me my tea in a flowered porcelain cup, drinking his own from an earthen mug an unlovely shade of brown. "I thought I'd give you the good china. It's for ladies." I took a sip.

"This is a very nice place," I said.

"Thanks." He reddened slightly. "We . . . we spent a lot of time on it. You know, fixing it up."

"Where is your girlfriend?" I ventured.

"She's at her parents' in Amersfoort."

"When is she coming back?"

Pete shrugged. "Tomorrow, I guess. Maybe Sunday."

"She has good taste," I said. My voice sounded strange to me, tinny, as if I were listening to myself on an answering machine. "It's a lovely home."

"Yeah." Pete picked a piece of lint off his shirt. "That's her thing."

"You can tell," I said. "I've never had that kind of touch . . . you know, knowing what kind of throw pillows to get. Having the right plates for things. And everything I have I ruin. Like people say they kill plants? I kill housewares. When I moved into my first apartment, I spent hours going to flea markets and garage sales, looking for these perfect objects. I've always had this thing about finding these perfect objects, like they're the key to something."

"To what?"

"To . . . *life*. I don't know."

"Are you sure you don't just like to shop?"

I shrugged. "Yeah, but that's the whole philosophy behind shopping, isn't it? You try to collect the possessions that seem to belong to the person you want to be, and you think you'll become that person. I remember I bought this old cookie jar from Mexico—orange, with big hand-painted flowers. And I had this art deco dressing table that I found in an antique store with the big mirror and wood inlays. The handles on the drawers were shaped like seashells. At a garage sale I got green lamps with red shades; they looked like jade. And in my mind, I saw it all so clearly, how beautiful all these things would look together, with the lamps on either end of the dressing table, the jar filled with hairpins and bracelets and, you know, pretty little things. But when I finally moved in and put them all together, it just looked all wrong. I thought it would be sort of whimsical and elegant, but it looked . . . well, it looked like a bunch of old shit someone had bought at a garage sale. Anyway, in two months, I'd lost the lid to the cookie jar and one of the lamps shattered, the other shorted out when I spilled beer on it. The seashell handles had broken off and the drawers of the dressing table were splintered." I sighed. "Anywhere I live for more than a month ends up looking like the inside of someone's coat pocket. Dark and filthy and covered with lint and crumpled paper and little pieces of dried-out tobacco. It's just the way I am."

Pete was staring at me intently. "It doesn't have to be."

"You're right," I said. "Maybe someday I'll find a lovely wife who makes a lovely home."

"I should go to bed," he said suddenly, although he didn't move away. "Do you . . . do you need some pajamas or anything? I could give you a T-shirt or—"

"I'm fine."

We stared at each other. I could hear his breath over the soft chorus of the boys' snores. When he spoke, the word matched it, shallow, asthmatic. I could hardly hear what he said.

"Kusje?"

The Dutch diminutive has a way of making a concept so innocent, so small. A *biertje* is just a harmless little beer, nothing that could cause you to make a fool of yourself or pass out in a pool of your own vomit. *Vriendje*, the word for "boyfriend," is literally a "little friend," conveying no trace of the volcanic chaos and cruelty lovers casually inflict on each other. A *kusje*, a little kiss; absent of anything adulterous or complicated, as innocent as a small child offering a dandelion to his mother. Just a little kiss. What was the trouble with that?Δ

He breathed it again. *"Kusje?"*

His mouth was warm. It left my lips with a trembling sensation of exposure. When I was little, my parents had a lava lamp in the basement, and my sister and I used to creep downstairs and stare at it, convinced that the pulsating, glowing bubble inside was alive and evil, plotting to break free and destroy us all. Now, clenching every muscle in my body against the strange, nauseous surge of lust that had welled up in response to Pete's kiss, I felt like that same bubble was inside me, gurgling swampily from my vulva to my rib cage and back again. *Hold it together, vulva!* I told myself sternly. *You're the last line of defense. If this thing gets out, we are all going to die.*

"We should go to sleep now," I said.

He cleared his throat gruffly. "You can come in the bedroom with me, if you want."

"I'm very tired," I said. "I really think I should go to sleep."

"Don't you want to sleep in the bed?"

"No!" I pressed myself painfully against the mound of blankets beneath me on the living room floor. "I like the floor! It's good to sleep on the floor!"

"All right, then. Sleep tight."

I sighed with relief as I heard the smooth click of the bedroom door locking behind him. He had taken me at my word, thank God. Pete was just a guy. A cute guy who reminded me of home. But he was also a guy with a *girlfriend*, a girlfriend who was probably a lovely person and had decorated this lovely apartment and had probably chosen the Laura Ashley–inspired duvet upon which I was now splayed, unclenching my now-aching genitals and practicing emotional self-mutilation over my brief and senseless urge to hastily fuck her boyfriend. Sighing, I gave my pelvic bone a disciplinary spank. As usual, I must have misread the situation. Probably Pete had just intended to give me a chaste little good night peck. Probably he had aimed for my cheek and missed. And as for his offering the bed, why, he was probably just being chivalrous. What a sad commentary, I thought to myself as I drifted off to sleep, blanketed by Arthur's soft snores from the sofa, that after all these tawdry adventures with uncircumcised Austrians, Swiss men seeking paid companionship, and polyamorous Italian oral surgeons/recreational rapists, I couldn't even recognize a true gentleman when he tried to put his tongue in my mouth.

I was a bit anxious when I arrived back at Jeroen and Mattijs's that morning, but it wasn't necessary. I apologized for being an asshole, sloppy, exculpating hugs were enthusiastically exchanged, and by the time Tommy phoned to ask if I wanted to meet up again that night for dinner, peace was fully restored.

"Pete's girlfriend is back," Tommy said. "She's coming to dinner."

"Did you meet her?" I asked, with false cheer. "What's she like?"

"Like a mom," Tommy said.

"Oh," I said, relieved but strangely deflated. It all made sense. There were a lot of guys—lost, arty types like Pete—who had those sort of very maternal girlfriends, solid girls who looked after them, saw that they ate, listened patiently and encouragingly to their endless, simultaneous litanies of self-aggrandizement and self-pity. I had never been very successful in my attempts to become such a girlfriend, being plenty self-aggrandizing/pitying myself. "Is she pretty?"

Tommy snorted. "I never wanted to fuck my mommy."

Dinner was at a noisy Thai restaurant near the train station. We had scarcely managed to arrange ourselves around the table before Pete's girlfriend, a broad, pleasant-looking blonde swathed in an enormous cardigan of fawn-colored wool, immediately commandeered the single menu card, instructing her foreign guests on what we would like best to eat.

"Tommy will prefer something spicy, I think," she was saying firmly. "Arthur, you will like the peanut sauce, but if you order this dish, you must not share any of it with Peter. Peter is allergic."

Across the table, Tommy caught my eye meaningfully. "Mommy," he mouthed.

The Girlfriend gazed at me coolly, biting her lower lip perplexedly before she looked back down at the menu. Half-standing, I leaned across the table, hoping to convince her that I was perfectly capable of selecting my own meal, when I felt a fly brush the back of my thigh beneath my skirt, lingering at the crease where my panties met my skin. I reached down to swat it away.

The fly was Pete's hand.

The lava-lamp sex demon in my belly sprang to life, fully lucid and screaming for blood, a wrenching surge of heat scalding my insides like a mouthful of boiling liquid. I had fallen in love before and didn't recall the sensation feeling so much like the symptoms of impending anaphylactic shock, but then, I had never before been seated across from my beloved's long-term girlfriend as she lectured me about the nutritive properties of shrimp pad thai. Panicked, I glanced sideways toward Pete, who smiled blandly as he plunged his hand past the sagging elastic of my underpants, cradling my trembling, sweat-beaded buttock against his cool palm. I thrust my knuckles against the edge of the table for balance as Pete's warm fingers edged steadily forward, creeping dangerously into the hollow of my thigh.

"Is it possible for you to eat pork?" the Girlfriend asked, cocking her head ruminatively to one side. "I know of course that many Jewish people like yourself will not eat it. Perhaps you can explain to me why this is? I have always thought it is really a shame for you, because it is a very nutritious and affordable meat."

"Excuse me," I croaked. "I'll be right back."

In the antiseptic safety of the single-stall bathroom I crouched over the toilet, gripping the sides with both hands to keep myself upright. I tried to meditate on the placid half-moon at the bottom of the bowl, forcing the cool, faintly urine-scented air in and out of my lungs, and when the urge to vomit had passed, I splashed some cold water on my face and smoothed my hair in the mirror over the sink.

There was a soft knock at the door.

"*Slechts een minuut,*" I stuttered. "Just a minute."

"It's me," Pete muttered hoarsely. "Please. Let me in."

My fingers trembled as I undid the lock. He catapulted toward me, and we thudded against the cool-tiled wall in a frantic embrace. Our mouths were speaking a private language our heads couldn't hope to understand, and when he moved his lips away to explore my neck, my face, my breasts, my own moved up and down in a pulsating circle, like a hungry bird, until he brought them back. The nauseous burning at the pit of my stomach was gone. Everything was right. His warm, piney breath, the cool skin of his neck against my burning wrist: It was all right, inevitable yet surprising, like a wild, perfect poem. There was no uncomfortable clinking of alien teeth, no embarrassing barrage of empty endearments, no unwelcome bearded friend hiding in tiny zebra underpants behind the door. There was, however, I thought as he unlatched my bra, something else, someone who was probably currently instructing her guests on the way to properly hold a set of chopsticks, someone whom I couldn't get out of my mind even as Pete's mouth closed tightly over my rigid nipple.

"Your girlfriend," I gasped, summoning all the remaining ragged fibers of my moral sensibility to wrench his head away from my breast, "is sitting right outside."

Pete sighed the broken sigh of the Deflating Erection. It was a sound I knew well, having heard it often in high school when I would casually mention that I was still a virgin. "I know," he said. "Believe me, I know."

"Well?" I said desperately. I needed his help. I was running on fumes here. I had about five more seconds before I no longer cared if I was going to hell. "Shouldn't that mean something to . . . to somebody?"

Pete clasped his hands roughly on either side of my face, and I threw my head back in an approximation of the poster from *Gone with the Wind*, a pose I had practiced in front of the mirror throughout the entire summer of 1989. This was the first time in my real life I'd ever had a chance to use it. "Look," he said throatily. "Things haven't been good between us in a long time. I told you. For months, I've been asking myself, why am I even here? Why don't I just go home? And now I know: It was because everything in my life so far, every decision I've ever made, everything that's ever happened to me, even meeting her, was because one day it would lead me to you." He brought my hand to his lips. "Don't you know what I mean?"

"Yes," I whispered.

It's always been easy for me to narrate certain sexual encounters, the kind that seem to become amusing cocktail party anecdotes even while they are happening, as if I can hear the cruel, titillated, gin-and-tonic laughter even while he's still ineptly fiddling with an obstinate zipper, a stubborn clasp. But to verbally express what happens during one of the real ones is almost impossible. You can use all the usual descriptive verbs—the melting, the burning—or revert to elaborate metaphorical sequences involving fire and water and tender pink flowers with dew-moistened petals. But the most eloquent statement I have ever heard on this matter was a medical study in which a group of scientists (Dutch scientists, by the way) found that at the pinnacle of orgasm, a woman's brain registers no activity at all. Her neural activity at the moment of climax is equal to that of someone in a vegetative state.

As we left the restaurant and headed to our bikes, Tommy pulled me roughly to one side. "Did you fuck him in the bathroom?"

"What?"

He narrowed his eyes. "Don't bullshit me. Did you *fuck him* in the bathroom?"

"No," I said truthfully. "I didn't." Tommy released my arm.

"Just do me a favor," Tommy said. "Don't fuck him until we leave. Will you do that for me?"

I softened a little. "Do you think she noticed anything?" Pete and the Girlfriend stood several yards in front of us, gazing at each other lovingly as he unfurled her bicycle chain from a rusty lamppost.

"No," Tommy said. "You weren't gone that long, and she was too busy telling Arthur how hot he should order his curry."

I took a deep breath. "I'm sorry. It must be awkward for you. I mean, she's a friend of yours."

Tommy guffawed. "She's not my friend! You and Pete are my friends, and as far as I can tell, she makes him miserable. And he can't stop talking about you."

"Really?"

"Dude. All fucking day he's asking me about you. What's she into? What's she like?"

"What did you say?"

"I said you were awesome." Tommy shrugged. "And that all the guys we went to school with were totally in love with you, but you were totally picky and intimidating."

I giggled. "Is that true?"

"*Fuck* no," said Tommy. "But like I said. He's my friend and you're my friend, and I can see what's happening. Just please don't fuck him before we're gone. It's the least you can do. I'm not that girl's biggest fan, but I'd feel awfully weird eating her oatmeal in the morning knowing I'm the ultimate cause of the demise of her relationship, you know?"

That was a Sunday. Early Tuesday morning, Tommy and Arthur boarded their flight home. By lunchtime, Pete was standing on the *welkom* mat of our apartment, holding a bottle of wine and a bunch of black-eyed Susans in a paper cone. That afternoon, even Helga didn't dare to bang on the floor.

My small collection of friends was not particularly encouraging about this new development in my life. While they managed to restrain themselves from emblazoning a scarlet *A* across my breast and dragging me in manacles through the town square, they nevertheless found ways to express their disapproval, with varying degrees of success. Over dinner one night, Jeroen and Mattijs told me the sad story of a female friend of theirs who had been involved with a married man for fifteen years.

"She is a wonderful woman," Jeroen said gravely. "Beautiful. Talented. She has everything going for her. But finally, the lies, the sneaking around, she cannot take it anymore. She tells him he must choose. It will be her, or the wife." Jeroen paused dramatically. "He chooses the wife, of course. And so she has no love, no baby, no nothing. And now she is forty-two, something like this, and she will be alone forever."

"She has been asked to write a book by a big publishing company," Mattijs piped up. "A novel of fiction based on this time. They give her quite a lot of money, actually. They think it will be a best seller." He stopped himself when he saw the look of feral glee spreading across my face. "Perhaps this wasn't the best example."

Beta Mattijs chose to convey his crushing disappointment in my lack of sexual morals as he was getting a lap dance at La Coquette, a hidden strip club in the red-light district where Antonio had brought us.

"You shouldn't fuck around with a guy who has a girlfriend," Beta Mattijs had said, as the naked teenager wedged between his legs swept into a deep bow, thrusting her buttocks brusquely against his forehead.

"You ought to be grateful." I quickly swiveled my stool so that my back faced the poles. The six-foot-tall Russian had again taken the stage, and she had already seized my mittened hand and pressed it to the silicone dome of her naked breast twice that night. I had a standing policy to remain completely bundled up at all times when in the red-light district, as I felt the sheer ludicrousness of my red mittens/yellow coat/green hat ensemble broadcast the fact that not an inch of the flesh below it was available for purchase. I looked like a big fuzzy traffic light. "If I had a real boyfriend, do you think he'd let me hang out here with you?"

Antonio fingered my sleeve. "I always like this coat. It remind me to Winnie-the-Pooh."

Beta Mattijs's girl jerked herself away from his visible erection to yell in a consonant-heavy language at the scrawny, olive-skinned boy who crouched against the wall, bathed in a jet of devilish red light. Without a word, the boy retreated dolefully into the darkened hallway leading to the alley. He could not have been more than ten years old. "My leetle bro-zer," said the girl regretfully, replacing her hand over the lumpy outline of Beta Mattijs's scrotum. "He eez supposed to wait outside."

Antonio stood up, knocking over his drink. "Here is boring. Let us go now instead to one sex show. On the Old Side for Burg's Wall* there is a woman who writes the word 'FUCK' on the stomach of a man with one Sharpie that she hold inside her pussy. While she does this, she is dressed like Cher."

"Why don't you call Summer?" I asked Antonio, once Beta Mattijs's dancer had tucked his moist twenty-euro note inside her studded codpiece and we'd pawed our way through to the street. I had met Antonio's American wife a couple of times before, and we had really seemed to hit it off. That was what I needed most of all, I thought, a girl to talk to. A nice, supportive *American* girl who would understand that I was just following my heart, which in the cheerfully amoral logic of the Hollywood romantic comedy was *the only thing I could do*. Summer would know that I wasn't the sadistic, Lycra-clad bimbo in this situation. I was the lovably neurotic Heroine saving the Hero from the suffocating embrace of the wrong woman! I had messy hair and a rickety bicycle and a coat made from the clumps of hair clogging the communal showers at the Jim Henson Home for Retired Muppets!

---

* Otherwise known as the Oudezijds Voorburgwal; see page 125.

Antonio looked uncomfortable. "Summer doesn't know I am with you tonight. I tell her about you and this guy." Antonio shrugged. "She doesn't like me to hang out with someone who does such a thing."

My cheeks flushed. "I see."

Hastily, Antonio patted my arm. "She likes you very much, really. She just do not trust you right now."

I couldn't blame her. While I was fully aware that my personality was cluttered with more than its fair share of bullshit, I had always prided myself on the thought that, beneath it all—beneath the hysteria and selfishness and periodic compulsion to symbolically immolate myself like a dull-witted, melancholic phoenix—I was essentially a good person. I didn't think I had it in me to knowingly hurt another person in any serious way. Now I had been tested, and I had failed. I was not a good person. I was a bad person who deserved bad things to happen to me, and yet here I was, for the first time in recent memory, incredibly happy. Sure, I felt guilty, but the guilt, to put it bluntly, was quite literally being fucked out of me. Every time the Girlfriend's face flashed before my mind's eye, Pete's hand would suddenly be down my pants. On the few days a week when Jeroen and Mattijs had classes to teach, we would lie on my futon in the living room for hours, staring mistily into each other's eyes.

"I want to marry you," Pete would say, trailing his fingertip over my collarbone and down the side of my breast. "I almost feel like you're my wife." If I experienced a pang of empathy for the girl who actually was like his wife, who shopped for his groceries and took his shirts to the dry cleaner, I slapped it back sternly. She was just some girl I had dinner with once, I reminded myself. I didn't even know her last name. "We'll live in Ireland. It's beautiful there, and artists don't have to pay income taxes. That's why Bono never gave up his residency."

Sometimes, Pete seemed susceptible to the same wrenching guilt I suffered from. On those days, after we had sex, he would cry, inching his body away from me across the fitted sheet, and I would have to comfort him, rocking his head against my breast until he stopped. It never took long. The guilt you feel over a bad thing that also makes you deliriously happy is the easiest thing in the world to assuage. If it wasn't, the world would be a very different place.

Lest I get too delirious, my mother called.

"Daddy and I are coming to visit," she said. "We'll be there the week before Thanksgiving. Try to eat some actual meals and do your laundry before then. I have no desire to relive the time you came home from college weighing eighty pounds and smelling like a homeless person."

"I thought you said you'd never come back to Europe after your honeymoon," I said, "when that French guy tried to make you pay for sitting on a park bench."

"The French are a bunch of sniveling anti-Semites," my mother said dismissively. "The Dutch are totally different. Besides, Northwest just merged with KLM and we can pay for almost the whole thing on frequent-flier miles. And Daddy can write the rest off as a business expense. It doesn't make sense *not* to come."

"Well, I'll be happy to see you."

She sighed. "Is there anything you need to tell me before we come?"

"What do you mean?"

"Well, you're not riddled with track marks and dancing in your underwear in some store window, are you?"

"No," I said. "Are you?"

"Don't be a smart-ass," my mother said. "I just want to know ahead of time, so I can brace your father."

"Actually," I said, "I'm wonderful. I've met someone and I'm in love."

"Oh? And what did his grandfather do during the war?"

"You just said the Dutch were different," I said. "And anyway, he's an American."

"What's he doing over there?"

This is where things got tricky. "He moved over here about a year ago to be with his girlfriend at the time. She's Dutch."

"Is he a drug addict? Why didn't he go home when they broke up?"

I took a deep breath. "They haven't actually broken up yet. They still live together. But it's basically over between them. He just has to do it the right way."

There was a long, terrible pause before my mother spoke. "You ought to be ashamed of yourself. You should be ashamed every single moment of every single day."

I tried to bring some levity to my voice. "It's sort of a dull background of shame with occasional intense flare-ups."

"Sounds like lupus."

"That's right," I said. "My relationship is like lupus."

"You know, you had a cousin who died of lupus," my mother said. "It was very, very sad."

"Mom," I said urgently, "I know this must sound terrible. But this is *for real*. All along I knew something had to happen, something was making me stay, and now I know what it was. I was supposed to find this guy. He says it was our destiny."

My mother let out a groan. "Oh, please. Will you give me just a small break?"

I was suddenly furious. "Do not quote lines from *Parenthood* at me right now! *Do not!* I'm telling you something important! *I have met the love of my life.*"

"I thought," my mother said, "that you went there to find your-self."

In a way, she was right. I *had* come to Europe to try to find myself, but how was that distinguishable from finding Pete? How else should we be defined but by the people we love? I had wandered, aimless, looking for something, and here it was. This was my purpose. This was my narrative. I'd be a fool not to grab onto it with both hands. I'd squeeze the life out of it before I'd ever let it go.

That year, Boom Chicago was throwing a huge Halloween party in the main theater. Though mainly intended as a friendly gesture to homesick American staff and friends, pretty much anyone was welcome; the irresistible urge of people to get dressed up in pumpkin costumes and make bad decisions with each other knows no nationality. The party was to have DJs, dancing, an open bar, and a costume competition with a cash prize, for which contestants were instructed to come dressed as "the scariest thing" they could imagine. After a few days of careful rumination, during which I considered the feasibility of going as a suicide bomber (too threatening), a broken condom (too sticky), and a malignant tumor (but how?), I settled on something sure to be a hit with this crowd: I would go dressed as "The Dutch Language." Mattijs let me have the pair of old wooden clogs he kept out on the balcony, and I bought a white T-shirt with long sleeves, white tights, a white skirt, and a white little Dutch girl cap from a souvenir shop, which I covered with all the Dutch words I knew, carefully lettered in black Sharpie. Pete came over a couple of hours before the party to help me get ready.

"I'm going to carry some extra Sharpies with me through the night and let people write Dutch things on me," I explained excitedly. "You know, like I was a cast. Or one of those autograph books."

Pete chuckled, fanning his hand over the phrase he had just

written across the back of my upper thigh. I twisted vainly, trying to read it. "What does it say?"

"It says, *Ik hou van jou*," he said. "I love you."

I seized his hands. "Come with me," I said. "Please. Just this once."

"I can't." He shook his head. "She's having a bunch of her girl-friends over for dinner." We almost never spoke the Girlfriend's name aloud when we were together. Pronouns seemed at once kinder and more dismissive.

"Perfect," I replied. "It's a girls' night. She doesn't need you there. Come on. I know you can't spend the night or anything, but . . . everyone is dying to meet you. Just tell her you're going out with some friends."

Pete looked sad. "That's the thing. She knows I don't have any other friends."

"No one?"

He shook his head again. "That's why I have you."

The party was packed. It seemed like every English-speaking expat in Amsterdam was there, and my costume was filled with obscene Dutch phrases and suggestions in no time. I refused when Luke the Promiscuous Australian offered me a tab of Ecstasy, but from the looks of the various configurations of sweaty goblins and witches writhing firmly against each other's bodies on the dance floor, it appeared I was the only one who had. When little Hattie, dressed in a slightly soiled toga and with pupils dilated to the size of peanut M&M's, came running over to tell me that her latest middle-aged lover wondered if I'd be interested in joining them in some kind of terrifying ménage à trois, I fled to the upstairs office, where Kat, resplendent in a very realistic devil costume, was furiously making out with a large bald man dressed as Albus Dumbledore.

"Is it okay if I use your phone?" I asked.

"Of course you can! I love you!" Kat shrieked plunging her red-taloned hands into the underpants of her magical companion.

Pete was furious when he answered. "What the fuck do you think you're doing?" I could hear the drops of his saliva sizzle against the receiver. "Why are you calling me here?"

"I just thought maybe you could sneak away and come to the party. Even just for an hour or something."

Pete snorted. "She's already fucking suspicious. She found your number in my cell phone a couple of days ago, and now she's telling all her girlfriends about this obnoxious American who has a crush on me. They think I don't understand them, but I do."

"I'm sorry," I whispered. "I don't mean to make problems for you."

He sighed. "Oh, come on. Of course you do. Listen, I'll meet you tomorrow in the park, okay? Don't call here again tonight or there's going to be trouble."

Kat and Dumbledore had moved into the supply closet. As I slowly made my way back down to the party, I could hear their whispered words of love through the half-shut door.

When I arrived at the park the next morning, Pete was waiting for me on our bench by the lily pond. He jumped to his feet when he saw me and enfolded me in a tight embrace.

"I'm so sorry," he said, when we came apart. "I hate having to do that to you."

"Do what?" I asked diffidently.

"You know. I wish it didn't have to be this way."

"It doesn't," I said, but Pete didn't seem to hear me.

"It's like I'm under fucking surveillance. She reads all of my e-mails, she listens to all my voice messages. If I leave the house, she asks me where I'm going a million times. It's like she doesn't trust me anymore."

"Right," I said. "I can see how that would be hard to understand."

"It's not just because of you. It's always been like this. It's only now that I see how fucked up it is." Pete suddenly seized my hand and pressed it to his face. "Please, please don't be mad at me. I need you. You're like the only thing in my life that reminds me I'm still *me*."

Pete had brought along his new digital camera to show me. As we sat on the bench for the next half hour or so, talking and cuddling, he took a steady stream of pictures.

"Stop it," I said finally. "I'm so hungover. I must look horrible."

"You look beautiful," he said, flipping through the photos. "God. Look at this one. Look at us." I leaned over to see the image. So this was what other people saw when they looked at us. A girl with a red scarf that picked up the rose in her cheeks, her brown hair curling tenderly around her jaw. The man gazed down into her face with a soft smile, his lips halfway to hers. We were a perfect vision of young love, a still from a romantic movie.

Pete deleted the picture.

"What are you doing?" I cried.

He looked at me, perplexed. "I have to delete them all, or she'll find them. She uses this camera too."

I wanted nothing more in that moment than to grab the camera out of his hands and thrash him repeatedly over the head with it, until man and machine both were reduced to unrecognizable pulp, but that wasn't going to do any good. Neither was screaming, or crying, or threatening, or anything I might have done at home. He might start to feel like I was more trouble than I was worth, and where would that leave me? Our affair had become the fragile symbol for this whole endeavor. If I left Pete or, worse, if he left me, I might as well pack my sad little duffel bags and go home, although as I desultorily cycled toward Boom for my afternoon shift, I thought that going home didn't actually seem like such a bad idea.

There was a dead pigeon in the alley where I parked my bike, lying on the cobblestones beside a large mound of gravel and silt. The streets of Amsterdam were littered with the carcasses of birds that had met a gruesome end beneath an oncoming tram or against the fender of a speeding bicycle, but this one was different. It lay perfect and uninjured, its wings intact, its beak slightly open. Stripping off one of my mittens, I picked up the little body in a sheet of crumpled tissue and set it carefully on the pile of gravel, where it wouldn't be crushed. If I were a character in a novel, the bird would be a symbol for something, the demise of my innocence, the impossibility of love. But this wasn't a novel, I reminded myself. It didn't mean anything. It was just a dead pigeon that had fallen from the sky.

I checked my e-mail in the office. There was a single new message in my inbox, and although it seemed unlikely, I was seized with hope that it was from Pete. Maybe he'd managed to save the picture and send it to me. Maybe he understood how much I needed him to be real.

"Dear Ms. Cheryl Pot," the message read. "We deeply appreciate your continued support for the work and ministries of the Reverend Jerry Falwell. Your generous Faith Partner gift helps us reach the lost with the Gospel of Jesus Christ through our worldwide television outreach and ministries."

They suggested a starting donation of $250.

Ten

SATAN IS ABOUT TO BEGIN THE CANDLE-LIGHTING CEREMONY

There is no Santa Claus in Holland.

Santa is jolly. Santa is too fat to ride a bicycle, and his obesity an unnecessary drain on the national health care system. Santa is financially generous for no logical reason. Santa is completely antithetical to the Dutch way of doing things.

In Santa's place is a tall, thin, and fastidious bureaucrat called Sinterklaas who dresses like Torquemada, the leader and spiritual godfather of the Spanish Inquisition. This attire is appropriate, as Sinterklaas spends most of the year in Spain. Unlike Santa, Sinterklaas does not keep elves in his employ. In Holland, elves (and their close relatives, the gnomes) live with their families in elaborate underground communities built in the roots of trees and lead rich and rewarding lives of their own. A Dutch elf would never agree to a life of indentured servitude making toys in Santa's workshop without a union wage, stock options, and six weeks guaranteed paid vacation, and anyway, Sinterklaas doesn't do toys. He doesn't get mail and he doesn't take requests. He pulls into Amsterdam harbor on his barge around the middle of November and begins a period of Inquisitorial observation that lasts about three weeks, until his feast day on December 5.

"Then, if you are found to be good," Mattijs explained, "Sinterklaas leaves in your shoe an orange and some chocolates in the shape of your initials."

"When do you get your real presents?" I asked.

Mattijs looked surprised. "Those are your real presents."

I was horrified. "An *orange*? What is this, *Little House on the Prairie*?"

"If you are found to be naughty," Mattijs continued, ignoring me, "you do not receive chocolates and candies. Instead, Zwarte Piet, who is the black servant of Sinterklaas, together with his assistants who are also black men, will beat you with sticks, put you in a sack, and take you away to Spain."

I felt it unnecessary to point out that we both knew a lot of people for whom being whipped by a group of forceful black men and whisked away to Ibiza was called a luxury vacation package. "And then what happens?" I asked.

"What do you mean?"

"What do the black men do with you once you're in Spain?"

Mattijs looked thoughtful. "I don't know," he said. "My mother never told it to me. I assume you are tortured, or sold into slavery. Whatever it is, it will be terrible." He waggled his finger at me playfully. "You had better be good!"

I had certainly better. My parents were arriving in Amsterdam the same day as Sinterklaas. If I was found to be naughty, I might easily be stuffed in a Samsonite garment bag by a couple of Jews and taken back to Omaha.

Christmas may not be a major commercial holiday in the Netherlands, but something had to fill the Santa void, and as Sinterklaas himself was about as cozy as a wax Victorian medical model, Zwarte Piet (or "Black Pete," for those of you not possessed with Yiddish-speaking relatives who habitually employed a similar-sounding adjective as a noun to describe the cleaning lady, the cast of *227*, and the Indian woman your cousin Justin dated) was the de facto face of the holiday. His pitch-black, bug-eyed visage was found on posters and wreaths in every shop window, the whites of his eyes bright and gleaming, his thick black lips stretched in a subservient grin. Zwarte Piet dressed in snug satin suits in vivid jewel tones. Large gold rings dangled from his ears, and he often wore a broad-brimmed hat trimmed with an enormous feather, which gave him the overall effect of a Renaissance-era Huggy Bear from *Starsky and Hutch*. The more enterprising shops boasted elaborate displays of three-dimensional Piet dolls, some in kneeling poses, their hands splayed wide, while others playfully thrust their exaggerated buttocks against the glass pane. De Bijenkorf, one of the city's poshest department stores, had even displayed a life-sized Piet climbing up the side of the building (according to legend, breaking and entering was his preferred method of getting into the house) but was made to remove it when the police received several phone calls from elderly neighbors reporting that some black guy was trying to break in through the third-story window.

"Doesn't anyone complain?" I asked Jeroen at the grocery store, fingering a cardboard table decoration with an illustration that would not have looked out of place painted on a chicken stand in Alabama in 1935.

He shrugged. "One year they tried to do instead a 'Rainbow Piet.' Some of the Piets were blue. Some were red. Some even were green. It did not become popular." He shook his head. "Now they say that he is black from the soot of the chimney when he climbs down it, not because he is African."

"I thought Piet comes in through the window," I said.

Jeroen shrugged again. "It's just a tradition for children."

"You *do* understand," I said, suddenly urgent, "that this would not be acceptable in America. You could *never* do this. *Never.*"

He smiled. "Yes, but things are different in Holland. We are not such a racist society as the U.S."

Apart from transforming the city of Amsterdam into a giant advertisement for the original *Jazz Singer*, the other great tradition of the season was to compose cruel poems about your friends and family members, and to read them out loud for maximum humiliation, while the children were feigning delight over their oranges. Inspired by the idea of informing loved ones, in verse, of the various ways they had failed you, I attempted some examples of my own:

> I wish my wife would lose some weight
> She is so very fat
> Our friends all giggle at my fate
> "Did you really marry *that*?"

"That's very good," said Mattijs approvingly. "But you must put in something also about the gift it will be attached to."

"I thought you didn't give gifts," I said.

"Sometimes," he said. "Something small and humorous. If it makes the poem more insulting."

I tried again:

> We dearly want a grandchild
> But our son says he is gay
> He claims that it is God above
> Who helped make him this way
>
> For sodomy is what he craves
> And bondage what he likes

Last Sunday he arrived for lunch
All outfitted with spikes

And so we give our special guy
These brand-new anal beads
We hope that they will satisfy
His prodigious anal needs.

It wasn't perfect; the rhyme scheme was a little inconsistent, and I wasn't sure about the inevitability of the second stanza, but a worthy effort nonetheless, and I felt confident to try one for real:

I dearly love my boyfriend
He is my heart, my life
But sadly there's a problem
He already has a wife

"No, no," he says, "not married, I—
It's just cohabitation
But we must be careful lest it end
In legal arbitration."

My parents tell me of their shame
My friends tell me to leave
But I find myself unable
What a tangled web we weave!

"Very good," said Pete dully, when I read it to him during one of our mornings on the futon.

I nestled my face against the warm skin of his neck. "It's not finished yet," I simpered. "It needs another stanza. And I'm not sure it says quite what I want to say yet."

He scowled. "I think it says it pretty well."

"What's that supposed to mean?"

"Rachel, come on."

I sat back on my heels. "What? What's wrong with it?"

"It's a little hostile for a Christmas card, that's all."

"They're supposed to be exaggerated," I said sullenly. "Like caricatures."

Pete relaxed a little. "It's cute. Cohabitation and arbitration is a good rhyme." He kissed the top of my head briskly, neatly dispatching any notion of more expansive nuzzling. "I've got to jet. I'm supposed to have lunch with her this afternoon."

"You're supposed to have lunch with me!"

He sighed. "Well, this morning she was going on and on about how we never talk anymore and we need to catch up, and the next thing I knew she was canceling her meeting, and I couldn't exactly tell her I was busy."

"You know my parents are coming tomorrow." I wielded this piece of information like a truncheon.

"Yeah? Why didn't you tell me?"

"I did," I said. "I told you at least four times." Pete, I had discovered, had an astoundingly poor memory. I had convinced myself that this was due to his prodigious consumption of marijuana—he was rarely without a ready bowl tucked into the front pocket of his backpack, where it could be easily retrieved and ignited the moment he stepped out of doors—but I was beginning to wonder if it wasn't something darker, like that he was stupid or, worse, just didn't give a shit about anything I said.

"Right," he said. "Do I get to meet them?"

"I don't know," I replied. "Do you think you'll be allowed out?"

Pete glanced longingly at his backpack. He was forbidden to smoke pot in the apartment, as the lingering smell made Jeroen nauseous. "Do they know about me?" he asked finally.

"They know you exist."

"That's not what I mean."

A sharp pain shot through the nerves behind my eye socket. I had a sudden, giddy vision of a tumor forming, shooting up majestically from the reddish murk like a mountain from the primordial sea. "If you mean have I told them that you have another girlfriend, then yes. They do."

"Why?" Pete looked pained.

"Because it's true! And if you're really as serious about us as you say, they're going to find out sooner or later. Besides, you don't know my mother. She should be a CIA interrogator. She gets this weird calm tone to her voice and you feel like you better tell her the truth because she already knows anyway."

Pete grabbed an apple from the fruit bowl on the table and set himself diligently to carving a hole in the side with a ballpoint pen. "I guess I should meet them then."

"If you think it's important," I said snarkily. "I wouldn't want to inconvenience you."

"Baby," he cajoled, setting down his newly formed apple bong. "Of course it's important to me. I love you. I want them to see that their girl is in good hands." He wrapped his arms around me tightly and pressed his lips to mine. I'd been with cuter guys, smarter guys, nicer guys. But there was something different about Pete. I think it was the sense that every time he touched me it could be for the last time. Like he was a soldier going off to battle, or one of those cancer patients in the movies who get sexier and sexier the closer they are to organ failure. "We'll have dinner," he whispered huskily, his fingers grazing the wire of my bra. "I've got my language class tomorrow night, so she expects me to be out."

"Okay," I said.

He stroked my lips with his finger before he pulled away to put on his jacket. "Are you working this afternoon?"

"I don't know."

"Skip. I'll come back over when I'm done." Pete got up, knocking the printout of my poem to the edge of the coffee table. I lunged for it before it hit the floor.

"You don't want to take this with you?"

Pete narrowed his eyes. "Nah," he said. "You know me. I'll forget to throw it away and then she'll find it when she's doing my laundry." He chucked me under the chin. "I do like it, though. It's funny as shit. You're a funny girl."

More Sinterklaas Poems to Share and Love

I got a little bit carried away writing mean poems to disappointing (and hypothetical!) family members and friends, so here are a few more. For a fun project, feel free to copy in calligraphy and pass along to someone special. It doesn't have to be a holiday. Why not let them know how you feel all year long?

TO A BELOVED MOTHER WHO NEVER LOVED ME*

> From the time I was a baby
> 'Til I'm ninety-three or four

---

* Not my real mother!

I always will be conscious
That you loved my sister more.
You trusted her with secrets
In her you did not doubt
You left her all your jewelry
And I was left without.

So when you open up this gift
I hope that you will see
A big fat lot of nothing
'Cause that's all you gave to me.

FOR A VERY SPECIAL ALCOHOLIC

Do you remember how you puked on stage
at high school graduation?
Or how you used to pee yourself
At each act of copulation?

I don't think I'll forget the night
You smashed up Rhonda's car
Or the time you gave a convict head
In that filthy roadside bar.

So here, my friend, my gift to you
For your ever empty cup
A nice big vat of whisky
Come on, you lush, drink up!

To a Favorite Fascist Cousin

Christmastime is almost here
And you can hardly wait
To gather 'round the fire with friends
And speak of those you hate.

Arabs, Muslims, liberals, blacks
Gays, a Jew or two
Immigrants—except for those
Who anteceded you.

For only Real Americans
In our fair land should dwell
But be patient; you'll see plenty of real
Americans in Hell.

Kraft Korner!

MAKE YOUR OWN ZWARTE PIET DOLL
Materials You Will Need
1 Ping-Pong ball
1 black marker
1 red marker
1 package white binder reinforcements
1 straight pin
Scraps of brightly colored fabric (stiff satin works best)
Gold wire
Black woolen pom-poms or trim (the kind people use to make toilet roll

covers shaped like poodles works well; in a pinch, you can also use
scraps torn from a Brillo pad)

Glue gun

An entitled sense that you can't be a racist because you went to a good
college

Several hundred dollars

Instructions

1. With the black marker, color the Ping-Pong ball all over, leaving a
   blank grin/grimace-like shape for the mouth, the wider and more
   grotesque, the better.

2. Color the mouth in with the red marker.

3. Place two white binder reinforcements where the eyes should be—
   the reinforcements are the whites, the middle is the dilated pupil.

4. Fashion a small hoop or circle from the gold wire and attach to the
   side of the Ping-Pong ball with the straight pin, forming an earring.

5. Glue the woolen pom-poms or Brillo pad to the top of the head,
   forming hair.

6. From the brightly colored fabric cut a body shape and glue to the
   bottom of the Ping-Pong ball.

7. If you like, you can cut a circle out of the same fabric and glue to
   the hair, as a beretlike hat.

Your Zwarte Piet is now finished. Take him to the mirror and make
him sing songs like "Mammy" and "My Old Kentucky Home" or
begin to develop a ventriloquist act in which he refers to you as
"Massah." Then slowly allow the realization of what you are doing
to seep into your being. Disgusted with yourself, throw the doll in
the trash bin or under the bed for the cat to eat and immediately
send the several hundred dollars to the Southern Poverty Law
Center.

•   •   •

I often expect to be overcome with emotion when I see my mother and father, brought to my knees by a wealth of nostalgia, shared memories, and unconditional love. Instead, our reunions feel a lot like the first day back at school after summer vacation. You show up in your special outfit, hoping that everyone will realize how you've changed, how you are now exactly the sort of person they want to invite to their parties/worship as a god/fingerbang in an urgent yet loving manner, but by fourth period, your hair is a mess, and you've realized that not only does your outfit not work quite the way it seemed to at home, Joe McDowell is never going to give you more than the most cursory of nods in a public place, no matter how many times he put his penis into your mouth over the summer. By the time the final bell rings, it seems like summer never happened at all.

"I don't understand," my father was shouting, "why it would kill us to stay in a decent fucking hotel for once. Are we that poor? Would it break the bank to sleep in a room with a goddamn window?"

"Fine, Marty," my mother hissed back. "Next time, you can plan everything. You can spend hours on the phone with the airlines. You can spend every lunch hour for a month going to pick up brochures from the Triple-A office."

"They have something called the Internet now," my father snapped back, "which would make your *sacrifice* a lot less impressive, if you could get over thinking the computer is going to burst into flames every time you touch it."

"Then call the Treasury Department," my mother shouted in response, "and tell them to fix the fucking exchange rate, because this windowless shithole is costing *three hundred bucks a night.*"

"I'm so happy to see you guys!" I exclaimed. "It feels like home already."

My mother turned her assessing gaze on me. "How much are you drinking?"

"A lot," I said. "That's what people do in Europe. They are all hedonistic alcoholics who have lots of indiscriminate bisexual sex when they're not busy denying the Holocaust and boycotting Israel."

Carefully, my mother gauged her response to my opening gambit. Would she parry with a snide rejoinder of her own? Or would she feign credulity at this clearly outrageous statement in an attempt to throw me off my game? After a calculated pause, she allowed herself no more than a barely audible "oy," leaving me with no choice but to change the subject. *Bien jouée, Maman.* Well played.

"We're having dinner with Pete tonight," I said. "He really wants to meet you."

My father blinked dumbly. "But I have to rent a bike."

"So rent a bike," I said, exasperated. "You go to a rental place and give them money. It's not exactly like getting a passport."

"I'm exhausted," my mother sighed theatrically, flinging herself on top of the bed. A small cloud of flaky dust rose with the impact. "Do we really have to do this now?"

"He made a dinner reservation," I said, beginning to feel desperate.

My mother opened one of her eyes. "Why? This is the only night he could get away?"

"What?" My father, ever late to the party, swiveled his head back and forth between his dueling women with utter bewilderment, as though he had just beamed in from some alternate dimension. "What are you talking about?"

"I told you," my mother said, not without some glee. "Rachel is this guy's *mistress.*"

My father cocked his chin quizzically in my direction. "Like a headmistress? A prop mistress?"

"A *sex* mistress." My mother spoke loudly, as if she were speaking to a deaf person, which in essence she was. My father is severely impaired when it comes to innuendo. Try to tell him a rustic joke about, say, a farmer and his three daughters, and you had better be prepared with an annotated copy of *Our Bodies, Ourselves* and the steely imperviousness to humiliation of a nursing home attendant dispatched to excavate the remains of some foreign object from the shriveled orifice of a still-frisky resident. "First there was the one in Vienna whose grandfather was probably Adolf Eichmann or something." (For the record, I had no recollection of telling her anything about this, which doesn't mean it didn't happen, but you see what I mean about her being in the CIA.) "Now there's this one, Pete, who has another girlfriend."

My father said, "Eichmann? I thought you said he was from L.A."

"No, no, no!" My mother's voice descended a winding staircase of tonal disgust. "Pete is the one we're having dinner with tonight. He's American, but he has another girlfriend here, whom he lives with."

"He's not living with Rachel?"

"No. He's cheating on the other girlfriend with Rachel. They're sneaking around behind the real girlfriend's back. I told you. Rachel is the *mistress.*"

"Oh," said my father. "*Ohhh.* I see. Well. That's not good."

"It's a disgrace," said my mother. "But anyway, the reason we have to have dinner with him tonight is because he probably made up some elaborate lie to cover for it with his real girlfriend, and we all need to jump so your daughter can keep sneaking around with him like some kind of cheap whore. Now do you understand?"

My father nodded. "That sounds fine. I really need to get a bike."

Having lost the battle but not the war, my mother announced that she needed a nap, so I accompanied my father to a bike rental shop a few blocks from the hotel. When we returned, she was wide awake, propped against a mound of pillows with a paperback murder mystery in hand.

"I don't know what the hell time it is," she said, "and I've got heartburn. I'll take a Prilosec and let's get out of here. I can't spend another second in this room."

I'm not sure how we settled on the Anne Frank Museum as our destination, but in retrospect, it seemed like the obvious choice. Carolina the Vampire was on the shift outside when we arrived, clutching a stack of Boom Chicago brochures to her black satin bustier, her eyes downcast. I greeted her with the customary three kisses and allowed her to inhale deeply next to my neck, but this did nothing to brighten her mood.

"I am in a very dark state," she explained. "Sebastiao speaks of nothing but leaving this place. The chimes of the church bells near our flat have grown unbearable to him. He says to hear every day this reminder of a false god is like his flesh is being slowly peeled off from his bones."

"Gee," I said, "that's too bad."

Carolina nodded solemnly and shifted her stack of booklets to her hip, pushing up one of her fishnet sleeves to reveal a series of deep cuts along her forearm. "Yesterday, I open my veins for him and he feeds all night on my blood, like he is my own child. But even this does not soothe him. I think he has grown tired of our love. In his e-mail I am finding messages from a girl we knew in Lisbon. Elena." She spat the name. "Sebastiao and I are not bound by sexual jealousies in the way of mortals. But this girl, I have known her before, in school, and she is listening all the time to the music of Nelly Furtado. I do not believe she is a true Child of Hell."

"Carolina, these are my parents," I said. "They're visiting for the week."

"You speak English so well," my mother said loudly. "Good for you."

Carolina flashed her fangs in thanks. "You should really go to the Jewish Museum while you are here," she said. "It doesn't get as crowded, and they have an excellent kosher restaurant. It is the best hummus I have ever had."

I'd been to the Anne Frank Museum several times, but until that afternoon with my parents, I had never realized the sheer awfulness of what she had been through. Say what you will about the horrors of the concentration camps, they might at least present some interesting networking opportunities. But to be trapped for *years* in five rooms with your family was a torment I could scarcely fathom.

I had long pictured hell as a never-ending Bar Mitzvah party at which you were forced to sit at a table with no one but your immediate relatives and forbidden from circulating among the other guests. To an infernal soundtrack of "Shout!" and "Play That Funky Music," dozens of adolescent boys approach you, asking you to slow dance to the catalog of Bryan Adams, but you are not permitted even the respite of their sweaty palms, and hesitant erections leaving warm damp patches on the metallic taffeta of your skirt. No, your mother has some very important things she needs to tell you about filing your taxes this year, and Uncle Bruce hasn't quite finished reading from the printout of Internet jokes about the Israeli-Palestinian conflict that he's brought along. There is no alcohol at this Bar Mitzvah, as Aunt Joyce was worried that it would "send a bad message to the kids." Your mother, having finished her lecture on the United States tax code, is now preparing to harass you about your health insurance, but not before she shares with the table a fun anecdote about the time you flirted unknowingly with your cousin Jonathan at a USY conclave.

You suspect she would find this a lot less amusing if she knew just how far things had gone with cousin Jonathan. Fortunately, she is cut off by an unearthly call to order over the P.A. system—Satan, flanked by a pair of singed demons and a hideous chicken with one enormous human breast, is about to begin the candle-lighting ceremony. This is my vision of hell. Poor Anne Frank. It must have been so much worse.

There was a rustling squelch of wet Kleenex as my mother dabbed at her eyes with the same tissue she had just used to wipe her nose. "Just imagine," she said, "what she could have accomplished if she had lived. Maybe she would have been a great writer, just like she dreamed. She wasn't so different from you, you know. Such a terrible waste."

"Which one's the waste?" I asked. "Me or her?"

My mother walked away. "That's your problem, Rachel. Everything isn't always about you. Oh my God!"

"What?"

"Come here and look. It's the most beautiful thing I've ever seen."

She was right. Anne Frank's toilet, which occupied a large role in her diaries as both a giver and a taker of life (on the one hand, there are few things more life-affirming than a really good bowel movement; on the other, if you flush, the Nazis will hear you), was an object of extraordinary wonder. The bowl is a masterpiece, a blue-and-white fantasia in Delft porcelain. An intricate pattern of scrolls and curlicues lapped the china rim and sides, and on the low shelf, where one's fresh excrement proudly suns itself before succumbing to the rising tide, was painted a pair of graceful lovebirds, their plumed tails entwined. It must have been nearly sixty years since they had last been covered with shit. I wondered whose it was.

•   •   •

Speaking of shit, Pete had reserved a table that night at a vegan restaurant. If he had hoped the gesture would help to curry favor with my meat-eschewing, teetotaling, nominally kosher parents, he was wrong, dead wrong. The restaurant he had chosen was run by Hare Krishnas, a group second only to Jews for Jesus in my mother's disapproval index, as the older brother of her childhood best friend had run off to join them immediately after graduating from high school, causing great disappointment for the family. As soon as the orange-robed waiter delivered our drink order I knew there would be trouble.

"What's this?" My mother examined the dark red liquid that Pete, in impressive Dutch, had ordered for her. "I don't want liquor."

"No, no, Mrs. Shukert, they don't serve alcohol here," said Pete. "Rachel already told me that you two aren't big drinkers so . . . it's pomegranate juice. Packed with antioxidants. They make it fresh."

My mother took a sip and made a face. "It tastes like a deathbed."

Pete forced a laugh. "That's funny! Like mother, like daughter, huh? I guess it must run in the family."

I looked down at the orange tablecloth, not trusting myself to meet his eyes.

"So, Peter," said my mother, "where does your real girlfriend think you are tonight?"

Pete glanced toward me nervously. I looked desperately to my father for help, but my father, holding his full glass of juice motionless at his lips, had clearly escaped to his happy place, which I imagined as a sort of New Urbanist space colony where placid asexuals in bike shorts spent all day discussing public transportation systems and the Talmud; in short, a place where none of us existed.

"Language class," I finally said. My voice was hoarse. "He's supposed to be at his language class."

"Hmmm," said my mother. She looked down at the menu. "I don't suppose he can tell me what a hoofgesmekterekten is?"

The attending Krishna flew to her side, his robes fluttering tensely behind him like the wings of a giant orange moth. "I'm afraid we don't have an English menu, but of course I can translate for you anything you wish."

There was a brief respite while my parents selected various arrangements of lentil-studded mush for our supper. As Waiter Krishna glided away on his ropey sandals, my mother mused, "I wonder if they all used to be nice Jewish boys here too, or if that's just America. I bet he's killing his parents, in any case."

Pete cleared his throat. "Listen, I want to say something."

"My stomach is not happy," my mother continued. "I just hope whatever I ordered isn't going to keep me up all night."

"Mom!"

Pete grappled at my thigh under the table. His fingers pressed painfully into my quadriceps as he spoke. "Look, Mrs. Shukert, Mr. Shukert. I know this isn't exactly an ideal situation, what's going on here. If I were you, I know I'd be worried. But I want you"—with an incongruous smile, he looked from my stunned father to my grim-faced mother—"*both* of you to know that I love your daughter. And I want you to know that regardless of my situation here, we have plans to be together, for a future together. You have my solemn promise."

"Piecrust promise," I whispered, before I even realized what I was doing. My father was uncomfortably saying something friendly and appeasing to my suitor, but my mother's eyes, green and shrewd as a clever cat's, darted toward me. She had heard. My sister and I had watched *Mary Poppins* together every day for a year. I could hear Julie Andrews's cut-glass lilt now: "A piecrust promise, easily made, easily broken." Slowly, I raised my eyes toward hers, expecting to see a bemused gleam of triumph. There was none. She looked like she was about to cry.

Pete left us at the end of the road, despite my halfhearted entreaties for him to join us somewhere for dessert; after all, he was expected home. As we walked across the park on the way back to the hotel, my father was kind. "Well," he said, "I think that was very brave of him to come right out and say that to us. That can't have been easy."

My mother walked a few steps apart from us, staring at the empty cement fountain in the center of the square. Tentatively, I reached for her hand. She let me hold it for a moment. It was as cool and soft as I remembered it.

"He looks like he works out," she said finally, before she drew it away. "I guess that's something."

We didn't see much of Pete that week. My parents wanted to spend their time sightseeing, which necessarily meant being out in public places, which Pete was loath to do with me in the best of times, for fear of running into someone he knew.

"Oh, come on," I would pout, when he refused to accompany me to a movie or the grocery store. "What are the chances?"

"High," Pete would say. "*Fucking* high. Think how often you run into people you know in Manhattan, and Amsterdam is, like, a fifteenth of the size. I guarantee you, one of these days we're going to run into someone. We could even run into *her.*" He shuddered. "She could decide she wants to stop off for some fucking French fries on the way home and suddenly I have no place to live."

"You're being ridiculous," I would reply. "And anyway, so what? Let us run into her. Tell her we ran into each other. Tell her you felt like grabbing a cup of coffee with someone who understands what it's like for you here. Or . . . here's an idea! Tell her the *truth*."

"I don't know," he would say, his voice breaking. "I don't know, I don't know, I don't know." And then he would start to cry, or grow angry at my unreasonableness, or throw himself at my neck, telling me how much he needed me, pleading with me not to give up on him. To be honest, it was getting pretty tiresome, and the break came as something of a relief.

Instead, we spent a great deal of time with Jeroen and Mattijs, whom my parents had met previously in New York and liked very much. Any lingering resentments between the boys and me quickly evaporated in the cozy haze of friendly chatter and parentally sub-sidized meals. Jeroen charmed the pants off my mother, feeding her choice tidbits about Amsterdam's Jewish heritage and traditional Dutch methods of soup-making. Mattijs arranged for his brother, a city planner, to show my father around some of the new projects his firm had in development on the reclaimed land north of the harbor. While my father coerced me into accompanying him on one of his relaxing six-hour bicycle journeys in the middle of a blinding sleet storm, the boys took my mother shopping in the Kalverstraat and defended her from the mocking laughter of the shop assistants when she politely requested to be shown to the Petites department.

Now, our merry quintet was making its way on foot through the crowded streets toward Centraal Station, hoping to make it in time to see Sinterklaas himself arrive in Amsterdam.

"Hurry, hurry!" Mattijs cried, striding ahead as fast as his tight pants would let him. "He will be here any minute!"

Jeroen ran to catch up, his eyes shining. Not for the first time, I was impressed by their boundless enthusiasm for the touchstones of childhood. When I had first arrived, they had treated me to a trip to the Efteling, the modest storybook-themed amusement park that played an integral role in the imagination of every Dutch child.

"Like Disneyland," I had said, except it had no rides, no recognizable characters, and nothing to buy. Instead, the park featured displays of mechanical flowers dancing in place to a wordless song and talking wastebaskets shaped like disembodied mouths that congratulated you audibly when you sorted your trash properly. *"Dank u wel!"* the wastebaskets bellowed, and Mattijs and Jeroen would squeal with delight. Perhaps that is what comes from spending one's whole life in a land of thatched cottages and gables of gingerbread and darling little sheep frolicking in meadows. The fairy tale never ends. In the village where Mattijs's parents lived, there was an honest-to-god *castle* with turrets and a moat, and a large stone in the town square where heretics, debtors, and other undesirables had been chained for the populace to scorn, spit at, and pee on, because that's what people did for fun in the days before reality television. By contrast, in Nebraska you could drive for miles without seeing anything but factory farms and herds of doomed cattle, and if you were lucky, a truck stop where you could buy a liquefied burrito and a fresh batch of homemade speed. It just gave you a different sense of what magic was.

"Sinterklaas, it's Sinterklaas!" Jeroen screamed over the cheers of the crowd. "Here he comes, on his boat from Spain."

"I have to go to the bathroom," my mother said, crankily. "My stomach. I think I'm about to—"

She was drowned out by a deafening ululation. From every corner and every lane, every alley and every byway, they careened, cavorted, tumbled, and teemed. Hundreds of them, maybe thousands, filling the streets, their eyeballs bulging, their monstrous grins flashing white behind their wide painted lips. There were old ones, shuffling along with walkers and canes and squinting at the spectators from beneath their kinky wigs; there were young ones, marching hand in hand, eyes wide. The limber ones turned somersaults and cartwheels, the bolder ones gyrated wildly, thrusting and arching their padded buttocks in an improvised jungle dance. There were thousands of Dutch people in blackface stretching as far as the eye could see. For the first and perhaps only time in my life, I was struck completely dumb.

"It is the *Zwartjes*!" Mattijs exclaimed. "The Zwarte Piets!" Gleefully, he plunged his hand into a large burlap sack proffered by a grinning man I believed I had last seen forcing himself on the Cameron girls in *Birth of a Nation*, and extracted a mass of sweets. "*Strooigoed*," he said, distributing the treats among us. "It's a tradition. *Pepernoten*, which are small biscuits of gingerbread, mixed with candies. You see? Everywhere, the *Zwartjes* are throwing it."

"And these . . . people," my mother said, gesturing at the unending stream of discrimination lawsuits caterwauling before her, "they . . . help . . . Santa Claus?"

"They are his slaves," Jeroen said helpfully. "Well, not slaves. People found this offensive, so now we say they are just good friends."

My father had turned pale. "I marched on Washington," he whispered. "I wanted to be a Freedom Rider." Weakly, he repeated this over and over again, like an autistic child rocking and moaning in self-soothing behavior. A female Piet, her green satin costume straining to contain her shelflike bosom, pelted him with a fistful of tiny cookies. He screamed.

Spinning around to avoid a similar barrage, I caught across the parade path a glimpse of a familiar backpack, a familiar jacket, a familiar head of rumpled hair.

It was the other Pete. My Pete.

I waved my arm wildly, trying to get his attention. He didn't see me. I was about to call out his name when a pair of hands in purple gloves snaked around his waist, hugging him tightly as a pink cheek appeared above his shoulder, pressed against his bare neck. It was funny; after all these weeks of care and caution, the avoiding of certain phone numbers and certain e-mail addresses and certain places at certain times of day, she had ceased to exist in my mind as an actual person with arms and hands and purple gloves. She had become a sort of metaphysical construct, like God. And yet, here she was, laughingly popping colored candies into Pete's smiling mouth, kissing him one, two, three times, on the cheek, on the chin, on the lips. As she pressed her face, rosy with cold, into his chest, they didn't look like an ill-suited pair nipping at the heels of heartbreak. They looked like we had in the vanished image in the display window of Pete's digital camera. They looked like two nice people in love.

I am allergic to oysters. When I eat them, my throat swells shut, trapping the surge of vomit and nearly choking me to death. This felt like that, except this time I *wished* I'd die. My mother sprang to my side. "Rachel?" she said loudly. "RACHEL! What is it? What's wrong?"

My voice, when it came, was a horrible hiss. *"Don't . . . say my name!"*

Her eyes followed mine. "Oy," my mother murmured. "Oy, oy, oy."

The only thing to do was make a run for it. I tore through the crowd, crushing mounds of cookies and candies with each fevered step. A man wearing a paper bishop's hat shook his fist at me as I knocked over his small son; in a blur of red in the corner of my eye I could see the child's lipsticked mouth contort unhappily in his soot-smeared face. Over the roar of the crowd, I could hear my mother screaming my name with increasing panic: "Rachel! Rachel! RACHEL!"

Why can't she shut up? I thought. I glanced up at the low gray sky. In a few minutes it would start to rain.

My mother was out of breath when she caught up to the low stoop where I was crouched, pressing my palms into my eye sockets. Timidly, she rested her hand on my clenched shoulder. "Do you want to talk?"

"Why?" The venom in my reply startled even me. My mother reeled back slightly, bracing herself for the worst. "So you can tell me you told me so? So you can tell me how wrong I am? How I should be ashamed of myself? How I'm stupid and I'm ruining my life? Because I know. Believe me"—my cheeks were suddenly drenched—"I know. I know. *I know.*"

"Rachy . . ." my mother began.

"DON'T! You don't have to tell me! I already know! I'm wrong! Everything I do is wrong!" A middle-aged woman with a glowing crown of pale hair stopped to frown at me. People don't yell in the streets in Amsterdam, not sober people. I didn't care. This was my mother standing in front of me. "I just want to be special," I whispered. "I just want to be the most important thing to someone. I just want someone to be on my side."

My mother grabbed my wrist. I tried to wrench it away, but I couldn't break her grip. Its strength was unearthly, like a superhero, like an adrenaline-mad woman lifting a pickup truck to free the baby trapped underneath. "*I* am on your side," she hissed. "You are the most important thing in the world to me. You always will be. I will *always*. Be. On your side."

"Let go," I whimpered.

"No," said my mother. "You are better than this. You are mine. Do you hear me? I love you, and you are *mine*!" Her face had turned a dangerous scarlet, and I suddenly felt afraid. Last Christmas, she had collapsed in the ladies' room of my father's office during a holiday party. The doctors said she had probably been born with the hole in her heart. Now she took medication: small yellow pills every night, one huge tablet at breakfast once a week, two aspirins daily to thin the blood. It was certain now, she had told me cheerfully as she lined the amber bottles up alphabetically on the windowsill beside the kitchen sink, one day she was going to die. Just like her parents. Just like everyone who had ever lived or ever would.

"I love you, too," I said.

She let go of my wrist and drew me to her. My mother is nearly six inches shorter than I am, but somehow, my head pressed against the familiar warmth of her clavicle. She wore the same Lancôme perfume I had chosen for her the Mother's Day I was eight and my father, in a panic, drove me to the department store and commanded me to pick something, anything. I felt proud that she still liked it.

"Just come home," she whispered fiercely, her breath tickling my earlobe. "I'll buy you the ticket. I want to. Just come home."

We trudged silently up the cobblestones back toward the parade route. She panted softly as we scaled the steep incline of the canal bridge before we reached the Prins Hendrikkade. "I hope they waited for us," she said. "Otherwise I don't know how the hell we're going to find them."

"It's okay," I said. "We'll be all right on our own."

Eleven

EVERYTHING IS GOING TO BE GREAT

Pete cried when I told him I was leaving.

"I don't understand how you can be so calm about this." His face was twisted into an angry ball as his shoulders shook up and down. I had an acting teacher once who tried to teach us to cry on cue by approximating the physical motions of weeping—the shuddering chest, the tightening of the larynx—with the idea that our muscle memory would take over and cause tears to fall. That was what Pete was doing now: making the shape of tears. "Can't you understand how hard this is for me? Why can't you think of me for a change?"

"I *am*," I protested. "I really think this is for the best. If I'm gone, it'll be much easier for you to end things and come home."

"If you leave I'll be all alone again."

I sighed. "No. You'll just have the space to do what you need to do."

Pete scowled, roughly wiping the nonexistent tears from his cheeks with the heels of his hands. "What I need is for you to stay here and be with me. That's what I need. Maybe I'm stupid, but I thought that's what you needed too."

It was December. The holidays were fast approaching, so when my mother suggested I come back to Omaha for a few weeks before I figured out my next move, I agreed. It was nice to be home. Like a lot of Jews, I'm a sucker for Christmas. My younger sister was on holiday from her first year of college, bubbly and newly adult, and we had a ball driving recklessly through the icy streets, oohing nostalgically over the familiar decorations, and posing on Santa's lap at the mall while my mother looked on.

Writing to Pete through his regular e-mail had always been something of a security risk, since his girlfriend had the password. I sometimes wrote him there anyway, taking care not to say anything that would arouse suspicion, but before I left Amsterdam, we had set up a special account for messages of a more private nature. I wrote him every day, telling him how much I missed him, how I was counting the days before we would be together for real. His correspondence was less frequent, but I figured that between work and having to find a way to end his relationship with a minimum of fuss, he had a lot on his plate. My mother, thankfully, had chosen not to ask any questions about the current status of my relationship.

"He said he'd try to end it with her before he goes home for Christmas," I would say, unprompted. "That's only a couple weeks away. The least I can do is be a little patient."

My mother would press her lips grimly together, like a pioneer woman surveying for the first time a barren homestead she is expected to turn into a home. "I've said all I'm going to say about it. When the circumstances change, I guess we'll start over with a clean slate." It was the best she could do.

It was the first night of Hanukkah, which fell that year about a week before Christmas. I was in the dining room, wrapping gifts, when the phone rang.

It was Pete, calling from Amsterdam. In my excitement, I

dropped the roll of festive paper I was holding, letting the crisp stream of blue and gold spill out through the slatted kitchen doors and into the living room.

"Baby! It's so good to hear your voice," I exclaimed. "I miss you so much! Just the time difference makes it so hard to get ahold of you. The connection is bad, I think. What did you just say?"

Pete was suddenly crystal clear. "I said, she *knows*."

I whooped. "You finally told her?"

"No, I didn't fucking tell her." His voice was glacial. "She found that e-mail account. She read *everything*."

A shiver went up my spine. This was not how it was supposed to happen, not at all. "What? How could she?"

In less than a minute, Pete's icy tone had turned to fire. "*How?*" he shouted. "How the fuck do you think? *You* did it. You sent e-mail from there to my regular account, and when she checked it this morning—*like she always fucking does, like YOU KNOW she always does*—she read it and she saw the address. That's how."

Desperately, I tried to think of what my last e-mail had said. I was sure it had been casual. Maybe a little too familiar, maybe I had signed off with "love" instead of a neutral dash or "XO." I might have mentioned that I missed him, but surely it was nothing that couldn't be explained away. She knew we were friends. Friends missed each other. I missed Jeroen and Mattijs already. "But how?" I asked. "How could she know the password?"

"Because," Pete said dully, "the password to both accounts is the same. I made it the same one because . . . because I knew I'd forget it otherwise."

"Oh," I said. "Oh dear."

"She read them all," he repeated. "Every single one of them. When I got home this afternoon, she was waiting there with her mother. Her *mother*. They practically had a fucking moving van waiting." He yelped out a slow, mournful sob. "I can't believe this is happening."

"What happened to the e-mails?" I said, suddenly panicked.

"What the fuck do you think?" Pete croaked. "She deleted them. They're gone."

Of course. Obliteration by technology. The more we communicate, the less permanent any of it is. I took a deep breath. None of that mattered. We would be a real couple now. This was my chance to show him how supportive and loving I could be. "Pete, I know this isn't how you wanted things to happen . . ."

"How I wanted things to happen? I broke her fucking heart!"

"I know," I said soothingly. "I know this is really hard. I'm really sorry this is the way things worked out. But maybe . . . just hear me out . . . maybe this is a blessing in disguise. I mean, at least it's out in the open now. You'll come back to the States. We'll be together, just like we talked about—"

"You did this on purpose," Pete said.

"I didn't!" I cried.

"You sent that e-mail from the wrong account on purpose. This is exactly what you wanted. You planned this all along. Didn't you?"

"No!" I was sobbing now, clutching the crumpled end of the wrapping paper to my breast like it was the body of my dying child. "It was a mistake! I swear!"

"I can't do this," Pete said darkly. "I just can't."

"But what about us?"

"I don't think you understand," he said. "My entire life has just completely fallen apart."

"But," I stammered, "I love you." It came out like a question.

Pete let out a short barking laugh. "So does she. I'm sorry, but I just can't fucking deal with you right now. I just can't."

· · ·

Several hours later, I was still lying facedown in the empty tub in the upstairs bathroom, my traditional spot for untrammeled weeping, when my mother knocked gently on the door.

"Go away," I moaned. "I promise I won't commit suicide."

She opened the door a crack and thrust the cordless receiver toward me. "It's Peter," she said, with a tone of disgust I had last heard her use when discussing Prince Charles's infamous tampon conversation. "Also, I would really like to take a bath, if you're all finished in here."

Pete was making sobbing noises across the line. "I'm so sorry. I was in shock. I love you and I can't live without you."

"I love you too," I wailed. With a gagging noise, my mother stalked off toward her bedroom.

"Listen," said Pete urgently. "I want you to fly out to L.A. after Christmas. We'll have almost two weeks together before I have to go back to Amsterdam and you go back to New York."

"You're going back?" I whimpered.

"Just for a month or so, to finish up some stuff and get my shit together," he promised. "Then I'll come back. If I send you a ticket, will you come to California?"

"Of course," I cooed.

"I can't wait to have you in my arms again, baby," Pete said tenderly. "You'll fly out New Year's Day. It's perfect. The start of a whole new life together."

Pete was true to his word. Two days later, I received a FedEx package containing a JetBlue voucher with a reservation printout.

"Maybe I was wrong," my mother said, prodding the voucher with her finger, as though it were an enormous coiled snake she'd been urged to pet.

"Of course you were," I squealed. "It was only natural for him to have felt a little worried at first. Pete's really sensitive. It must have been terrible for him to see her so . . . you know, so *devastated*. But he loves me. And everything is going to be great."

At first, everything *was* great. Pete picked me up at the airport in Long Beach and we fell into each other's arms, kissing under the palm trees to the roar of diesel jets, just like in the movies. The first few days together were a blur of sex and food, midnight dips in the hot tub and cuddling around the Christmas tree, gazing into each other's eyes. Lauren, one of my closest friends from New York, was also spending the holidays with her family in L.A., and the three of us spent several happy hours together on the boardwalk at Venice and lying out by the pool. Lauren was known among our friends as a notoriously finicky judge of character, and I was thrilled that she and Pete seemed to hit it off. Pete's parents, while understandably taken aback at the radical change in personnel, soon began to warm up, as did the small army of tiny dogs that roamed their house, pressing themselves against my ankles until I would scoop them up and cradle their quivering, manicured bodies against my chest. Pete, on the other hand, was becoming increasingly distant. At first I pretended not to notice his growing antipathy, figuring it was yet another blip in his ever-changing moods that would quickly correct itself, but his coldness soon became impossible to ignore. He spoke to me less and less. Sometimes, as I got dressed in the morning or fixed something to eat, I noticed him staring at me oddly through narrowed eyes, as if I were some strange apparition he wasn't sure anyone else could see. Finally, I snapped.

"What is the matter with you?" I said irritably. "Why are you acting like this?"

I expected him to protest, to claim that he wasn't behaving oddly at all. Instead, he said, "It's just weird. Don't you think this is weird?"

"What's weird?"

"This. *Us.* I mean, here you are, acting like you're my girl-friend..."

"I *am* your girlfriend."

"Are you, though? Do you think we're maybe pretending to be something we're not?"

I firmly wiped back the frustrated tears that threatened to spill down my cheeks. "Two nights ago, when we were sitting in front of the tree with the dogs, you told me you couldn't wait to grow old with me. You said that was how it would be for the rest of our lives."

Pete's voice was devoid of emotion, as though something had suddenly reached inside and detached his soul, as neatly as pulling a plug from a socket. I felt as if I were listening to a robot as he said the words I had been dreading for the past five months. "This isn't working out. I think you should go somewhere else."

I felt like someone was strangling me. "You mean, like, right now?"

"I'll drive you to Lauren's if you want," he continued. "I just think you shouldn't be here."

As I silently climbed out of the car in Lauren's driveway, suitcase in hand, Pete stopped me. He kissed me long and tenderly on the lips. "You look beautiful," he said. Then he pulled out a digital camera from his jacket pocket and took my picture. "Look," he said, show-ing me my likeness in the viewfinder. My eyes were moist and wide with hurt, my lips slightly parted in bewilderment. Looking at that picture was like taking a bullet. I thought I'd rather claw my eyes out than look at it again. He smiled. "That's you, loving me."

"Erase it," I hissed. "Now." Pete just kept smiling as he drove away.

• • •

"Rachel, that guy is a *sociopath*." Lauren's eyes flashed with fury as she slammed the empty vodka bottle down on the kitchen counter, on which the full contents of her parents' liquor cabinet was spread. "I'm serious. He is sick in his fucking *mind*."

"I thought you liked him," I said miserably, pouring the last of the Scotch down my throat and thanking God that Lauren knew me well enough to bring out the booze. I've never been one to drown my sorrows in a carton of Ben and Jerry's. Not when good old-fashioned grain alcohol nourishes the body *and* the soul.

"Whatever. He's fun. He's cute, I guess." Lauren considered the peeling label on a barnacled bottle of peach schnapps before reaching instead for the cognac. "But he is seriously fucking crazy, and possibly emotionally abusive."

"I don't care," I said weepily. "I just want him to want me back."

"Then you're as sick in the head as he is." Lauren abandoned the cognac and seized both of my hands in hers. "*Listen*," she said urgently, only slurring slightly. "You deserve better than this. You deserve someone really good."

Suddenly, I felt very angry. I snatched my hands away. "Why?" I asked sharply. "What have I ever done that was good? I'm a shitty person, in a lot of ways. I was a complete asshole to Jeroen and Mattijs. I cheated on Sam. Maybe I don't deserve better. Maybe this is exactly what I deserve."

"Please," Lauren said furiously. "You weren't an asshole to those guys. You're just *messy*. And you cheated on Sam after he had moved to L.A. without you, and it happened one time, and you were a total mensch about it and told him what happened so he could make his own decision." Lauren is the only Gentile I have ever known who can use Yiddish words completely convincingly during the course of conversation. She slid a glass over the counter to me, filled to the brim with Seagram's Canadian rye. "That is completely—I stress, *completely*—different than carrying on a serious affair for months with someone while you've been living, basically *married*, to someone else for five years."

"Six," I said gloomily.

"Even worse," said Lauren. "And then, when the person you've been living with finds out and dumps you, you beg the other person to drop everything and come be with you, only to throw them out of your house and *completely humiliate* them for *no reason whatsoever.* What you did to Sam was not very nice, but it was *normal.* A totally normal thing that often happens in relationships that are already falling apart. What Pete has done, on the other hand, is *fucking pathological.*"

I was somewhat surprised by her vehemence. Lauren was usually so rational, so evenhanded. But I had to admit she had a point.

"Look. I don't mean to let you off the hook for getting involved with Pete. It's certainly not one of your finer moments. But you're not a bad person, Rachel. Deep down, you're actually pretty good. BJ, Mattijs, Jeroen, me: We all already know." She patted my head fondly. "I'm afraid you're just going to have to accept it."

I thought about going back to Omaha, but there didn't seem to be a point. I didn't feel up to explaining it all to my parents just yet, and I was going to have to return to New York eventually; all of my stuff was there. Lauren was heading back in a little over a week, so I pushed back my ticket so we could travel together. The official explanation was that I wanted to recuperate and make the most out of my vacation, but really, to my secret shame, I wanted to stay out there as long as possible in case Pete changed his mind. If Lauren or her family guessed this, they were kind enough not to say anything.

Lauren and I were at the airport, waiting to check our bags through to JFK, when a voice mail came through on my mobile phone. It was from Pete. Tearfully, he begged my forgiveness, saying he had made a terrible mistake. He loved me more than anything in the world, and it was only the space of the past week that had made him realize how much he needed to be with me. He still had to go back to Amsterdam to sort some things out, but he'd come back to me in New York the second he was done; that is, if I would have him. I listened to the message several times, with increasing rapture, and forced the phone to Lauren's ear so she could listen too.

"You see?" I said triumphantly. "His head has just been in a weird place. Everything happened so fast. But now that he's had a little time to figure things out, everything is going to be great."

Lauren just rolled her eyes. "Hurry up. We've got to get through security or we're going to miss the plane."

Pete called every day my first couple of weeks back in New York. Then the calls began to taper off, and soon, they stopped entirely. The sole person I confided in was Lauren, who was the only one of my close friends who had met Pete and therefore the only one I felt could really understand.

"He did say he had a crazy cell phone bill last month," I mused in her kitchen in Brooklyn one afternoon, as she cooked us one of her special budget lunches of black beans, tortillas, and kale, "and the time difference can really make things tricky, especially if he's been working a lot."

"Mmmm," said Lauren, stirring her beans impassively.

"You know what?" I said brightly. "It's the off-season and there are some awfully cheap airfares right now. I saw one just the other day for like four hundred bucks. Maybe I should just fly over there and surprise him."

Lauren looked at me skeptically. "Where are you going to get four hundred dollars?"

"I have money," I said defensively. "I have some savings bonds

I got for my Bat Mitzvah that are about to mature. How awesome would it be to surprise him like that? It would be so romantic."

Lauren carefully put her wooden stirrer down on the spoon rest and turned to face me. "I have to tell you something," she said gravely.

"Okay."

"I never wanted to tell you this; I just couldn't see a good reason to at the time. But now I think it's important."

I felt my heart thud against my chest. "What is it?"

Lauren looked hesitant. "You have to promise not to get mad at me. Please."

I clenched my jaw. "Just tell me."

"Maybe you should sit down."

"I'm *fine*."

"Okay." Lauren licked her lips nervously and rubbed her hands a couple of times against her jeans. "You remember that last time we hung out with him in L.A.?"

"Oh yeah," I said. "At the Thai restaurant. You were suddenly worried you had eaten something with peanut sauce and had to go home." Lauren was deathly allergic to peanuts; practically all she had to do was look at a peanut and she'd blow up like a balloon. The ever-tactful BJ had once given her as a gift a giant jar of Jif from which he'd removed the label and replaced it with one marked "DEATH."

"Right. Well, I didn't actually think I'd eaten anything with peanuts," she said. "I left because . . . "—she cleared her throat—"you got up from the table, remember? I think your sister called or something and you went outside to talk to her. You were gone for maybe ten or fifteen minutes. Pete and I were just at the table, chatting, and I remember telling him some stupid story about those kids I used to babysit, and he laughed, and then he told me how awesome he thought I was. I guess I was flattered. And then"—awkwardly, she cleared her throat again—"he leaned over the table, and looked really deep into my eyes, and said he knew this must sound crazy, but he felt just, like, incredibly drawn to me. He said it was almost like this mystical feeling, and he'd had it since he first saw me. And I was like, 'But Rachel, you love Rachel,' and he said he felt like maybe the only reason he had met you and been through all this stuff with you was so that he would one day meet me."

Lauren thrust her hands in the air, her fingers spread plaintively in a sort of bewildered apology. I wanted to scream at her, shake her, force her to say she was lying, but I knew she wasn't. It was all too chillingly, heartbreakingly familiar. "What did you say?" I whispered, feeling the blood drain out of my cheeks.

"Nothing! I didn't say anything! I was horrified. And then you came back in and he just put his arm around you and acted like nothing had happened. I thought that maybe I'd imagined it, or he was joking, or maybe he was just, I don't know, like really New Age–y or something and he didn't mean it like that. And then, just as I was calming down, I suddenly felt his hand on my leg."

"Of course," I whispered, "of course."

Lauren looked close to tears. "That's when I got up and said the thing about the peanuts. I just . . . I couldn't be there. I couldn't sleep that night. I didn't know what to do. I figured you needed to know, before you got any more involved with this guy. But I was terrified to tell you, and then, like, the next day he dropped you off at my house. You were already so upset and I thought there was just no reason to add to it, you know? Since it was over anyway. But now . . . look, Rach, I want you to know that I *get it*. When he said that to me, for a second, I felt kind of . . . well, he just exudes this kind of rectitude . . . and it's very seductive. But he knows what he's doing, okay? He's a terrible person. Probably a sociopath. They say one percent of the population is. That's one in every hundred people. You're bound to date one sooner or later." A pleading note crept into her voice. "You can be mad at me if you want. I'll understand. Just please, please don't talk to him anymore."

I felt as though I were a million miles away, staring down at the earth through an atmospheric fog. "I guess I better not cash in any of my Bat Mitzvah bonds."

Lauren forced a smile. "Do you still want some kale?"

I don't remember exactly what happened after that. I don't remember if I ate the kale or didn't eat the kale. I don't remember when I left the apartment, or what I did after that, or where I slept, or if I did. I know I didn't faint. But everything went black just the same.

There are as many different kinds of broken hearts as there are broken bones. There are the hairline fractures, which, while painful, are ultimately nothing more than minor inconveniences that disappear without a trace. There are simple fractures: clean, complete breaks that once healed leave the bone stronger than before. Comminuted fractures: a hundred tiny shards from a hundred tiny hurts, likely to crumble at any moment but invisible from the outside. And compound fractures, the worst of all, when the bone is roughly snapped in two with one jagged edge thrust through the skin of the mangled limb. The kind of break inflicted in dungeons by professional torturers. The kind that leave you with one leg shorter than the other, marked for life, a hobbling, mangled mess doomed to a lifetime of pain. That, I thought, was the kind of broken heart I had.

When I first got back to New York I slept on the couches of sympathetic friends, but after about a month I found a share on Craigslist, hauled my stuff out of storage, and moved in. The apartment, which I shared with a couple of affable cokehead waiter/musicians and a quiet girl with a schizophrenic cat, was advertised as a converted storefront, although "converted" was a relative term. What was now my bedroom had once been the window display. It was cordoned off from the main room with a plank of crumbling drywall, but the street-side wall was still made of glass.

"Is it shatterproof?" I asked.

"I don't know," said my new roommate. He wiped his nose. "I guess you could cover it up with a big piece of wood or something. But don't make any holes in the frame. The landlord won't like it, and we think he might be in the Mafia."

The previous occupant of my display case had covered the glass with the cloudy permeable paint that shops use in their holiday windows to create the illusion of snow. I figured that was good enough for me. I might freeze to death or be cut to ribbons in the night, but all I really needed was a place to cry.

Every day, I staggered home from my temp job, peeled off my hideous business-casual ensemble of wrinkled blouse and brown paisley skirt my grandmother had bought me at the Limited in 1995, lay facedown on my bare mattress in my underwear, and cried until I fell asleep. Invisible in my frosted case, I could make out the silhouettes of Life's Great Pageant as it passed by: weary workers marching joylessly home from the subway, drunks reeling out from the bar next door, fumbling with their trouser zips before urinating against the windowpane, mere inches from my tear-stained face. Once I watched as a male figure hoisted a female companion against the windowpane and fucked her with deep, heaving thrusts until he shoved her aside and ejaculated spectacularly across the glass.

My friends sometimes stopped by to bring food and make sure I hadn't killed myself, but I didn't want to see anyone. Their faces, while kind, were like a reproach, a reminder of my foolishness in the face of cooler heads, and the shame would start a fresh flood of tears. I cried for Pete, for who I thought he had been, for the future I thought we would have. I cried for myself for being so stupid in so many truly astonishing ways. But most of all, I found myself crying for her, the Girlfriend, the woman whose existence I had struggled mightily to ignore. She had had a life with him, a home, a future. Despite my hurt and hysteria, I was lucid enough to know that what I felt was nothing compared to what she must be going through. I could barely remember what she looked like, but I cried for her all the same. And when I thought I was all cried out, I cried more, because it was a habit now. I didn't know what else to do. I was exactly where I had been before I had ever gone away: broke, living with strangers, unloved, alone. But then at least there were exciting things on the horizon: a promise of work, of love, of adventure. Now I had no prospects at all. I was twenty-four years old and felt as though I'd already lived my whole life.

It was early spring when I stopped crying. I was down to a single quilt when the shrill ring of my cell phone roused me one morning. I hoisted myself out of bed, tipping over the top section of the tower of milk crates full of clothes I had instead of a closet, and staggered to the living room. The phone was lying under the coffee table, next to a wrinkled copy of *Guitar World* and a cardboard orange juice container that had been left undisturbed for nine days. On the small screen was an unfamiliar number, beginning in a +31 20. It was the code for Amsterdam. It had to be Pete.

"Oh no," I said aloud. I wouldn't answer. I'd flush the phone down the toilet. I'd hide it in the sink under the stacks of moldering dishes. I'd make a tiny coffin and bury it under a tree in the scrubby soil of McCarren Park. "Oh no."

"Dude!" my roommate bellowed from behind his bedroom

door. "It's seven in the fucking morning. Answer your motherfucking phone!"

I took a moment to compose myself before I answered. Naturally, I wanted to sound cool, collected, like I might have a naked and perhaps famous man in my bedroom waiting to do morning sex things to me. "Hello?"

"Darling!" Mattijs's voice crackled over the receiver, loud and bright and unmistakable.

"Mattijs!" I said. "Is that you?"

"Of course! Such a silly little person you are. Who else would be calling you from Holland?"

"Hello, darling!" There was a muffled click as Jeroen seized the extension. "I miss you, sweetie!"

"I miss you too," I said truthfully.

"Has Mattijs told you yet?"

"Of course not," Mattijs said, indignant. "I am waiting for you."

"Tell me what?" I asked. "What's going on?"

"We have wonderful news!" Jeroen said.

"Wonderful, marvelous news!" echoed Mattijs. "You must come back to Amsterdam!"

"I can't," I said. "I miss you and everything, but I can't. I don't have any money, and I'm just starting to feel—"

"We have at last gotten the funding for the play!" Even from across the sea, the force of Mattijs's voice made the end table and everything on it quiver. I lunged for the remote control and clutched it like a talisman.

"You did?" I squeaked.

"YES! All the money we asked for to make the performance! I told you the Dutch government will do such a thing! There is no George Bush in Tiny Brave Holland!"

"Will I stay with you again?" I asked.

"No!" Mattijs said. "God forbid! We love you, darling, but never again."

"We have found your own apartment," Jeroen added solicitously. "It will be paid for by our company. And also of course you will get a salary and a bicycle, and we will book your aeroplane flight."

There was a bloodcurdling howl as the schizophrenic cat bolted to her favorite hiding place inside one of the kitchen cabinets. Girl Roommate, who was the owner of the cat, had explained when she moved in that mental illness was extremely common in tortoise-shells. "She's harmless," the girl had said, "but sometimes she needs to hide somewhere. I think it keeps out the voices." The cat relieved herself inside the cabinet, among the pots and pans and other implements never intended to come into contact with animal waste. This was understandable, as Girl Roommate rarely if ever remembered to change the cat's litter, but that didn't make it any less disturbing. Now, none of this was my problem anymore. No more cat shit in the pans, no more people showing up for band practice at four in the morning, no more sobbing alone on a mattress while strangers practically came on my face. I was needed elsewhere.

"We begin rehearsal in six weeks," Mattijs was saying. "Will you be ready?"

"Six weeks?" I laughed. "I can leave tomorrow."

"You will see," added Jeroen. "This time, everything is going to be great."

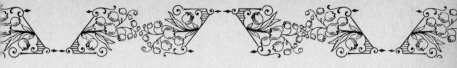

SEIZE THE PICKLE FIRMLY AND NEVER LET IT GO

On the ten days a year that the sun shines in Amsterdam, there is no place in the world more beautiful. The day I arrived was one of them.

Mattijs and Jeroen met my train from the airport, and as we emerged, laden with baggage (both figurative and metaphoric) from the hazy concrete tangle of Centraal Station and into the familiar crush of bicycles and clanging tram cars, befuddled tourists and striding commuters, spinning outdoor racks of postcards and small white stands selling soft drinks and herring, I felt a sense of unexpected well-being come over me. It felt like coming home.

"Everything is just the same," Mattijs said. "Nothing ever changes here."

"I haven't been gone very long," I said.

He shrugged. "It wouldn't matter if you had. Amsterdam is always the same, until at last we float away into the sea."

We went straight to my new place in the Jordaan, a traditionally working-class neighborhood to the north that like London's East End had once been home to legions of lusty fruit-sellers, fishmongers, and other musical poor people, and was now overrun with pale and forbidding art galleries, shops selling complicated eyewear, and shiny North American expats looking for overpriced authenticity far away from home. The apartment Mattijs and Jeroen had found for me, however, was not one of those nominally refinished, drastically marked-up abodes. It belonged to a friend of a friend, a photographer who was spending the next six months living with and photographing the native peoples of the western Sahara and was willing to sublet his place for a song.

"It's very small," Jeroen warned as he unlocked the door at the top of a steep, dark flight of narrow steps.

"His furniture and things are still here, of course," added Mattijs. "But when we saw them, we thought maybe they would be kind of your taste."

The bedroom had an iron four-poster bed draped with a conical canopy of white mosquito netting. The windowsills were lined with pots of lavender, and the walls of the kitchen were hung with cast-iron pans coated in cheerful red enamel. There was a small brocaded ottoman next to the wood-burning stove, and a bell-shaped art nouveau light fixture painted with a pretty pattern of orange leaves dangled over the lacquered writing table in the living room, emitting a warm glow. And best of all, I didn't have to share it with anyone.

"I love it," I said. "It's perfect. It's the apartment I've always dreamed of."

Jeroen gave me a hesitant grin. "I'm glad, darling. The only thing that is a little bit bad is that there is no telephone, no television, no Internet, and no refrigerator."

I laughed. "You should have seen the place where I was staying in New York. I used to try to feel better by reminding myself that Nelson Mandela lived for twenty-seven years in an eight-by-eight-foot prison cell, but then I remembered that at least he wasn't paying eight hundred dollars a month for it, and I would get depressed again. We did have a refrigerator, I guess, but I stopped using it when the toilet broke and my roommates started peeing in the vegetable drawer. So it's all a matter of degrees."

The boys stayed a few more minutes before they left me alone to unpack. Across the street, framed by a large picture window, a shirtless old man played a halting version of "Edelweiss" on the trumpet. I leaned out the window and applauded when he had finished, and he gave me a dignified little bow before disappearing from the window, his trumpet in hand.

After I unpacked, I put my suitcases away in the closet in the hall and walked to the Internet café down the street, where you could check your e-mail or make long-distance phone calls from individual booths. The café smelled strongly of stale tobacco and the oniony tang of unwashed armpits. Under a laminated poster advertising low rates on calls to Rabat, Sana'a, and Riyadh, a group of elderly men in djellabas sat smoking, playing backgammon, and eating candied dates and raisins from foil packets. I had a pocketful of change I had been saving from the last time I was in the country, and from the very fat man behind the cash register I bought a chocolate bar and a white ticket with a seven-digit pay code and settled into one of the Plexiglas phone booths to make my calls. I left a quick message on my mother's voice mail to let her know I'd arrived safely. Then I dialed Antonio.

"I have just now seen the film *White Chicks* of the Brothers Wayans," he said. I had barely even identified myself. "You have seen this film? Is *amazing*. These two black guys, all the time they are dressed up like the sisters of Hilton. I wish I had made this film myself for the Venice Biennale."

"Aren't you surprised to hear from me?" I asked. "That I'm back?"

Antonio said, "You were always coming back."

"Are you still the captain of your ship?" I asked.

"No," Antonio replied. "I crash into a bridge. The passengers have to make one emergency evacuation onto the sidewalk."

"Oh my goodness. I hope no one was hurt."

"Oh, no, no," Antonio said, seemingly unaware of the sarcasm in my voice. "But of course, they take the boat from me. For repair. After this, I become one panty salesman."

"Excuse me?"

"Panties. From my backpack, I make one business selling the underpants for a woman to wear beneath her clothes. They are sent to me from my friend in Argentina, who is designer of underpants. But nobody wants. Then I begin one business selling empanadas, but my business partner he is deported back to Chile. So now I am running one illegal cinema, on the Prinsengracht. The room I have is once one illegal casino run by this man who is one Uzbek. I think maybe he is front for the terrorist operation, but I meet him through the Hare Krishna, and he give me the key to the building. I put in one screen, one film projector, and I show there DVDs from America. Each night, a different film. To watch the film costs three euro. One beer is two euro. The popcorn I provide myself."

"That's very generous of you," I said.

"It is not," Antonio corrected me. "Each night I go to the movie theater on the Rembrandtplein and they give me in one garbage bag the leftover popcorn of the day. The Dutch, they hate to waste."

"Ah."

"Tonight I show *Morvern Callar* of Samantha Morton. Also I show two episodes of *The Simple Life* of Paris Hilton. I wish I could show *White Chicks*," he said mournfully, "but it is here in the theater. Come early and you will be my guest. I will make you pay only for beer."

"Great," I said. "I'll be there."

Antonio said quickly, "Are you still with the guy?"

"What guy?" I asked, with pretended innocence.

"The guy with the girlfriend. I can't remember his name."

"Pete," I said flatly. "No. That's all over."

For the past couple of months, I had managed to push Pete from my thoughts. Maybe it was Antonio's reminder of the tortuous back-alley abortion that had been our eight-month relationship, maybe it was being back here, but there he was again, as impossible to ignore as a shrieking car alarm in the middle of the night and just as painful. Maybe I was a glutton for punishment, or maybe I wanted to confirm what I already knew, or maybe I was just being affected by Dutch parsimoniousness and didn't want the extra minutes on my call ticket to go to waste. Whatever the reason, after I hung up with Antonio, I dialed Pete.

"*Met* Peter."

"Hi," I said. There was no response. "It's Rachel."

"Oh, hi," he said smoothly. "What's up?" There was nothing in his tone to betray that I was anything other than a casual acquaintance who had happened to ring him up out of the blue. I remembered that first night at the Thai restaurant, his bland, vacant smile as his hands clawed at my panties under the table.

"I'm here," I said. The receiver grew damp with the slick sweat of my palm. "In Amsterdam."

"Oh yeah?" he replied, with the same empty friendliness. "Since when?"

"Since . . . since I am," I said.

"Well," he said. "That's great."

I disguised the wobble in my voice by loudly clearing my throat. "Anyway, I just thought I'd call and let you know I was here. So just in case we run into each other or something, it won't be a surprise."

"Actually, I'm glad you called," said Pete. "It's good to hear from you." Warmth was creeping into his voice. Maybe I had just caught him off guard before.

"Do you want to . . . I don't know . . . meet up sometime?" I ventured. Why was I doing this? Why? Why? "It might be good to talk . . ."

"I'd love that," Pete said.

"Great, so—"

He interrupted me. "I really want you to meet my girlfriend."

I fought the urge to bash my head against the door of the phone booth until the Plexiglas was opaque with blood and brains and gore, or until the old men at the front of the store looked up from their backgammon, whichever came first. "I've met her," I said. "Remember?"

"Oh no!" Pete whooped, as though I had just told him a wonderful joke. "Not her! I haven't seen her for months; we don't even speak anymore. No, I met someone else. An English girl. She's amazing . . . actually, she reminds me a lot of you. I really want you to meet her."

"I don't want to meet her," I said.

"Rachel," he said, lowering his voice to the melodramatic rasp I remembered him using when he had something Very Important to Say, like *I love you* or *She knows* or *Do you need me to pull out*. "We're getting married. She's going to be my wife."

The laughter erupted from me like an explosion of soda from a shaken can. It reverberated through the call center, drowning out the muttered words of affection in the other booths, the staticky pleas from Guyana and Tangiers for money and shoes and blue jeans. The old men looked up. One of them, a bearded ancient in a crocheted skullcap, shook a large, walnut-like fist at me. Another angrily thrust a giant, work-roughened forefinger to his lips, but I was helpless. I slumped against the door of the booth, clutching the Formica counter for support, gasping for air. "Rachel? Rachel? Are you still there?" Pete's voice, brimming with syrupy concern, wheezed from the drooping receiver. "Please don't cry. I should have told you in person. I didn't think you would take it so hard. But really I think you should be happy for me."

This set me off again. I fell to my knees in convulsive mirth, like I was being tickled mercilessly by an omnipotent set of fingers. The man in the skullcap threw up his hands and marched over to the cash register to complain. "Rachel?" Pete called. "Rachel! Are you still there?"

At last, I was able to speak. "No," I said.

Pete sounded confused. "What?"

"I'm not still here," I said. "Good-bye, Pete."

Later that night, as I made my way to Antonio's, I was still giddy. Pete's hold on me, my lingering sadness, my lingering shame, all of that was gone. It was as if someone had switched the light on after an endless night and I finally saw that all the monsters that had menaced me in the darkness were really just a hatstand, a billowing curtain, an open closet door. Here I was, back in Amsterdam, with a second—actually, a *third* chance to make a go of it, to return changed and better. This was the third act, where everything gets resolved. The heroine rides off bravely into the sunset, proud and alone. I had an apartment, a salary, a job, a *purpose*. This time would be different. This time I was going to stay on the motherfucking horse.

Antonio greeted me at the door and led me upstairs to a dim room filled with several rows of cozy-looking sofas. Immediately, I stubbed my toe hard on an unseen ottoman and howled in pain. "Why is it so dark in here?" I moaned. "Can't we turn a light on?"

"I don't know if these couches and things have ever been cleaned," said Antonio. "I keep it dark so you cannot tell they are filthy."

"Classy joint," I said.

"If you want, when the movie start, I will give you one newspaper to sit on," Antonio said magnanimously. "Free of charge."

"Where is everybody else?" I asked. "It's almost nine o'clock already."

"It is possible I fuck up," said Antonio. "It is possible I have put the wrong date on the e-mail. In ten minutes if still no one arrives, we will lock up and go to Habibi. They have for me some hash."

"Is Abdullah still there?" I asked. I had missed the jovial bartender who had spent so many evenings catering to us, doling out napkins and paracetamol while undulating his chubby hips happily to one of the cassettes of oud music he liked to play on the ancient boom box behind the bar.

Antonio shook his head. "No. About two months ago, he disappears and Fahim take over the bar. Fahim say Abdullah leaves to go back to business school, but I hear one rumor that he is left to make jihad."

"Wow," I said, thinking of Abdullah's bouncing bottom, his childlike fondness for Malibu rum. "That's unexpected."

Antonio filled me in on the doings of our former colleagues. Kat had met a rich scion of the minor English aristocracy and moved with him to London, where she was hoping to break into PR. Hattie's parents had forced her back to Auckland after her most recent abortion, but not before she managed to infect a wide swath of the waitstaff of the Leidseplein with a particularly virulent case of chlamydia. "Is not her fault," said Antonio reasonably. "A woman cannot tell that she has this disease. How she is to know what she has done?"

The Portuguese vampires had officially ended their relationship with some sort of self-composed ceremonial sex rite. Carolina, the female vampire, had returned to Lisbon; Sebastiao, the male, had stayed on, living with a group of polyamorous Belgians who shared a squat in North Amsterdam with a group of loosely affiliated Hare Krishnas who were big in the illegal gambling industry (the same Hare Krishnas who had introduced Antonio to our unseen Uzbeki benefactor), until he went broke and went home.

"What about Mattijs?" I asked.

"Gone," said Antonio, matter-of-factly. Beta Mattijs, it seemed, had been felled by a severe attack of psoriasis that had sent him back to his rural hometown on the German border, which was near a special spa where he could receive treatment.

"Oh no," I said. Beta Mattijs, in his way, had been a real friend. Now he was lying in a saltwater pool somewhere with armies of tiny fish feeding on his necrotic flesh, and I hadn't even sent him an e-mail. "That's terrible. I can't believe I've fallen so out of touch."

"At Boom Chicago it is always like this," Antonio reassured me. "Each year it is the same. The old people leave, and the new ones come to take their place. I am the only one who remains."

The doorbell rang. Antonio let out a cackle and leapt down the stairs, returning with three men in tow. "They are here for the film!"

Beaming, he sprang into action immediately, collecting money, opening beers, and distributing paper bowls of popcorn and carnival tickets torn from a heavy roll hidden beneath the counter as the three men stood at the bar, smiling awkwardly, looking as though they were wondering just what they had gotten themselves into. I felt like I should be a good hostess, and turned to the man I stood the closest to, a dark-haired guy who looked a few years older than me.

"Hi," I said, a little too loudly. "My name is Rachel. What's yours?"

Gamely, he shook my outstretched hand. "I'm Ben," he said politely. "It's a pleasure to meet you."

Clasping his damp palm against my own, I gave this Ben a quick once-over. He was a couple inches taller than I was, with a swimmer's powerful arms and broad shoulders beneath the faded red jersey of his T-shirt. His hair, not as dark as I had thought at first, was cropped close, and the reddish stubble along his jawline shone with a veil of sweat. His eyes were deeply set, but even in the darkness I could tell they were a very bright blue. And then there was his nose: Prominent but rough-hewn, and tactile, like a plaster cast of a Rodin still bearing the molded finger marks of its maker, it pointed toward an ethnicity altogether more familiar than those often seen in this cheery city of Nordic bridgeless wonders. My family had once gone to New York City on a summer vacation and my one-year-old sister plucked a sour pickle from the metal bowl on a table at Wolf's Deli and refused to let it go. She held on to it for hours as we dragged along through the city streets, oblivious to the scent of garlic and brine infesting the clothes of anyone who came close to her. I remembered her sleeping in my father's arms in a sweltering subway car. Her hands dangled limply around his neck, but her grip was unyielding on the gherkin growing warm and wrinkled in her tiny fist. For my baby sister, at least at that moment, that pickle was the *thing*, the perfect object, the answer to everything. The world was the pickle, and inside the pickle was the entire world. I congratulated myself for this pleasingly Buddhist train of thought and, quite strangely, felt an electric urge to seize this stranger's nose like my sister had that pickle. I wanted to grasp it firmly in my fingers and never let it go.

Ben looked at me strangely. "Is something funny?" He had an accent I couldn't quite place, not quite English, not quite Australian.

"What?" I gasped. "No. Why?"

"I don't mean to be rude, but you're grinning at me like a maniac. Is everything all right?"

Mortified, I forced the overstretched edges of my mouth back into place. That I used my hands for this purpose did not, unfortunately, help me make the case that I was not, in fact, a loon. "Ben," I said. "I like the name Ben."

"Really?"

"Yes," I pressed on, determined to convince him that I was a normal person who hadn't been fantasizing about gripping his proboscis like it was a lump of peat dug from the riverbank of an ancestral home, like the red earth of Tara. "You know, it's a Scrabble word. A 'ben' is an inner room or chamber. And backwards, of course, it's 'neb,' which is also a useful Scrabble word meaning the beak of a bird." I blinked rapidly several times, to make my sudden emergence onto the autism spectrum complete. I knew a lot of people who were nervous talkers, but I seemed to have invented nervous Asperger's. "It's just a very nice name."

Ben looked bemused. "That's interesting. It's so common. I would think to be really attached to a particular name it would have to be something strange, like Melchior or Algernon."

"Or Ernest?" I said.

"Well, I thought that one was a bit obvious. By the way, my admittedly glancing familiarity with the more prosaic work of Oscar Wilde is the product of a first-rate colonial education, not because I'm a homosexual. I'm not a homosexual."

"I didn't think you were," I said, "until you started talking about your colonial education."

Ben chuckled. "We did occasionally get paddled by the head-master for particularly egregious misbehavior, but I managed to escape with my sexual desire for women intact. I *am* very comfortable around homosexuals. I lived for years with my best friend and his husband in South Africa."

"Me too!" I said excitedly. "With my best friend and his husband too, here in Amsterdam. Although they're actually both kind of my best friend."

"Mine split up," Ben said. "It was terrible. I almost felt like my parents were getting divorced. Again." He shook his head ruefully. "You'll have to excuse me. I'm not usually this forthcoming with people I've just met, but I'm very, very stoned."

I decided to change the subject. "Did you say South Africa?" There had been dozens of South African families in town when I was growing up, all Jewish: the Mirvishes, who lived up the street from us; the Rabinowitzes, who had moved to Omaha when I was in the fifth grade. Shayna Rabinowitz, the eldest of the Rabinowitz family, had entered my class, and we had for a time been quite good friends, although I remembered her chiefly now for her fanatical devotion to the movie *Grease*, and particularly to the actor Jeff Conway, who played the second male lead. "Keh-neh-kie, he's mah boy-frehnd," she would sigh during the animated opening credits, her plummy vowels inflected with a staccato African rhythm that to me sounded terribly exotic. As a strictly Zucco/Travolta girl myself, her ardor for his sidekick was no threat to me. We spent many hours in our sleeping bags whispering overheatedly about what it would be like once we were married to our respective T-Birds. What kind of disgusting acts would we be expected to master in order to keep our bad boys happy? Natalie Posner, a mutual friend, had recently informed us of the existence of something called a "blow job" after seeing Shelley Long perform such a thing on her on-screen lover in the movie *Outrageous Fortune*. The sheer mechanics of such an act had caused both of us to recoil, but Shayna bravely said: "Ah don't keh. If that's what Ah hef to do to mehk Keh-neh-kie mah boy-frehnd, then Ah just do it and eat a hahd candy ahf-teh to tehk aweh the tehst of wee."

"Is that where you're from?"

"Yes," said Ben. "From Cape Town."

"Are you on vacation?"

"No." Ben offered me a cigarette. I don't usually smoke, but I took it anyway. "I've lived here for the last couple of years. I work in advertising." He gestured toward the other men. "We all work at the same agency. That's how we heard about this. A guy at our office knows Antonio's wife."

Ben introduced his companions. The guy in the scarred leather jacket was Paul, the new IT guy who had just moved from Brooklyn—not the Brooklyn of converted warehouses and vegan cupcakes that I inhabited, but the real Brooklyn, where people had their last names scrolled in wrought iron on the gates outside their vinyl-sided row houses. This was Paul's first time in the Netherlands, and it had made quite an impression on him already. "I can't believe it," he said, shaking his head. "Everything you gotta know a guy for back home—dope, girls, whatever—here it's all legal. How the hell is anyone supposed to make a living?" The other guy was Linus, a taciturn Swede (aren't they all?). A cigarette dangled from his lower lip as he stared sullenly at a dark spot on the carpet.

"Stop talking the shit," growled Linus. "I have a hangover it's killing me. Start this fucking film already."

After the movie, we were hungry, and Ben said he knew a late-night brown café on the Berenstraat that served decent food until two a.m. Antonio begged off, saying his wife would be waiting up for him, so the four of us went off without him. The meal was re-laxed and comfortable; even Linus seemed more at ease, throwing back beers and laughing hysterically at visions no one else seemed to see. When the check arrived, Ben grabbed it.

"I've got it," he said.

"Are you sure?" I asked, hugely relieved. I wouldn't start getting a salary until rehearsals began on Monday. And also, was this a date now? Were we on a date?

"Of course," he said. "It's my pleasure."

We said good-bye outside the restaurant. Paul and Linus each kissed me good-bye three times in the Dutch way—foreigners pick that up quickly—and went to unlock their bikes. Ben and I stood looking at each other under the awning. As usual, it had started to rain.

"Well," I said, trying to sound cool. "I had a really good time."

"Me too," said Ben. "I'll see you around."

That was it. No "let's do it again sometime," no "here's my number." Not even a perfunctory kiss on the cheek. As I climbed on my bicycle and pedaled home through the rain, I was oddly crestfallen. It wasn't like I was looking for romance, we seemed to enjoy each other's company. It would have been nice, at least, to have made a new friend.

I didn't have a lot of time to brood. We started rehearsals for the play the following morning. My dialogue was in English, the other actor's in Dutch, which was proving something of a challenge. I had started sleeping with an English-Nederlands dictionary under my pillow, as if the words would seep into my head by magic as I slept. The days were long and tiring (and noticeably devoid of the pe-riodic breaks demanded by American Actors' Equity), bookended by fifty-minute bicycle rides each way. One afternoon, a couple of weeks after that first night at the cinema, I was cycling furiously home from rehearsal, trying to beat the rain, when the pedals jammed, tipping me onto the damp pavement. The hem of my jeans had caught in the chain, which pulled from the ring and cut deep into my shin. Cursing, I ripped the bloody fabric from the flanged spokes as I tried to reattach the chain, watching bleakly as the bicycle grease seeped into my wounds. In another five minutes I was going to get uremic poisoning, and just to put the icing on the cake, it was really starting to pour. I considered ditching the useless bike and limping the rest of the way home to die, when I saw a familiar figure ambling nearby. It was Paul, the IT guy from Brooklyn I had met the other night, and I threw myself shamelessly into his path. As it happened, Paul had once worked as a mechanic back in Hoboken, and in about thirty seconds flat, he had fixed my bike and asked me to have dinner with him on Friday night. I wasn't really interested (and I wasn't planning on dating for a while anyway), but I felt it would be impolite to refuse.

When Friday rolled around, Paul picked me up at my apartment, and for lack of a better idea, we wound up at a terrible tourist Italian restaurant down the block, eating reheated pizzas and overdone pasta smothered in orange cream sauce. After dinner, Paul asked if I wanted to get a drink, suggesting we try the place that had just opened on the Rozengracht, a sprawling edifice of glass and chrome that would not have been out of place on one of the most loathsome corners of the Meatpacking District in New York. We'd feel right at home.

The place was packed, but I managed to snag a snug corner table while Paul pushed his way through to the bar, returning with a tray of drinks and an ashtray. When his hand had suddenly made its way under the table to my knee and begun the inevitable journey up my thigh, I excused myself to go to the bathroom. I was standing at the sink, rubbing away a dribble of stray mascara with the side of my finger, when I heard a mighty flush and a familiar figure appeared from out of the polished chrome stall.

"Hello!" said Ben. "Fancy running into you here!"

"Oh my God," I said. "I'm in the men's room, aren't I? I am. I'm in the men's room."

"Yes." Ben's mouth twitched. "In the future, you might consider the presence of urinals as a sign that you're in the wrong place. But don't worry. There's no one in here but me, and I won't tell."

"I'm here with your friend Paul," I said.

"I'm here with Linus," he said. "And a lot of other people from our office. We invited Paul, but he mentioned today at work that he was seeing you."

"It's not a date," I said. "Just friends. You know. A friend date. You know, like when no one else wants to take you to prom."

Ben said, "I have no idea what you are talking about. Aren't you having a nice time?"

"I am. He's just not my type."

"He seemed awfully excited about seeing you."

"Really?"

"He wouldn't let Linus or me hear the end of it. I told him I didn't know it was a competition."

I bit my lip. "I don't want to hurt his feelings. Maybe I'll just tell him I'm not into white guys."

Ben laughed. "That's very tactful."

As I watched him calmly rub soap into his hands by the communal sink, I realized I had known all along that I would see him again. For years, I had had chronic nightmares, often so frightening that even as a teenager I was terrified to go to sleep. To comfort myself, I would close my eyes tightly and picture in my mind's eye people who were important to me, envisioning them standing in front of a variegated beacon of light, like the still at the beginning of a Disney cartoon, when the featured star—Mickey or Donald or Goofy—stands in front of a backlit pinwheeled background, arms outstretched. Sometimes I still imagined that I saw this kind of animated halo, as with a sixth sense, around certain people when I first met them, and that these people, invariably, would have some kind of impact on my life. I had felt it around Mattijs. I had seen it with Antonio. It was behind BJ the first time I saw him at college, in his pointy little French boots, arching his back to advantageously display his round ass in his snug corduroy trousers. And it was there around Ben. As he passed me I caught a whiff of his aftershave, a touch strong but clean and cold like the scent of sweet water.

"Come on," he said. "Let's go find your boyfriend."

Linus the Swede was sitting at the table with Paul when we got back, tucking heartily into our stockpile of drinks. After marveling over the amazing coincidence of running into each other again, the four of us went to join the large group that Ben and Linus had come in with, a friendly mixture of Americans, Australians, and Brits who all worked together at the same ad agency. After a few drinks, someone suggested that we head over to the Paradiso, the famous nightclub in a former Renaissance church. Normally I would prefer to be strapped to a dental chair while a meth-addicted hygienist scraped plaque from my teeth with a razor blade than to go out to a nightclub. Nightclubs seemed to me to be designed in direct opposition to the things I found enjoyable, such as audible conversation, easy access to affordable alcohol, and not being groped by sexually fluid strangers brandishing glow-in-the-dark bendy sticks like bolo whips. I had "gone dancing" once in New York as a wide-eyed college freshman and was promptly spotted, befriended, and drugged by a group of oily youths from New Jersey. Luckily, I was able to make my escape before losing consciousness and being gang-raped in the back of a Cadillac Escalade, but after spending the next day and a half in the NYU health center with an IV up my arm, muttering things, I swore to myself I would never set foot in a nightclub again.

"Sure," I said. "That sounds like fun." I was eager to be where Ben was, and to be honest, I was equally eager not to be alone with Paul.

"Will be great," declared Linus. "Tonight they are playing some sweet yungle beats."

"Yungle?" I whispered to Ben.

"It's the Swedish accent," he whispered back. "Today he was talking about how he tried to work out at the yim, except all they were playing on the stereo was Yanet Yackson and Yustin Timberlake, so he grabbed his yacket and left."

"As would I," I said. "I would yump in my yeep and drive away."

"Not me," said Ben. "I would yog."

On the way to Paradiso, with Paul and Linus bringing up the rear of the line and huddling over a shared joint (or yoint), Ben and I naturally fell into step together.

"What's your last name?" I asked.

He narrowed his eyes slightly. "Never mind."

"Why?"

"Why do you want to know?"

"No reason," I said. "Just curious."

He sighed. "It's long and Jewish. You wouldn't know it."

"Try me," I said.

It was about three in the morning when we first kissed. I was bopping around foolishly with the others in a large circle, as though we were a group of teenagers at a high school dance, when I noticed Ben was gone. I found him standing outside in the stairwell, smoking a cigarette. I asked him for a drag, and the next thing I knew we were slammed against the wall in a crushing embrace. How this happened, I can't tell you. It wasn't an independent decision. I didn't kiss him. He didn't kiss me. But there we were, kissing all the same.

"What about Paul?" I murmured, clinging to Ben's fragrant neck. "It's not nice to just sneak out on him like this."

"No," said Ben. "It's not. But he'll have to understand."

"What if he doesn't?"

"Well, then I guess he'll really fuck up my computer. But I think you might be worth it."

When I woke up, it was late afternoon. Ben was still asleep, his cheek crumpled and cherubic against the fluffy white duvet. "Club Duvet," he had called it that morning, as we indulged in yet another postcoital cuddle tangled up in its comforting cloud. "Membership: two."

"Me and you," I had echoed sleepily, snuggling my face against the warm rug of his chest.

Now, as he lay snoring softly, I admired his face, creased and pink with sleep. The tiny mole under his right eye, the velvety patches of skin beside his bristly sideburns, his neat perfect ears. I wanted to take a whole ear into my mouth, to fold and crush it between my dry lips, feel its coolness, its pliability, like a slab of silken eraser rubber. I settled for gently rubbing his earlobe with the tip of my finger. He let out a defensive snort, flopped over on his stomach, and stuck his ass in the air. Most of Club Duvet went with him.

I got out of bed and at once began to investigate the contents of the apartment. The standard-issue Ikea furniture, the unruly stack of action movies beside the DVD player, the dirty dishes in the sink: all blessedly devoid of a woman's fretful touch. I rushed to the bathroom, throwing open the cupboard doors like someone possessed, searching wildly for a stray tube of lip gloss, a hair clip, a fresh smudge of mascara on the ceramic lip of the sink. Not so much as a tampon in sight.

"What are you doing?" Ben was blinking sleepily in the doorway, wearing a T-shirt and a pair of olive-green underpants with an enormous hole in the front, through which one of his ruddy testicles, gleaming with a fine prickling of golden hair, was visible.

"Oh, you know," I said quickly. "Just cleaning up and getting ready to go."

Pouting, he scratched the sweet soft patch beside his ear. "Aren't you hungry?"

"A little," I confessed.

"I thought maybe I'd order some pizza. And I have a bunch of movies. We could watch them. I hate watching movies by myself." I followed him back into the living room, watching as he opened the Dutch doors that led out to the garden. It was lined with rose hedges, healthy but overgrown, dotted here and there with tight buds. They were dying on the stem. Someone should prune them, I thought. It wouldn't take long, and they were desperate to bloom. They just needed someone to cut back the thorns and help them along.

"It's about to storm again," Ben said, closing the doors again and drawing the filmy white curtain back. "You can't go out in this. You should stay."

When the pizza arrived, we sat across from each other at the big glass table in the dining room, staring at each other as we ate. Flecks of crust fell from his lips onto his shirt. A slice of prosciutto dangled from his mouth like a second tongue.

I didn't leave that night, or the next morning, or indeed until late Sunday afternoon, when I actually had to be somewhere. Mattijs and Jeroen had taken a booth for their fledgling theater company in the neighborhood art fair, and I had promised to sit there with them, talking to passersby and generally acting as an advertisement for the show. Still dressed in my clothes from Friday, which Ben had thoughtfully run through the washing machine, I was chatting up a biblically shod couple visiting from San Francisco when from the corner of my eye I caught a glimpse of Ben, dressed in a Peppermint Patty–esque ensemble of flip-flops and greenish military jacket, accepting brochure after brochure from an unusually animated Mattijs.

"Hello." He smiled at me sheepishly, when I had finished with the San Franciscans. "I was just in the neighborhood, and I thought I'd see if you wanted to get some ice cream or something."

"Really?" I said, grinning. "You were just in the neighborhood?"

"Well, I do *live* in the neighborhood," said Ben. "And I really did want some ice cream. But if you're going to insist on shaming me and calling me out on what little game I have, then yes, fine, I did mostly just want to see you."

"Did you see that nice English boy who was talking to me yesterday?" Mattijs crowed when I turned up at rehearsal the next morning in the same (albeit again freshly laundered) outfit I had now been wearing for four days. "He was really kind of good-looking, and so interested in all the things I was telling him."

"I know," I said. "That's the boy I was telling you about. For me. Mine."

"Oh." Mattijs looked thoughtful. "I went on and on about our funding plans for maybe thirty-five minutes."

"I know," I said. "In Dutch."

"Well," said Mattijs. "He must really like you if he listened to that."

• • •

It was midnight on my grandmother's birthday by the time we finished rehearsal, but the time difference was on my side. The call center was deserted. Even the elderly backgammon players had gone home for the night.

"I'm so relieved to hear from you," my grandmother said. "We never know what to think. You read about all these terrible things, with the war and all these suicide bombings all the time."

"Grandma," I said, "I'm in Amsterdam. It's about as far from Baghdad as Omaha is from Anchorage."

"I understand they have a lot of Arabs there, though, isn't that right?"

"They do," I said, "although they seem to spend most of their time buying pistachio nuts and checking out young women in short skirts. You know. A lot like Grandpa when he goes to the supermarket."

"Don't tease your grandma," she scolded. "Have you met any nice boys in Amsterdam?"

A pleasant flush crept over my face. For once, I had a good answer. "As a matter of fact, I have. I met someone. I've only been seeing him for about a month, but . . . I don't know. I have a good feeling about him. I'm excited."

She hesitated. "He doesn't have another girlfriend, does he?"

"No, Grandma," I said. "He's got a couple of boyfriends though. Although that's really just for the money."

"Hush your mouth," Grandma said. "So? Tell me about him. Is he American?"

"No," I said.

Her voice caught slightly. "Is he Dutch?"

"No . . ."

"It's okay if he is, you know," she said quickly. "The Dutch are nice people. You know, they were very good to the Jews."

"He's not Dutch."

She sounded impatient. "Then where is he from?"

"Oh," I said with a cruel chuckle. "He's from Africa."

There was a full minute of silence on the other end as my grandmother swiftly went through all five stages of the Kübler-Ross cycle of grief: Denial, Anger, Bargaining, Depression, and, finally, a tacit, conditional Acceptance. At last she managed to peel herself off the country-blue tile of her living room floor (the plush wall-to-wall carpets having recently been stripped in favor of more traction-rich surfaces that were less likely to send a careless or clumsy old person prematurely to the glue factory) and croak as politely as possible: "Where in Africa?"

Cameroon, I longed to say. *Botswana. The People's Republic of Congo.* But facts were facts, and I loved my grandmother. "South Africa," I said.

"Oh!" A cautious note of hope crept into her voice. "What's his name?"

"Ben," I said.

"Ben?" My grandmother caught her breath. "As in Benjamin?"

"That's right."

"Ohhhhh. And what's his last name?"

I braced myself. "Abramowitz," I said.

Her scream of joy rattled the booth, reverberating throughout the call center. The guy manning the cash register woke up, wiped his Kit Kat–stained fingers on the hem of his caftan and rushed over. "Madam," he said, knocking urgently on the Plexiglas pane. "Madam, are you all right?"

"I'm fine," I said. "It's my grandmother. She just found out my boyfriend is Jewish."

"Oh." He sniffed. "And so she is upset." His English was perfect.

I said, "I'm going to call my mother now."

"You could have killed her," my mother scolded, when I told her what had happened. "She's old. If she had a stroke, it would be on your head."

"If we get married," I said, "I'm not going to change my name. I mean, Rachel Shukert is one thing, but Rachel Abramowitz? It sounds like I'm someone's ninety-three-year-old bubbe who sits around the nursing home eating prunes and telling you stories about 'ven I vos in de camps.' I just don't think I'm prepared to sound that oppressively Jewish. What if we have to go to a Muslim country sometime? Or the South?"

My mother sighed. "Either way, Rachel, I'm not buying my dress yet."

I hated when she was noncommittal like this. "Come on. I know you have an opinion. Just tell me what you think."

She sighed again. "You were always boy-crazy. Even when you were a baby. Practically as soon as you could walk you were chasing Danny Kagan around the rec room of the synagogue. You were the sluttiest toddler I ever saw."

"Thank you," I said. "What a nice thing to say."

"By the time you were about six or seven, though, you started asking me, did I think you would someday get married? And if so, to who? Do you remember what I used to say?"

"You would say that somewhere far away, while I was growing up, some little boy was also growing up," I said.

"No," said my mother. "I said that somewhere, maybe somewhere very far away, a little *Jewish* boy was growing up at the same time as you. And one day, maybe when you were least expecting it, you would meet him and he would be the one for you."

"I remember."

I could feel my mother's satisfied smirk all the way across the ocean. "I would say South Africa is pretty far away, wouldn't you?"

"I have to go," I said. "He's waiting for me."

"Oh yeah? How late is it there? Is he taking you someplace nice?"

"We're going to Club Duvet," I said suddenly. "The hottest club in town. It's impossible to get into. They hardly let anyone in."

"Good," said my mother. "See that it stays that way."

How to End This Book

Now that we have come to the end of the story (not to mention the end of the number of pages that one can fairly be expected to read in the service of a relatively conventional narrative), it seems to me that there are many ways I could end this book.

My first idea was to flash years forward to the present day: Ben is my husband; we're mostly happy; we bicker about money and taking out the trash; we have one cat and no children. But I wanted to leave something to the imagination and, also, not rip off the ending of the last Harry Potter book.

I thought of ending with a cinematic accounting of the futures of my characters, imagining them in freeze-frame with their fates spelled out below them in unyielding white type, like at the end of *Animal House*: Mattijs and Jeroen are still together, running a successful theater and film company; Antonio divorced his wife and still lives in Amsterdam with his girlfriend and their three-legged terrier; Pete once called Rachel out of the blue while she was having a picnic in Union Square Park with BJ, asking if they could meet for coffee. She refused. His current whereabouts are unknown.

But I have lost touch with the great majority of the people who figure into this story. I have no idea what happened to them, how they look back on this time or the experiences we have shared, or if they even remember me at all. This, I think, is entirely as it should be. Their stories are their own, not mine. I suppose it's nice to catch up on Facebook, to click through photo albums full of weddings and babies, vacations and expanding waistlines, but all this constant contact, the updates, the *corrections* are the enemy of memory, which is all we have to make stories with. These people were important to me at a crucial time in my life, and I want them to stay there, symbols in the half-true myths I have concocted as a way of giving shape and sense to my experience. I know this is selfish. But if I held even a fraction of the same significance to them, I hope they feel the same way about me.

So, I guess I'm just going to conclude more or less the way I began.

Leaving the Grand Tour

Step 1: The End Is Also the Beginning, or Quit While You're Ahead
Knowing when you've had enough is a great skill. I've heard it said that in literature there is no such thing as a happy ending; there are only happy intervals. (To be honest, I read this in Rue McClanahan's autobiography, but if you think I should attribute it to Tolstoy or something in order to make myself sound smarter, then fine, it's Tolstoy.)

If you can go for long enough without washing your hair, it eventually gets clean again. If you stick it out long enough, you're bound to stumble across a happy interval, and sometimes the best endings are also beginnings.

Maybe the beginning is a new love; maybe it's a new job, a new place. Maybe a posh valet-type person has tracked you down to tell you that the entire British royal family has perished in a freak electrical accident and that you are the sole heir to the throne. (John Goodman fans will recognize this as the beginning of the 1991 film *King Ralph*, but wasn't it also an end? An end to just plain Ralph?) An end is nearly always the beginning of something. And a beginning, in its hopeful way, is always a kind of end.

Ben and I had been seeing each other for a few months. The play, which had opened to good reviews, decent attendance, and modest success, was about halfway through its run, my visa would expire when it closed, and it was time for decisions to be made. Ben and I usually met up for drinks after the show at a bar near the train station on the Zeedijk; I liked it because it was one of the only places in town that would make American-style cocktails. One night, as we stumbled out of the bar before going back to his place, Ben squatted on the ancient stone stoop outside, produced a large pouch of loose tobacco from his pocket, and began to roll a cigarette. I sat below him on the bottom step, noticing for the first time the number 1679 carved into the cornerstone, the year the façade must have been built. I traced the numbers lightly with the tip of my finger. I remember thinking that being in love changes your sense of yourself on the space-time continuum. How many countless other pairs of lovers had in the past four-hundred-odd years sought a private shadow on these same steps? How many others had heard, in the clutter of languages that had once been spoken in Amsterdam, in Flemish or Frisian or Spanish or Yiddish or French, some version of what Ben was about to say to me?

"I think I love you," said Ben. He looked down a moment, to where my fingers still lingered in the roughly carved year. "No. I know. I love you."

I caught my breath. "I love you too."

"So," he said, "how can we be together? How can I convince you to stay?"

"I couldn't if I wanted to," I said. "It doesn't have anything to do with you. It's the law. But the longer I'm here, the more I realize this isn't really where I belong. There are things I want to do, and I can't do them here. If you want to be together," I continued, "you'll have to come with me."

Ben flicked a speck of tobacco from his lips. "Fine. Then I will."

"I don't need to be rescued," I said.

Ben took my hands. "Look. I don't know exactly what you want. I don't know exactly what I want. But what I don't want is to wake up in ten years, alone, knowing that I kept a job but let my life disappear." He took my hands. "Rachel Shukert, you are the one for me. I know you have dreams of your own. I want both of us to get everything we want. But you . . . you are my big break. You are the thing that makes everything else possible. Do you know what I mean?"

I knew, as I looked into his earnest, loving face, that this was my happy interval. It was the end of an era, an end that was also a beginning.

Step 2: Reconciling with Your Family

You would be surprised at how far showing up in Omaha while involved in a marriage-track relationship with a well-mannered, gainfully employed, age-appropriate coreligionist who is on paper virtually identical to whomever they would have arranged for you to marry a hundred years ago in the shtetl will go toward dispelling any doubts your parents may still harbor about the viability of your future. This may make you understandably angry. What about your own achievements, talents, and identity as a human being? This argument, while high-minded, is ultimately futile. Your parents have long since ceased to be impressed by you. And while the ensuing parental ecstasy over this new, unexpected addition to their lives may be infuriating, bear in mind that breaking up with a loving and supportive partner because the idea of him pleases your mother is almost as arrogant as doing the same because of some idea you have about "not needing to be rescued." Sometimes it's okay to make other people happy.

Step 3: Restoring Health to Your Bank Account

These are troubled times. If the Department of Labor can't tell you what to do, neither can I. If while reading this book you unexpectedly inherited the throne of a minor European kingdom (see *King Ralph*, above); became the drug-addicted/sexually abused/political-pundit child of a prominent public figure; were tapped, out of the blue, as a long-shot vice-presidential candidate; or were forcibly conscripted as a child soldier into a brutal insurgent militia, you could maybe get a book or TV deal. Otherwise, I'm afraid you'll have to temp like the rest of us.

Step 4: Some Final Words

At the end of *The Wizard of Oz*, Dorothy wakes up in her bed back in sepia-toned Depression-era Kansas, surrounded by Auntie Em and Uncle Henry, their three concerned farmhands, and Professor Marvel, the blustery mustachioed neighborhood fortune-teller who has dropped by to see how she's doing. They ask her what she's learned from the experience. Dorothy replies:

"Well—I think it's that if I ever go looking for my heart's desire again, I won't look any further than my own backyard. Because if it isn't there, I never really lost it to begin with. Isn't that right?"

That seems to be the conventional wisdom at the end of so many books and stories like these. That all the wandering was really for nothing, because Kansas is where you belong. You're better off safe in your bed, surrounded by people who care about you, and anything you can't find there you never needed anyway.

Well, with all due respect to Dorothy (and, naturally, to the friends of Dorothy), I strongly disagree. A backyard is nothing but a little patch of dirt and rocks and sky. And the world is a vast, terrifying, and wonderful place, filled with things we don't yet know we need. Nothing comes to us until we leave our little patch of dirt and go find them.

To put it another way: There's a Buddhist saying that when you travel, your soul takes a few days to catch up with you, and when you return, it takes a few days to make it back. I've always thought this was a beautiful thought, but I've realized that I don't think it's true. I think that, rather than our souls being finite entities floating about in some great, metaphysical airport terminal, anxiously checking the board for our flight information and skimming last week's issue of *The Economist* while polishing off an economy-sized bag of Skittles, we travel to search for our souls. Everywhere we go, every experience we have, we find another little piece that leads us to the next, like a clue in a treasure hunt. Each little piece of soul we find gets layered on top of the last one. Layers of sediment, forming a mountain. Can a mountain ever be finished? Can a soul? I guess it's finished when we are. Or when we stop looking for the pieces. Whichever comes first.

All right! Enough of this dippy meandering into the queasy realms of the spiritually abstract. Let's peel ourselves gingerly out of the sticky sitcom hug we're locked in, curse at each other until we feel comfortable again, and sit back for the brief but thrilling conclusion of *Everything Is Going to Be Great*.

Thirteen

THE END OF
THE BEGINNING

Mattijs and Jeroen came over to Ben's place—now our place—the night before we left Amsterdam for good, armed with a case of cheap rosé and several boxes of generic-brand tissue.

"They are for you, darling," Mattijs said, presenting them to me with a little flourish. "For all the crying you are going to do because you miss us so much, and whatever is left over, Ben can use for when he is masturbating."

"Thank you," I said, "but I plan to wait until we've been together at least a year before I stop having sex with him entirely."

"What was that?" Ben called from the kitchen. "Did you say something about me?"

Mattijs's bellow, as always, was deafening. "I was just saying that some of the tissue is for you, in order for you to mop up your extra semen when you are masturbating all the time because Rachel won't have sex with you anymore."

Ben emerged from the kitchen looking admirably composed, holding four open bottles of wine by their necks. These he passed round, one each. Between my clumsiness and his general obliviousness to all matters concerning the household, all the proper glasses in the house had long ago succumbed to the lure of the Dumpster, like lemmings waiting calmly to hurl themselves into the sea. "I just shouldn't marry her," he said. "There's an old saying that Jewish princesses don't believe in sex after marriage."

"We met the Happy Hooker!" I said brightly, changing the subject. After Ben's last day at work, we had decided to take the time that remained to do all the things we had always wanted to do in Amsterdam, figuring it might be a while before we had another chance. Over the past week we'd been to all the museums, taken a nighttime canal cruise, and arranged to spend a night at the bed and breakfast run by Xaviera Hollander, the infamous former madam and best-selling author.

Jeroen gasped in delight. "What was she like?"

"Amazing," I said truthfully. "She walks around all the time in a housedress and full makeup, and when you check in, she gets the money right up front, just like a whore. The very first thing she asked me was if my tits were real. We shared a bathroom with a seventy-five-year-old Hungarian transsexual named Susan."

Ben shuddered. "I saw Susan without her teeth in."

"Susan had one of the first sex change operations, in Helsinki," I continued. "She said she hasn't had an orgasm since they cut it off in 1955."

Jeroen laughed. "How does this come up?"

"Oh, you know," I said. "In the morning, over toaster strudel."

"Tell about the bedroom," said Ben.

"Oh!" I said excitedly. "Well, I told Xaviera I was planning to write about it, and she said we could have the special room for the same price as one of the small ones. So we get upstairs, and it's just sort of a regular bedroom, and then we realize what makes it special." I paused dramatically. "The entire room is made up for three. Three sets of pillows, three washcloths, three towels, three ashtrays. Three of everything, and only one bed."

Jeroen smirked. "Well, darling, with your history, maybe that makes sense."

Ben said, "Is that a crack about that little episode with the old Nazi Austrian photographers, or a reference to the humiliating love triangle that everyone knew was doomed but her?"

"The threesome—*aborted*, by the way—was with the fake Italian dentists," I snapped. "There was only *one* old Austrian photographer, and his father was maybe the Nazi, not him. I have no proof. Only speculation."

Mattijs started to sniffle.

"What?" I asked.

"Nothing," he whimpered. "I'm just so happy you two found each other, that's all."

The four of us stayed up all night, finishing the wine. Mattijs and Jeroen were in rare form, generously treating the entire neighborhood to a shouted rendition of "Against All Odds" and other beloved Dutch folk songs* as we finished up our last-minute packing. As I tossed assorted bits of moving detritus—scraps of paper, random electrical cords—into the big black carrier bags for the garbage, it occurred to me how much I was going to miss this place. Not just Amsterdam, but *this* place. I had probably moved apartments at least fifteen times in the past five years, with not a hint of regret. But this was the kitchen where I tried to bake Ben a birthday cake using Duncan Hines cake mix ordered specially from the States, only for my confusion about conversion into degrees Celsius to render it into a kind of chocolaty cudgel suitable for beating potential intruders into a frosting-covered pulp. This was the garden where I had pruned the thorny climbing roses until my arms were covered in welts, had planted the doomed hydrangea now dying beside the fence. This was the bedroom where Club Duvet had first

---

* See page 173.

received its charter. This had been more than just another apartment. This had been our home. It was only natural to feel a little sentimental, which perhaps is why I suddenly found myself in the middle of the room, bellowing along with Jeroen and Mattijs to a phoneticized version of "Take Me Home" as we clutched each other like drowning men, heads thrown back in ecstasy. Phil Collins and pink wine make fools of us all.

Dawn was breaking when the boys finally said good-bye. Ben went to the kitchen to give us some privacy. In the front hallway, I held them both for a long time.

"Be good," said Jeroen. "Take care of each other."

"Thank you for the Kleenex," I choked. It was all I could say.

"Darling," said Mattijs, "it was always our pleasure."

A couple of hours later, Ben and I were woken from our snatched bit of sleep by the deafening saxophone of Phil Collins's "Sussudio" thundering through the apartment. Our upstairs neighbor, in a demonically brilliant act of retribution, had placed his speakers facedown on the floor, playing at full blast the very music with which we had tormented him throughout the night. Ben leapt naked from the bedclothes, shrieking obscenities at the ceiling and shaking his fists like a man possessed. I was more philosophical. "I guess we've worn out our welcome," I said. "It's always good to know when it's time to go." Ben's bad mood didn't lift, however, until the taxi arrived to take us to the airport. In his final act at our former home, he swapped out the nameplate next to the buzzer of the offending neighbor for a small slip of paper he had neatly labeled:

A. CUNT #2A

"There," he said, standing back to admire his handiwork. "Now we can leave."

•   •   •

I turned to watch out the back windshield as we pulled away.

"What's the matter?" Ben said crossly. "Tell me you didn't forget your passport."

"No," I said. "I just wanted a last look. And honestly, I keep expecting to see your irate neighbor come running after us with a shotgun. It seems so anticlimactic to just pull away quietly in an early morning taxi. I feel like there should be some big finish. A shootout in the streets."

"Cheer up. We've still got a chance of being killed by terrorists on the plane. Oh for fuck's sake," he said, taking in my ashen face and shaking hands. "I'm kidding. I'll bet you fifty bucks we're not killed by terrorists."

"I'm not taking that bet," I whimpered. "The only way I can win is if we're both dead."

"Technically," said Ben, "but some would argue that even if you lose, you still win, because you're alive. Wouldn't that be true?"

I looked into his face, his gentle, mocking eyes, his lips pursed in an expression quizzical and endearingly simian, like when a baby hands you a chunk of banana from its mouth and stares at you challengingly until you give it back. I reached for his hand. "You know, Ben," I said, "I think there was a time when I might have argued that point with you. But now, yes. I think it's true. I think you win if you're alive."

My hand still in his, I turned to look out the window. Against the gray sky, I saw my reflection looming over the city as we drove by: the fleets of bicycles smoothly clipping over the bridges and under the quays, the houseboats and the barges, the gabled stone houses leaning toward each other over the canals, whispering the secrets of centuries. It lingered there, faint and porous, a double exposure, a ghost in the corner of a picture postcard. Then the morning sunlight broke through the clouds, and it was gone.

ACKNOWLEDGMENTS

It is sometimes so difficult to express true thanks in person, let alone tell people how much they mean to you, that I am always grateful whenever I have a chance to do so in print, assured I won't spoil the moment by sounding inadvertently sarcastic or looking sheepishly down at my shoes.

First of all, I want to thank my editor and publisher, the awesome (in the godlike sense of the word) Carrie Kania, for her unparalleled patience, support, and insight. She is very simply the best, and I feel incredibly lucky to have been taken under her wing. I am also eternally grateful to everyone at Harper Perennial, especially the wonderful Brittany Hamblin, Amy Baker, Alberto Rojas, Erica "Precious" Barmash, Calvert Morgan, and my darling Joseph Papa. And to Robin Bilardello, who is a talent to be reckoned with.

Huge thanks to Rebecca Friedman, my agent and friend, who has provided me with such devoted encouragement over the years that I often think there must be something wrong with her. Thank you also to Adam Korn, who has always believed in me. Big thanks to Kaya Chwals, Christian Schaub, and Hettie Veneziano for not asking too many questions when I asked them how to say "rape" in various world languages, and to the brilliant Rachel Friedman, who draws a mean pair of underpants.

Thank you to BJ Lockhart, Lauren Marks, Stephen Brackett, Peter Cook, Michael Schulman, Nick Jones, Reginald Veneziano,

Evan Cabnet, and Julie Klausner, who have all listened to me freak out countless times over the years and only rarely betrayed their annoyance, and also to Jesse Oxfeld, Daniel Nester, Ron Hogan, Jason Boog, Leonard Beugher, Elisa Beugher, Timothy Schaeffert, Rachel Kramer Bussel, Mike Edison, Mike Albo, Joshua Neuman, Will Doig, Pete Smith, Liz Meriwether, and Beth Black. Thank you to David Rakoff for being so incredibly kind, and to Colin Shepherd for the delicious insider factoids.

Gratitude beyond gratitude to Arjen Hosper and Martijn Vorstenbosch. Without them everything would have been TERRIBLE.

Thank you to my parents, Aveva and Marty Shukert, who have always let me do things they knew were bad ideas, and to Ariel Shukert, who is my sister and no one else's.

And most of all, thank you to Ben Abramowitz, for taking me away from all this. I hope it was worth it.